The School on the Hill

A History of the Bellefonte Academy Cougars

2016

By Ralph Gray

Cover by
Bill Ammerman
State College, Pennsylvania

Special thanks to
"Mr. Bellefonte Football"
Harry Breon
Bellefonte, Pennsylvania
For his extensive research

Direct all book inquires to
Ralph Gray
P.O. Box 408
Millheim, Pennsylvania 16854
Phone: 814-349-5740
Email: RNK12161@verizon.net

Introduction

Bellefonte's founders, James Dunlop and his son-in-law John Harris recognized the importance of quality public education and transferred the ownership of land reserved for an academy to a board of trustees created when the school was incorporated on Jan. 8, 1805. In 1806 the State provided $2000 to erect a suitable building, providing that 6 poor children receive a free education for 2 years.

The original 2-story structure was built on a limestone bluff overlooking the Big Spring. The north and south wings were added in the 1840's and a brick addition was added in 1873. Due to the lack of qualified teachers, the Academy closed its doors during the War of 1812 and the Civil War.

Quarterly tuition was based on the courses taken. Greek and Latin cost $5, Mathematics $4 and English $3. Geography and all the sciences were also offered; and there was an extra charge for fuel during the winter. By the mid-1850's the Academy was competing with the Bellefonte public school system.

Fire destroyed the upper floor in July of 1904 but restorations were made in time for the fall term. The structure was completely destroyed by fire in 1913, but was re-built 200 ft. long with stone from the hill on which the Academy stood and the enlarged building opened 6 months later for the 1913-14 school year.

In 1910, construction began on an athletic complex on E. Bishop Street; and by 1912 it consisted of ball fields, a cinder track, tennis courts, a skating rink and swimming pool. Revenue generated from athletic events benefited the Academy.

A fire on May 30, 1921 in the attic could not be extinguished by the Bellefonte Fire Companies due to the lack of water pressure. The Lock Haven Fire Co. arrived in 45 minutes and saved the building from complete destruction. The borough council promptly purchased a pumper for the firemen. The students were taken into private homes and classes resumed at Bellefonte H.S. The school carried $22,000 of insurance, but damages exceeded $30,000.

The nearly bankrupt school was sold for $3500 on Sept. 14, 1934 to a private group at a Sheriff's Sale by the mortgage holder. The majestic building stood empty until 1939 when a fire at Bellefonte High necessitated classes being held there. In 1946 the Academy was converted to 33 apartments by owner Harry Tanney; but was completely destroyed by fire on July 14, 2004.

Tom Songer of the Torron Group was interested in building a residential development on the Academy grounds, but the plan fell through in July of 2006.

This book contains a brief Academy history and a list of prominent attendees. It is a history of the sports program introduced by Headmaster James P. Hughes in 1890 and its rise to national prominence under the leadership of his son, James R. Hughes. Academy personnel who made a major impact in sports are also featured in this work which extends through 1932 with a strong emphasis on football.

Established in 1910, the Hughes Athletic Field consisted of 8 acres enclosed by a wooden fence, with a baseball/football field surrounded by a quarter mile cinder track. There were upper and lower tennis courts, and a 323 x 80 ft. concrete swimming pool with a bathhouse. The pool, 6.5 ft. deep at one end and 3.5 ft. at the other, became an arc-lighted skating pond in the winter.

iv

Table of Contents

James P. Hughes   James R. Hughes

Chapter 1
Football at the Academy

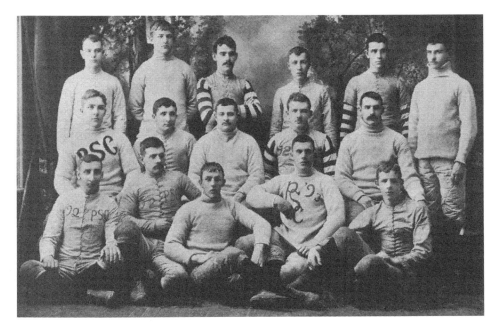

1890 Pennsylvania State College 2-2 Football Team
First row, L-R: Stephenson, Bohn, Aull, Fay, Atherton. **Second row:** Cartwright, Dale, Reed. Hildebrand, Hile. **Third row:** Mattern, Lloyd, McLean, Belt, F.K. Mattern, Yocum. **Wins:** Altoona (68-0), Bellefonte (23-0). **Losses:** Penn (20-0), Franklin & Marshall (10-0).

On Thanksgiving Day, November 27th, 1890, a team from Penn State College played a squad representing Bellefonte and the Academy composed of former college players and "Bellefonte boys". James R. "Uncle Jimmy" Hughes, an instructor at the Academy, had been out of college for 5 years, but was permitted to play right end for Bellefonte. Hughes continued to play for the Academy and the town team for a total of 13 years; becoming the team captain and quarterback.

The starting eleven for **Bellefonte**: Centre-Bush; Right Guard-Aull; Right Tackle-Rothrock; Right End-Hughes; Left Guard-Fearon; Left Tackle-Shadd; Left End-Dale; Quarter Back-Foster; Half Back-Orbison (Captain); Half Back-Cruse; Full Back-Mitchell.

After the opening kickoff at the Bellefonte athletic field, a defensive struggle ensued for the first half; but the Penn State team was able to push across a touchdown as a result of a series of brilliant runs for a 6-0 lead.

In the 2nd half, Bellefonte made a valiant effort and made strong inroads into State territory; but they ultimately weakened and were unable to score, losing their only game 23-0.

As was the custom of that time, the home team was expected to provide the visitors with a guarantee of money, presumably to cover expenses. Therefore, an admission fee was charged at the gate; but a majority of the fans jumped the fence and enjoyed the game without paying. Consequently, the players had to dig deep into their own pockets or beg to make up the difference.

The management issued a warning to the Bellefonte citizens: "Next year there will be some fun with those fence-climbers, and don't you forget it."

Note 1: 1883-97, touchdown 4 pts.; field goal 5 pts.; kick after touchdown 2 pts.; safety 2 pts.
Note 2: From 1895-1922, the Bellefonte Academy Football Team was 112-65.

1891—Record 2-0

Four or five weeks prior to game day Saturday, Nov. 21, the Academy football team directed by James R. Hughes and the Bellefonte High School football team coached by Charley Houck were preparing for an clash that would determine the champion of the town. The battle was brutal, as nearly every man that played in the 2:30 clash had a black eye, a bloody nose, a leg injury, or an arm in a sling. The Academy scored 2 touchdowns and kicked 2 field goals in the first half; and added 2 more TD'S and a FG in the second tor a 38-0 victory. The high school team put up a plucky fight, but could not stop the heavier Cougars. The Academy band played "Annie Laurie". The play of Shaffer, James & Ed Hughes, and Harry Gerbrich stood out for the Academy, while Charley Dorworth played like a tiger for the high school. The lineups: **Academy:** Green, C; Holtz, LG; H. Hoy, RG; E. Hoy, LT; Clark, RT; Thomas, RE; Gerbrich, LE; J. Hughes, QB; E. Hughes, RH; Shaffer, LH; Loeb, FB. **High School:** White, C; Hamilton, , LG; H. Gerbrich, RG; Cruse, LT; Hylman, RT; Dorworth, LE; McCalmont, RE; Curtin, QB; McClain, LH; Houck, RH; H. Houck, FB. Referee—Charley Houck. Umpire—George Bush. The young ladies of the Academy were out in full force and helped encourage the players.

In a 2nd game with the high school, and the Blue and Gold clad Academy squad used a cross pass of over 50 yards on the last play of the game to win, 8-6.

1892—Record 0-1

The Bellefonte Academy got trounced 24-0 by a State College Picked Team.

Mansfield, Pennsylvania was the site of the first night game in college football history. Electric lights were installed and Mansfield State Normal and Wyoming Seminary played to a 0-0 tie on September 18, 1892.

1893—Record 2-1

Philipsburg handed the Academy a 28-0 loss.

The Cougars got revenge on Thanksgiving Day before a crowd of 600 under fair skies. Philipsburg took the 2:30 kickoff and moved into Academy territory but lost the ball on downs. Bellefonte promptly drove downfield and scored on a Curtin touchdown. Hughes' kick made the score 6-0. A few minutes later, Paul Cruse ran for a Cougar tally, but it was called back. On the next play Cruse dashed 62 yards for a score, but Hughes' placekick was wide. Philipsburg got on the board in the 2nd period when Barnes stole the ball and ran to pay dirt. Hugh Taylor tallied on a 7-yard run for Bellefonte after Orbison took the ball out of the Philipsburg punter's hands and raced across the goal for an 18-4 halftime lead. Rothrock of the Cougars scored 2 touchdowns in the 2nd half; and Bush tacked on the 2-point placekick, giving the Academy a 28-4 victory.

Academy Captain Paul Cruse got 11 men together to play a Bellefonte town team; but the town team lacked players, so Lester Shaffer and Ed Cowdrick of the Academy joined the town squad. Shaffer tried several end runs, but the Cougar's Lute Hughes stopped him every time. Minutes after the Academy scored a touchdown and added a 2-point placekick, the town team used the Princeton play[1] and center wedge to push across a tally before the first half ended, reducing the Academy lead to 6-4. A long end run produced another Cougar score and the placekick was added. The town team then tallied on a line plunge but fell short, 12-8.

---

[1] Catching a forward pass and running with the ball.

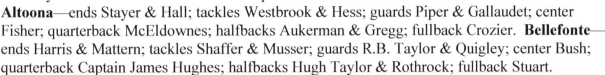

1894—Record 1-1

The Academy suffered a 16-0 loss at Altoona's Lakemont Park. The visitors fought a tough fight in the first half, but succumbed to the Altoona squad in the 2nd half. Gregg had 2 scores and Capt. Aukerman added another. Placekicks were made by Crozier and Atherton. The lineups:

Altoona—ends Stayer & Hall; tackles Westbrook & Hess; guards Piper & Gallaudet; center Fisher; quarterback McEldownes; halfbacks Aukerman & Gregg; fullback Crozier. **Bellefonte**—ends Harris & Mattern; tackles Shaffer & Musser; guards R.B. Taylor & Quigley; center Bush; quarterback Captain James Hughes; halfbacks Hugh Taylor & Rothrock; fullback Stuart.

At the Glassworks Meadow, located on the road to Coleville, the Academy topped Williamsport, 6-2. A large crowd in a slow drizzling rain witnessed the teams slosh in the mud for 4 quarters. In the first half, Williamsport scored a safety for a 2-0 edge. The 2nd half saw Bellefonte drive the ball down the field; but Shaffer fumbled the slippery ball. Teammate Dorworth picked it up and ran for a 15-yard touchdown, and Hughes tacked on the placekick. The lineups: **Williamsport**—ends Shaw & Thompson; tackles Bruner & Page; guards Greer & Farles; center Wilson; quarterback Young; halfbacks Captain W.C. Stone & McIntire; fullback Seaman.

Bellefonte—ends Charles Dorworth & L. Hughes; tackles Eldridge & Mahaffey; guards Meek & Quigley; center White; quarterback James Hughes; halfbacks John Henderson & Ed Hughes; fullback Shaffer.

1895—Record 2-2

The Penn State Freshmen took the measure of the Academy at Glassworks Meadow Field in Bellefonte, 10-8. John Henderson scored for the Cougars on an 8-yard run and J. Curtin tallied from 5 yards out. Penn State also scored 2 touchdowns, but a successful 2-point placement made the difference. The lineups:

Penn State—ends Rees & Miller; tackles F. Dimmie & Boyd; guards Barnes & Stern; center Ruble; quarterback Ewing; halfbacks Captain Shoffstall & Pollock; fullback D. Widner.

Bellefonte—ends Lane & Rothrock; tackles L. Hughes & Eldridge; guards Roan & Cochran; center Rulofson; quarterback Captain James Hughes; fullback Hastings.

In a 3 p.m. game at Glassworks Meadow against Philipsburg High, the first half was scoreless. After the intermission John Henderson and J. Curtin scored touchdowns; a placekick was successful, and Bellefonte had a 10-0 victory.

On November 16th, a 3 p.m. game with Williamsport High resulted in an 18-0 loss for the Academy at Glassworks Meadow. Williamsport ran all over Bellefonte in the first half, scoring on the initial drive of the contest. The Cougars played stronger in the 2nd half.

Photo at right: Bellefonte's Glass Works Meadow.

To promote the health of each student, games of Ball and Tennis, Bathing, Fishing, Coasting and Skating, were recommended. A well equipped gymnasium and suitable athletic grounds were within a five minute walk of the Academy.

1896—Record 3-3-1

Wins for the Academy came at the expense of Philipsburg High (20-0), and Bellefonte High (10-0 & 2-0). Bellefonte High also tied the Cougars 4-4. Losses were to Williamsport (6-0), Penn State Freshmen (8-2), and Lock Haven Normal (16-0). In the 10-0 BHS win at Hecla Park, Prof. Roy Mattern, a former starter at Penn State, played for Bellefonte High. In the 4-4 tie, both teams used first stringers in a game which was supposed to be a scrub match at Hecla Park.

Ben Rich, 21, formerly of Bellefonte, was killed playing football for the Tyrone club in a 22-0 loss to Bellwood.

1897—Record 4-1-1

In a 0-0 tie with Lock Haven Normal, the Academy played a strong defensive game and was close to Lock Haven's goal line when the game ended. The contest was played in 20 minute halves at Lock Haven.

At Driving Park in Philipsburg, the Academy lost, 10-0. In the first half, Curtin had a long run, but fumbled; and a Philipsburger picked up the ball on his 20-yard line and ran 80 yards for a touchdown. Reuban Mull scored for Philipsburg on a 40-yard scamper in the 2nd half behind great blocking.

In a 2nd game with Lock Haven Normal, Cummings took the opening kickoff for the Academy and ran 85 yards for a touchdown. The Cougars also scored a safety and had a 2nd touchdown called back. The 2nd half saw Curtin score from 7 yards out after a drive consisting of end runs and line plunges making the final score 10-0. The game was played at Glassworks Meadow in Bellefonte at 3 p.m. Admission was 25 cents for men, 15 cents for ladies.

The game scheduled with Williamsport High School was cancelled.

Bellefonte topped the Penn State College scrubs twice, 8-0 & 4-0. The first game was at Glassworks Meadow with Maurice Otto and John Henderson scoring touchdowns. None of the placekicks after touchdowns were successful.

Philipsburg came to Bellefonte's Glassworks Meadow and went away on the short end of an 8-0 score on a rainy day. Reuban Mull, the Philipsburg ace, sprained his ankle.

On December 16th, the Academy Football Banquet attracted 16 people. The Captain and Team Manager was James Hughes.

Note: From 1898-1903, a touchdown was 5 pts.; field goal 5 pts; kick after a touchdown 1 pt.; safety 2 pts.

4

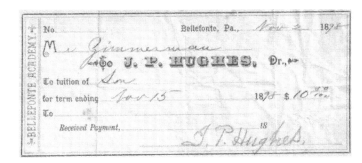

1898—Record 2-1-2

The Fall Term at the Academy started on Wednesday, September 7th.

The 1898 Blue and Gold **Bellefonte Academy Cougars**: Palmer, left end; Decker, left tackle; Garbrick, center; Teller, right guard; Potter, right tackle; Twitmire, right end; Cummings, left halfback; John Henderson, right halfback; Cassidy, fullback; Captain James Hughes, quarterback. The Academy used Princeton and Penn offensive plays.

Against Altoona High, the Academy put 11 points on the board in the first half at Bellefonte before 500 spectators; and the Maroon and White equaled that total in the 20-minute 2nd half for an 11-11 deadlock. Cummings of the Cougars had a 3-yard run for a touchdown, and Captain Hughes kicked the extra point. Cassidy later went over from 10 yards out, but the point-after was missed. For Altoona, Wherle scored on an 11-yard run, and Andy Farabaugh hit pay dirt on a 17-yard scamper. L. Farabaugh had a successful placekick.

The Central Pennsylvania Railroad provided the transportation to Williamsport for a 2:45 game played in a strong wind. With the wind at his back, the Cougar's Palmer ended the initial drive of the contest with a 50-yard touchdown. Hughes kicked the point-after. The Academy, led by John Henderson, mounted another drive which ended at Williamsport High's 3-yard line after a Fleming fumble. In the 2nd 20-minute half, Bellefonte stopped a drive by the home team; but Williamsport later went to the Cornell formation[2] and Vail scored with 9 minutes left. He tacked on the PAT for a 6-6 tie.

In a 2nd meeting with Williamsport High at the Glassworks Meadow, 500 fans saw John Henderson and Potter each score touchdowns with Hughes kicking the extra points. Prior to the Saturday game, Henderson was helping a farmer thresh in a nearby field; and Hughes showed Henderson's boss the broken cheekbone that he had sustained in the previous Williamsport tussle. The flabbergasted farmer talked to the other workers and they agreed to postpone the job until Monday. John Henderson promptly starred in the 12-0 victory over the visiting Millionaires.

A crowd of 500 at Waverly Field in Altoona witnessed a Bellefonte Academy loss to Altoona High School, 6-0. Andy Farabaugh scored early into the contest and L. Farabaugh kicked the point after. Halves were 20 minutes in length.

Bellefonte had its own way with Lock Haven Normal at home in front of a large crowd. On the first play after the kickoff, Lock Haven fumbled and Palmer picked up the loose ball and returned it for a touchdown. Palmer had 3 scores on the day, Henderson had 2, and Cummings had a touchdown reception on the Princeton delayed pass in giving Lock Haven its only loss of the season.

---

[2] A tackle was used in the offensive backfield to ram the line ahead of the ball-carrier.

George McGee

George McGee—One of the major success stories in sports, George played halfback on the Bellefonte Academy football team and centerfield on the baseball team from 1899-1902. He was a member of the Penn State College scrub team his first 2 years; but when the starting fullback was injured, George got his chance against rival Dickinson and scored 2 touchdowns in an 11-0 victory. He took over the starting job at fullback and was outstanding in the secondary, where he was known as a fierce tackler. He lettered in 1904-1905 and captained the team in his senior year. In 1909 he was a Graduate Advisory Coach at Penn State.

1899—Record 1-3-2

Altoona High School took the measure of the Bellefonte Academy twice—10-0 & 5-0. In the first half of Game 1, Kelley drop-kicked a field goal from 35 yards out, giving the Maroons a 5-0 lead. In the 2nd half, Andy Farabaugh scored on a 50-yard run; but the placekick failed, making the final score 10-0.

In the 2nd game, Wherle made the only touchdown for a 5-0 Altoona victory.

The Penn State College scrubs scored a safety against the Academy and won, 2-0. Most of the game was played in State College territory.

Bellefonte's big 6-0 victory over the Penn State freshmen caused bells to ring and horns to blow. Maurice Otto broke his leg above the ankle; but teammate Miller had a 65-yard touchdown jaunt. Mac Curtin kicked the point-after.

The Preps tied Potts College twice—5-5 & 6-6. In the first deadlock, all the scoring took place in the 2nd half. Joe Twitmire of the Cougars capped off a 90-yard drive with a 5-yard run. Mac Curtin missed the PAT. Potts put the pigskin over the goal at the end of a 25-yard push, but couldn't convert the point-after.

The 2nd tie with Potts took place in Bellefonte before 2500 spectators and was played in 20-minute halves. Cougar signal-caller Miller engineered a scoreless first half on a field that had been roped off by the local police. The Academy took the 2nd half kickoff and marched down the field with Joe Twitmire covering the final 15 yards. Mac Curtin's placekick was good. Later, with Curtin in punt formation, his kick hit a teammate, giving Potts the ball on the Academy 25. Wheland tallied several plays later for Potts with only 8 seconds left in the game and the extra point was good, tying the score at 6-6.

Along with Joe Twitmire, Curtin, and Miller, George McGee, Dreibelbis and Wilbur Twitmire starred for Bellefonte. Wheland and Vail stood out for Potts.

6

1900—Record 3-3-2

Several hundred fans witnessed a 0-0 tie with Dickinson Seminary at the Bellefonte Fair Grounds. The stars for the Academy were Randolph Hoy and Austin Eadon, who caught a cross pass and ran 40 yards before being tackled.

Bellefonte lost to Altoona High 12-0 at Waverly Field in Altoona before 300 people. Altoona scored 2.5 minutes into the game when Greer hit pay dirt from the 4; and a Maroon fumble at the Academy 20 ended another first period march. Altoona's Fair turned a Cougar fumble into 5 points in the 2nd half; and the game ended with the ball in Bellefonte territory. Wingard kicked both extra points.

In a re-match with Dickinson Seminary, the Academy came up short, 11-6. All the scoring took place in the first half; and Twitmire scored a touchdown for the Cougars. Dickinson's English & Hill scored touchdowns for the Seminarians and Grove kicked a PAT. In the 2nd half, Bellefonte drove to Dickinson's 6-inch line, but couldn't punch the ball over.

The **Academy** lined up with: Randolph Hoy, LE; Babb, LT; J. McGee, LG; Stevens, C; G. McGee, RG; Fleming, RT; Mahaffey, RE; Cassidy, QB; Joe Twitmire, LH; Austin Eadon, RH; Curtin, FB.

A 4:00 game with the State College Preps resulted in an 11-0 Bellefonte win. The game was played in 20 and 15-minute halves. Curtin and Joe Twitmire scored touchdowns and Cassidy kicked a point-after-touchdown.

A 2nd contest with Altoona High was played in Bellefonte. The Blue and Gold rushed for more yards than the visitors; but lost 2 fumbles in the shadow of the Maroon goal post and had to settle for a 0-0 deadlock.

Bellefonte topped Lock Haven Normal, 5-0 at Lock Haven in front of 2000 spectators. J. McGee scored the Academy touchdown in a game played in 20-minute halves.

The Academy used line bucks by Smith and Joe Twitmire along with long gainers on end runs to down Williamsport High School, 16-5. 200 fans braved the rain at the Bellefonte Fair Grounds and saw mudders Twitmire, Maurice Otto, and Smith score touchdowns. Cassidy kicked a point-after. Lane of Williamsport scored the visitors' touchdown after recovering a Bellefonte bobble.

The Penn State College scrubs defeated the Academy 5-0 by scoring early using mass plays. However, Bellefonte was able to stop the State reserves on their own 3-yard line later in the first half. In the 2nd half, Bellefonte's Smith had a long run, but State turned back the Cougars at least 3 times in their own territory.

1901—Record 4-3-1

The Altoona Athletic Club ruined the Cougar opener, 12-0. Wellar and Spindlemeyer tallied touchdowns; and Wingard kicked 2 placements. Bellefonte was outplayed by the visitors who were much heavier and stronger.

In a very rough game with Williamsport High, the Academy was victorious, 18-0. Williamsport's manager stated the Bellefonte players were not responsible for 3 serious injuries to his players—Weiss sustained 3 broken ribs, Kline had a shoulder broken in 2 places, and Campbell suffered internal injuries. Donald Mahaffey and George McGee scored touchdowns, Keichline scored a point-after, and the Blue and Gold tacked on a safety.

500 fans witnessed a Bellefonte 6-5 win over the Penn State College scrubs at Beaver Field. Heck scored the Reserves' touchdown; and Rand Hoy had a 90-yard run for a Cougar counter. Keichline's kick for the extra point was the game winner.

The Academy could not be stopped in a game against Lock Haven Normal as Joe Twitmire, D. Mahaffey, G. McGee, Taylor, Keichline, and Killen tallied for Bellefonte. Carson chipped in 5 extra point placekicks for the Cougars.

In a 2nd game at Beaver Field, Bellefonte topped the Penn State College Reserves, 5-0 on a Saturday morning.

Dickinson Seminary handed the Academy a 15-5 loss as Ames, Cramer, and Andrus hit pay dirt. G. McGee crossed the goal line for Bellefonte.

1902—Record 2-0-2

Although a 33-0 Bellefonte victory over Philipsburg High School was an extremely clean game, one gridder sustained a severe cut in the head, and another had to be carried off the field with a badly damaged leg. Long end runs combined with Leathers & McCandless bucking the line, Maurice Otto & Joe Twitmire's line plunges, and the all-around team play of the Cougars made the difference. Twitmire had 2 touchdowns, McCandless & Heinle had one each, and Keichline tallied touchdown runs of 15 and 85 yards. Keichline tacked on 3 extra points in a contest played in 20-minute halves.

A rematch with Philipsburg was a 0-0 stalemate. Near the end of the 2nd half, Bellefonte's Mahaffey scored a touchdown, but it was called back due to a penalty.

The Academy played a State College Town Team twice—the first game was won by Bellefonte 2-0 as the result of a safety. The 2nd confrontation ended 0-0 due to a missed field goal by Gephart of the Cougars on the last play of the game as the wind took the attempt to the left of the goal post.

**1903—
Record 4-2**
Despite the rain, a good-sized crowd showed up at the Bellefonte Fair Grounds and witnessed a 20-0 Academy victory over Philipsburg.

1903 - FOOTBALL TEAM.

1903 Bellefonte Academy Cougars

Sauers, John Weaver, Gephart, and Leathers each scored touchdowns.

In a slugfest against Lock Haven Normal, Academy fullback John Weaver was roughed up, and some players were knocked out of the game. Lock Haven was led by 190-pound fullback Caldwin who ran for 100 yards and scored on a 3-yard run near the end of the first 20-minute half. Bellefonte was stopped one yard from the goal in the 5-0 loss.

A 2nd game with Lock Haven Normal ended in a 5-0 Rivertown victory. Niles had a 35-yard touchdown scamper for the only score of the contest.

Bellefonte hopped on Houtzdale to the tune of 12-0, scoring a touchdown in each half. Heinle and Sauers hit pay dirt for the winners.

1903 Ford

The Cougars travelled to Bellwood and came away with a 2-0 win. Keichline's punting was the difference in the game, as one of his kicks was dropped by a Bellwood receiver, who picked it up and circled into his end zone where he was tackled for a safety.

The rematch with Bellwood was at Bellefonte; and the Blue and Gold Cougars again came out on top, 2-0. The game between the 2 schools was nicely played.

The Academy Manger was Fred Weaver, and the Cougar Captain was Elliott Van de Vanter. William Louder was a member of the team.

Note: From 1904-1908 a touchdown was 5 pts., field goal 4 pts., kick after touchdown 1 pt.

9

1904 Bellefonte Academy Football Team

1904—Record 4-3-1

A downpour turned the Bellefonte Fair Grounds into a sea of mud; but the Academy boys made some long runs in defeating Philipsburg 5-0. Roelof had an 18-yard run for the only score.

A small crowd gathered at Driving Park in Bellefonte and witnessed a 17-0 Williamsport High victory over the Cougars. The powerful Millionaires were led by Crooks, Hines, and Braddock, who scored touchdowns; and Hogland, who booted 2 extra points. John Weaver, Captain Gutelius, and DuBarry played well for Bellefonte. Williamsport had disposed of Elmira, New York, by a 6-5 count.

In a game played at Bellefonte in 20 & 15-minute halves, Altoona High succumbed to a powerful Academy ground game which amassed 300 yards. The Cougars put 18 points on the board in the first half, with Johnny Weaver, Mortimer Miller, Gutelius, and Roelof accounting for all the scoring in the contest. Weaver also made 3 successful placekicks in the 28-0 rout.

After a scoreless first half, Roelof scored on an 18-yard run behind some fine interference in downing the Philipsburg YMCA, 5-0.

A large crowd enjoyed both the weather and a great game in Bellefonte as the Blue and Gold topped the Bellwood Athletic Club, 5-0. The touchdown was the result of an 18-yard run by Gutelius.

In a game played in 20 & 17-minute halves, the Penn State Scrubs took the measure of the Academy, 6-0. The State Reserves scored 5 minutes into the contest, and Dodge kicked the point-after. The lead held up until the 2nd half when the Cougars closed the gap with a touchdown; but the score was nullified by a penalty.

Bellefonte Fairgrounds at Red Roost

Bellefonte played Williamsport High tough in the first half; but the Billtown Boys were relentless with their end sweeps in the 2nd half, and put 10 points on the board. Van Dusen scored the touchdown, and Crooks booted a 30-yard field goal.

Altoona was the scene for a rematch with the Maroon Railroaders which was played before a large crowd. Line plunges and end sweeps by the Cougars accounted for over 200 yards rushing, led by John Weaver with 2 touchdowns. Bellefonte's Roelof had a tally and Gutelius kicked 2 extra points in the 17-0 win played in 20 &15-minute halves.

On Thanksgiving Day, the Academy entertained the Bellwood Athletic Club; but had to settle for a 0-0 deadlock due to Bellefonte touchdowns being called back in each half by the officials.

John Jacobs was a member of the 1904 Academy football team.

1905 Record: 3-4-1

On September 22, the Academy football eleven was scheduled to play against the Penn State varsity at Beaver Field. Owing to the crippled condition of the Bellefonte team, their manager was compelled to call the game off.

Bellefonte High School defeated the Academy 2-0, scoring a safety. The townspeople enjoyed the victory so much that a rematch was scheduled; and the cross-town rivals played to a 0-0 tie.

In a game played in 20-minute halves, Snow Shoe topped the Academy 6-4 on a 5-yard touchdown run by J. Parks and an Osman point-after kick. Musser booted a 17-yard field goal for Bellefonte.

A 2nd game with Snow Shoe resulted in a 22-0 trampling by the Academy due to the Bellefonte players changing positions.

Oakley Pantall of the Academy accounted for all the points in a 9-6 victory over Philipsburg. He had an 11-yard run for a touchdown and kicked a 22-yard field goal for the Cougars. The game was played in 20 & 15-minute periods. In the 2nd meeting with Philipsburg, Johnny Weaver scored on a 6-yard run and Oakley Pantall tacked on the point-after in a 6-0 Bellefonte shutout.

The Bellefonte Fairgrounds was the scene for a showdown between State College High School and the Academy. Dubany and McKeever of the Academy were out with injuries; and the visitors blanked Bellefonte 11-0.

The Bellefonte Academy took on the Pennsylvania State College scrubs; and the State reserves pinned a 35-0 loss on the Blue and Gold gridders.

Rothfus

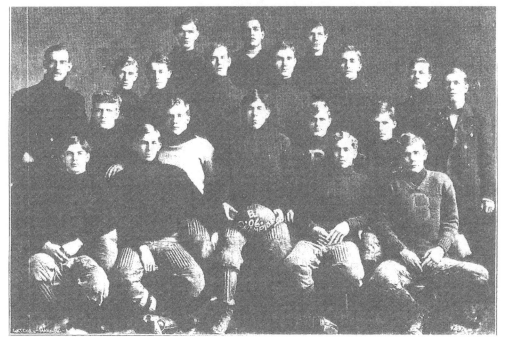

1906 Champion Foot Ball Team
1st row (L-R): Fullerton, Seyler, Capt. McCarthy, Louden, McCaslin. **2nd row:** McCreight, Tompkins, Pantall, Pentz, Mgr. Van Allen. **3rd row:** Coach Walker, Armstrong, Mitchell, Row, Dunsmore, Doepkin, Munch. **4th row:** Smith, Shenk, Lyon.

1906—Record 6-3

The 1906 **Academy** roster: Captain Clyde McCarthy; LH-Francis Tompkins; FB-John Weaver; QB-Charles Fullerton; RE-Frank Armstrong; RT-Edward Lyon; C-Robert McCaslin; LG-Don McCreight; LT-John Dunsmore; LE-Oakley Pantall; RH-Guy Smith; T-John Penty; T-Albert Doepkin; E-Ray Acheson; E-George Row; HB-Frank Seyler; QB-Bill Louden.

Central State Normal of Lock Haven got the best of the Academy, 5-0; as quarterback Bastian scored on a 25-yard run. The game was scrappy with lots of disputes and was played entirely in Bellefonte territory.

In a contest with Lock Haven High School played in 20-minute halves, the Academy dominated behind the line bucking of Captain Clyde McCarthy and John Dunsmore; and the running of Oakley Pantall, Francis Tompkins, Ray Acheson and Guy Smith, who scored a touchdown apiece in the 31-0 trouncing.

A game with Goodwill of Philipsburg was played in a sea of mud, but resulted in a 5-0 Cougar victory.

The rematch with Goodwill resulted in a 10-0 Bellefonte win.

Minds

Playing on Dickinson Seminary's field in Williamsport in 20-minute halves, the Academy topped Williamsport High, 5-0. Oakley Pantall had an 8-yard touchdown run; but several Cougar scores were nullified. Previously the series between the 2 schools stood at 3-3-1.

The Blue and Gold Academy boys blocked 2 Williamsport High punts which were recovered in the end zone for touchdowns by Oakley Pantall and Robert McCaslin, respectively. Pantall closed out the scoring with a 15-yard field goal for a 14-0 win.

Bellefonte Academy got revenge against Lock Haven Normal in a game played in 20-minute halves, 10-0. Oakley Pantall had a field goal and a point-after placekick; and John Weaver scored the touchdown. Central State's defense held the Cougars scoreless in the 2nd half.

Penn State College trimmed the Bellefonte Academy, 12-0.

Dickinson Seminary tamed the Cougars to the tune of 27-0. Rothfus had 100 yards rushing and had touchdowns runs of 8, 30, 15, and 20 yards. Minds tacked on a tally with a 5-yard run. Dickinson Seminary was a prep school for Methodist Dickinson College of Carlisle beginning in 1848; and was a predecessor of Lycoming College of Williamsport

1906 Notes: A game with Baltimore U. was cancelled. Several Academy boys went turkey hunting; and Townsend and Fraser bagged a gobbler. The professional Canton Bulldogs spent time in Bellefonte and practiced daily at Penn State College under the tutelage of State football coach Tom Fennell.

1907 Central State (Lock Haven) Foot Ball Team

1907—Record 2-4-5

A large crowd at Columbia Park in Altoona watched a 0-0 stalemate between the Academy and Altoona High.

Against Indiana Normal, the Bellefonte boys won 4-0 on a 2nd period field goal by Oakley Pantall which travelled 22 yards.

In the 2nd quarter of a game with Williamsport High, Cougar Clyde Oberlin recovered a Billtown bobble in the end zone for a touchdown. The lead held up until the final period when an Academy fumbled punt was recovered by the visitors; and Kinley crossed the goal line from the 3-yard line. Painter kicked the point-after for a 6-5 Williamsport edge. Bellefonte promptly drove the ball down the field, but time ran out on the Blue and Gold.

In a 55-minute contest with Dickinson Seminary, the Academy fell behind in the 2nd period when Skeele had an 11-yard touchdown romp and Williamson kicked the point-after. Bellefonte drove to the Dickinson 1-yard line near the end of the first half; but failed to score. In the final quarter, Warren Elsey picked up a fumble and returned the ball 8 yards for a Cougar touchdown. Oakley Pantall booted the extra point to make the final score 6-6.

Indiana Normal hosted the rematch with the Academy which was knotted at 0-0 at the end of play. A 50-yard field goal attempt by Oakley Pantall hit the crossbar, but took a fortuitous Indiana bounce.

Kiskiminetas (Kiski Prep) put 25 points on the board in the first half with Stone (5- yd. run), Smith (20-yd. fumble return), Lytle (2-yd. run), and Fanker (7-yd. run) accounting for the touchdowns. McKean hit pay dirt from 1-yd. out in the 2nd half; and Lytle kicked 4 points-after in a 29-0 shutout of the Academy. Bellefonte was in the shadow of the Kiski goal post 3 times in the 2nd half to no avail. Quarterback Devin lead the Cougar ground attack. Lyon sat out with an injury.

Lock Haven Normal racked up 20 points in the first half, with Thomas (2 tds), Webb (1 td), Peck (1 td), and Benan (1 td) doing most of the damage. The Havenites added 12 more to the scoreboard in the 2nd half which included a Parsons field goal. Bellefonte was completely outplayed in the 32-0 defeat.

The Blue and Gold attained a moral victory in tying Kiski Prep, 0-0, at State College. Kiskiminetas was the recognized champion team of western Pennsylvania[3].

A 2nd game with Altoona High resulted in an 11-0 Bellefonte triumph. Wayne Smith and Oakley Pantall scored touchdowns for the Academy.

Lock Haven Normal upended the Cougars 5-0, pushing across a touchdown in the 2nd quarter. The game ended in dispute.

The Williamsport Gazette stated that the Bellefonte-Williamsport contest was the best game played there in years. The visitors jumped out to a 6-0 lead in the 2nd period; but the Billtown Boys punched across a touchdown near the end of the game and booted the extra point for a 6-6 tie.

---

[3] Dispite overtures from the Academy for the next 6 years, Kiski refused to play Bellefonte.

1908 Foot Ball Team. 1st row (L-R): Struble, Hayes, Boyd, Shields, Wyckoff, Thomas, Sleppy. **2nd row:** Yocum, McCandless, Elliott, Albert Schenk, Philliber. **3rd row:** Stevens, Mugele, Elsey, Louden, John Wagner, Dave Succop, Al H. Wilson, South, Dillon, Mahoney, Capt. Smith, Hess, Oberlin, Drake, Eisenbeis, H.F. Wright, Mgr. Abrams, Coach Charles E. Hall.

1908—Record 10-2

The opening game with Penn State College drew 1500 fans, who witnessed a 6-5 Bellefonte victory in a contest played in 15-minute halves. State's Harrington scored a touchdown in the first half; and with 3 minutes left in the 2nd half, Coffey Dillon returned a State punt 40 yards, tying the contest. Warren Elsey kicked the game-winning extra point. PSC was at mid-field at the game's end. State went on to defeat Grove City, Geneva, West Virginia, Bucknell, and Pittsburgh while losing to Carlisle, Penn, Cornell, and Navy.

Punxsutawney High School was an 11-0 victim of the Academy in game played in 20 & 15-minute halves. Coffey Dillon hit pay dirt along with Captain Wayne Smith, a native of Punxy, who returned a Woodchuck fumble 23 yards. Oakley Pantall booted the point-after.

The first 10 minutes of the Altoona High game was played on an even basis; but the Cougars proceeded to put 23 first half points on the board in winning 43-0. The Blue and Gold defense limited Altoona to 23 yards of offense; while Coffey Dillon poured it on, scoring 5 touchdowns. Captain Wayne Smith and Elliott also tallied touchdowns; and Clyde Oberlin had 4 place-kick points. Smith also chipped in with a 23-yard field goal to cap off the scoring.

A Coffey Dillon 15-yard fumble return for a touchdown in the last quarter enabled Bellefonte to upend Williamsport High, 5-0. James Foresman and Albert Shenk suited up for the Cougars.

The Dickinson Seminary-Academy game had a 3 p.m. start and attracted a very large crowd. Coming in, the Seminarians had disposed of 2 opponents by scores of 90-0 and 69-0; but Bellefonte scored 14 first half points by attacking Dickinson's flanks and coasted to an 18-4 triumph. Coffey Dillon, along with Wayne Smith and Claude Wyckoff scored touchdowns. Dillon missed 2 field goals but made all 3 extra-point kicks. The play of Smith stood out; and the Cougars celebrated the win with a bonfire.

1908—cont.

The Academy trailed Altoona High 5-4 at the end of 3 quarters; but the 4th belonged to the Cougars. Coffey Dillon and Wayne Smith had touchdown runs of 50 and 5 yards, respectively, for 8 second half points and a 12-5 victory.

Doran hit pay dirt 3 times in leading Bellefonte over Indiana Normal, 15-0.

The Blue and Gold Cougars put a touchdown on the board in the 2nd period, tacked on the extra point, and held on for a 6-0 win over Punxsutawney High.

Bellefonte tallied 12 points in the first 20-minute half in a rematch with Indiana Normal and posted a 17-6 win. Coffey Dillon scored 2 touchdowns and kicked 2 extra points, while teammate Wayne Smith added a 5-pointer. L. Smith scored Indiana's td and the point-after.

The Cougars scored in each of the 15-min. halves at Philipsburg in a snowstorm that dumped 2 inches onto the field. Despite the slippery and muddy conditions, Coffey Dillon (3 yds.) and Clyde Oberlin (7 yds.) scored touchdowns and Dillon kicked a point-after for an 11-0 win.

The rematch with Philipsburg High was played in 25-minute halves in Bellefonte; and the Academy rang up a 29-0 victory. The Cougars tallied 24 points in the first half, led by Coffey Dillon with 2 touchdowns and a 30-yard field goal. Dillon scored his 100th point of the season in the process. Injuries beset Wayne Smith and Wyckoff; but Clyde Oberlin filled in admirably with 2 touchdowns and a point-after. Wright rounded out the scoring with a 22-yard field goal.

Wayne Smith and Coffey Dillon got injured in a 2nd game with Williamsport High; and the Billtown Boys upended the Academy 22-0. Weise accounted for 4 touchdowns and Henninger kicked 2 points-after. Many Bellefonte starters got injured; and the Cougars were hopelessly outplayed and not able to cash in on a couple of scoring opportunities. Dillon totaled 20 touchdowns during a very successful season for the Blue and Gold.

Note: In 1908, kickoffs were initiated from the middle of a 110 yard "gridiron".

The forward pass was legalized in 1906, but by 1908 it was still a risky play. If the offense touched a forward pass and then it was freed, touching by another offensive player was considered illegal, and the ball was given over to the opponents.

A team had 3 downs to gain 10 yards to begin a new series.

1909 Bellefonte Academy 5-2-1 Champion Foot Ball Team.
Front row, L-R: Lee, Condo, Claude Wyckoff, Captain Dillon, Sleppy, Negley, Hess. **2nd row:** Foster, Locke, Boyd, Weston, Reiter, Beattie, Thomas, Eisenbeis, Bauer. **3rd row:** Assistant Manager Newell, Yocum, Fisk, Doane, Gray, Wingerter, Smith, Weaver, Louden, McBride, Sprague, Mahoney, Coach Evans, Manager Bill Entrekin.

Bellefonte opened up with Bucknell Academy and was victorious by a score of 47-2. Captain Coffey Dillon skirted the Bucknell ends with success, scoring 4 touchdowns. Big guns Smith & Weston had 3 tallies between them and Beattie caught a forward pass and ran 30 yds. for a score. Dillon kicked 7 extra points.

The next game was at Indiana Normal and played in a downpour; but the Academy prevailed, 5-0. The field was so bad that a player who fell would slide 10 to 15 yards on the slimy ground, and some places on the field had 3 or 4 inches of water. Negley of the Cougars recovered most of the slippery balls. Dillon made the only score of the game on a run around left end in the first half. Neither side could run the ball in the 2nd half due to the field conditions.

Dickinson Seminary of Williamsport invaded Bellefonte on October 23rd; and due to the drizzling rain, only straight football was played. The Cougars were outweighed 15-20 lbs. per man; but fought the Billtown Boys to a 0-0 tie.

Bellefonte won the next contest by a 6-0 count over the Anderson College team of Altoona. Anderson had held Kiski to a 0-0 tie and defeated Lock Haven Normal 3-0. Dillon The Blue and Gold were in Altoona territory most of the game and missed 3 scoring opportunities; but Weston got around the end for a 3-yard touchdown and Dillon tacked on the extra point kick. Sleppy's punting kept Altoona at bay. Smith and Louden were injured.

Outweighed 20 lbs. to a man, the Academy was trounced 24-6 by Lock Haven Normal. Down 11-0 in the 2nd period, Dillon ran back a kickoff and lateraled to Weston, who registered a touchdown. Dillon kicked the point-after. The River Boys were led by Fleming with 3 touchdowns, Thomas with 1; and scored a 2-pt. safety. Red Smith tackled well and Sleppy was adept at punting for Bellefonte.

The Cougars of Coach Evans travelled to Lewisburg on November 13th and beat the Bucknell Reserves, 22-2. Bellefonte was able to run the ends as well as through the line as Dillon tallied 3 touchdowns while Weston (40-yard pass) and Reiter chipped in one each.

1909—cont.

Dillon booted 2 extra points. The Bison points were the result of a safety. The game was played in the morning due to the Bucknell-Dickinson contest being scheduled in the p.m.

At Altoona on November 20th, key Cougars Smith and Louden were injured in the first half and taken out of the game with Anderson College. Crippled players for the opposition were replaced with 4 heavy men from the Osgood Athletic Team of Altoona. In the waning moments of the contest, Captain Dillon replaced right end Beattie with Foster; and Altoona exploited that terminal for a touchdown in winning 5-0.

In the most important game of the season, Bellefonte entertained a strong Osgood team of Altoona before a large and appreciative crowd on Thanksgiving Day and came out on top, 24-0, despite Smith and Louden being out of the game. The Blue and Gold used the forward pass to great advantage and put 20 points on the board with Coffey Dillon and Purcell A. Beattie scoring 2 touchdowns apiece. Dillon tacked on 4 extra points by placekicks in a game played in 25-minute halves. The lineups:

Bellefonte (Sub.)	Pos.	Osgood	
Beattie (Foster)	RE	Hayes	Touchdowns—Dillon 2, Beattie 2.
Eisenbeis	RT	Hoffman	Goals—Dillon 4. Time of Halves—
Locke (Weaver)	RG	Crum	25 minutes. Referee—Bush.
Boyd (Doane)	C	Tipton	Umpire—Heverly. Field Judge—
Lee (McBride)	LG	Campbell	Bower. Head Linesman—Otto.
Condo (Fisk)	LT	Fultz	
Negley (Bauer)	LE	Williams	Mr. James R. Hughes, Headmaster
Sleppy	QB	Kelley	at the Academy will hold a banquet
Dillon	RH	Richards	for the Lettered Men in the near
Weston	LH	Gherrit	future, as has been the custom.
Evans	FB	Carboy	

The Athletic Association awarded the letter "B" to the following varsity men—LH Capt. Dillon; FB Smith; RH Weston; QB Negley; RE Beattie; LE Sleppy; LT Condo; RT Eisenbeis; LG Lee; RG Louden; and C Boyd. The letter was also given to subs Locke, Hess, Thomas, and Bauer. Manager Entrekin will be succeeded by Newell '11, of Pittsburg for the 1910 season.

Purcell Adolf Beattie was elected captain for the 1910 season by the lettered men of the football squad. "Cocky" Beattie hailed from Moundsville, West Virginia.
Note: From 1909-1911, a touchdown was 5 points, a field goal 3 and an extra point placekick 1.

In the 1911 football season, Penn State beat Pitt 3-0 on Thanksgiving Day in Pittsburgh to finish at 8-0-1. Red Smith, a 1910 Bellefonte Academy graduate played for the University of Pittsburgh. Al Wilson, a 1908 Academy grad, and Richard Weston, a 1910 Academy grad played for Penn State College.

On March 30, 1911, a "gingermath" was held at the Track House to arouse spirit in the student body. Every Academy student attended. Coach Kimble and all the athletic teams were featured. On May 13, 1911, the Track House was the scene of a dance attended by 20 couples.

On November 30, 1911 a gingermath was held at the Frat House for the purpose of arousing spirit in the football team. Speakers were Captain Quigley, Colonel Taylor, and Senator Heinley. A pledge was drawn up by Mr. James Hughes for the team to refrain from smoking and eating between meals. All members of the football team signed. Speeches by Coach Weller and "Mr. Jimmy" Hughes concluded the event.

Kimble

1910—Record 7-0-2

Not only was the Bellefonte Academy undefeated, but the Cougars captured the Pennsylvania State Prep Championship as well under the tutelage of new head coach I.C. Kimble of Newark, Delaware.

Purcell Beattie was elected captain with the condition that he would relinquish the captaincy to Wayne Smith, should Smith return to the Academy. Smith, from Punxy, did return in 1910.

Smith

10-minute quarters were the norm for the 1910 season as the Blue and Gold travelled to Williamsport on October 8th to take on old rival Dickinson, a Methodist Seminary. The Seminarians took the initial kickoff and methodically marched to the Academy 30 where Hodgson booted a field goal for a 3-0 lead. Bellefonte got on the board in the 2nd period as a result of long end runs and passes; and Coffey Dillon hit pay dirt from 11 yards out. He added the point-after with a placekick for a 6-3 victory. Officials Thomas, Shultz, and Kline were busy during the contest due to frequent infringement of the new rules.

Dillon

The Cougars used the forward pass effectively in defeating the Bucknell Academy Reserves 17-3 on Saturday, October 15th at Lewisburg. The teams were evenly matched in weight; and Bellefonte scored touchdowns in the first 3 quarters to bury the Bison. Dillon, Beattie, and Negley scored for Bellefonte; and Dillon booted 2 extra points. Bucknell resorted to trick plays all afternoon; and scored on the last play of the game, as Nichols kicked a 40-yard field goal.

Weston

On Saturday, October 10th, at newly-constructed Hughes Field in Bellefonte, the Cougars upended Indiana Normal 15-5. Indiana drew first blood with a McCreight touchdown in the opening period; but Ruffner's placekick went awry. Using off-tackle plays and end runs, Bellefonte's Wayne Smith scored a touchdown on a run of 5 yds; Harry Symes had a 50-yard run for a score; and Dillon kicked a 25-yd.

Negley

field goal along with 2 extra points on the wet field.

Coffey Dillon set the tone for a Saturday, October 29th game against the Tyrone YMCA by running back a kickoff for a 100-yard tally. Weston had touchdown runs of 20 and 11 yards; Symes ran 65 yards for one; and Negley had another. Beattie kicked an extra point. Dillon added 4 placekicks in the 30-0 rout on a very cold day.

Beattie   On Saturday night, October 29th, a bonfire was held on the diamond in Bellefonte celebrating 3 straight Cougar wins. The pile of boxes was lit by the Hon. John K. Tener, who made a brief speech; but rain prevented more speeches as the crowd scattered. Bellefonte High also celebrated a big win over Philipsburg.

Indiana, Pennsylvania was the scene for Game 5 of the 1910 Cougar schedule; but the Academy had to settle for a 0-0 tie with the Normal School due to an injury to star back Coffey Dillon.

The next Saturday, Bellefonte took on Lock Haven Normal and scored 2 first half touchdowns to put away the Riverboys, 12-0. Yocum, at 150 pounds, filled in admirably for Dillon on offense and showed great tackling skills on defense. Smith tallied on a 22-yard pass, and Weston had a 40-yard run. Weston added 2 extra point kicks—the first one at a bad angle into the wind.[4]

Game 7 took place at the Lock Haven Normal field and resulted in a 3-3 tie. In the 3rd period a Negley forward pass to Weston carried to the Havenite 20, where Dillon made good on a 20-yard field goal, having missed on earlier one. Fleming hit a 25-yd. field goal for Normal with 10 min. left. The entire Academy student body made the trip and saw a game which featured good defense and many punts.

The scheduled game with the Bucknell Reserves was postponed; so the Penn State Forestry School filled the opening on Thanksgiving Day and fell to Bellefonte, 6-0. A 30-yard run by Beattie set up a touchdown pass from Negley to Beattie in the 2nd quarter. Most of the Cougar yards were gains from forward passes while the Foresters used direct and fake line plunges. Beattie kicked the point-after.

Manager Stahl of the Academy made arrangements with Bucknell to play the game that was scheduled for Thanksgiving Day; and the Cougars prevailed by a score of 6-0, having pushed across a touchdown in the first quarter against the Bison Reserves.

On Saturday, November 5th, the Second and Third Floors of the main Academy building clashed arms in a most exciting football contest. The Third Floor came out on top by a score of 10-0.

The 3rd Floor lined up with RE Bassett; RT Chambers; RG Bubb; C Chartner; LG Vaughan; LT J, Taylor; LE Tiffany; QB Meredith; RH J. Brenneman; FB Fisk; LH Neely. 2nd floor: RE Stead; RT Myers; RG Shiber; C Maltby & Loh; LG McClave & Elliott; LT Oscar Deitrich; LE Heathcote; QB Smith; RH Elliott; FB Piper & McClave; LH Phillips.

"Pink" Reiter refereed and Robinson was the umpire. K.N. Chambers played a phenomenal game at right tackle. Tiffany and Neely scored the touchdowns; and little "Irish" Meredith saved a touchdown by tackling Smith, who had broken loose and was dashing to pay dirt. Smith was hoisted onto the shoulders of 2 of his teammates for about 5 minutes. Hopefully, there will be another such game next Saturday.

Hess

Locke

Taylor

Symes

Eisenbeis

Gamble

---

[4] According to rule, the kick had to be attempted at the point on the goal line where the touchdown was scored.

1910 Bellefonte Academy 7-0-2 Pennsylvania State Prep Championship Football Team
First row, L-R: Stead, Reese, E. Eisenbeis, Fiske, Crouse, Deitrich, Loh. **Second row:**
Robinson, Phillips, Foster Doane. Capt. Wayne B."Red" Smith, Grisbaum, Irwin, Yocum, Boas.
Third row: Asst. Mgr. Edward Maltby, Symes, Dillon, Hess, Negley, Per Eisenbeis, Gamble,
Benjamin Taylor, Leroy Locke, Dick Weston, Beattie, Coach Kimble, Mgr. Arthur F. Stahl.

The Record:

Bellefonte	6	Dickinson Seminary	3
Bellefonte	17	Bucknell Academy	3
Bellefonte	15	Indiana Normal	5
Bellefonte	30	Tyrone P.R.R. Y.M.C.A	0
Bellefonte	0	Indiana Normal	0
Bellefonte	12	Lock Haven Normal	0
Bellefonte	3	Lock Haven Normal	3
Bellefonte	6	State College Foresters	0
Bellefonte	6	Bucknell Academy	0
Total	95		14

At right is the **Bellefonte Academy Varsity Letter** earned by Samuel M. Hess of State
College, who played football for the Cougars in 1909-10. Sam graduated from Penn State where
he was a manager for the freshman baseball team. The Hess Field Complex in State College is
named for his brother, John Michael Hess.

Boyd, a 3-year student who got into hot water at the Academy circa 1910, was penalized
with 1000 lines to commit to memory; and the friend who accompanied him in his escapade was
given 500 lines. Boyd refused to comply and went home to Chicago despite the pleading of
Headmaster James R. Hughes, who wanted him to stay at Bellefonte and graduate.

The 1910 football team included Frank Seyler, Ward Fleming, and substitute Gray.

20

Indiana Normal 0, Bellefonte Academy 0

On Saturday, November 12th, 1910, Bellefonte played its second game with Indiana Normal, this time on Normal's field, the game ending with neither side having a score to its credit.

Indiana claimed a safety which would give them 2 points; but Bellefonte disputed their claim, and their stand was backed up by the decisions of recognized football authorities of Penn State College and Princeton University.

The question arose over a play which came off in this manner: Weston was carrying the ball on Bellefonte's 3-yard line when he was tackled and the force of the tackle carried him over his goal line. The whistle, instead of being blown when the runner ceased to advance, was blown after the ball was down, the runner having been forced back 3 yards after the ball had ceased to go forward. The official, seeing the ball over the goal line in possession of a Bellefonte man gave Indiana a safety.

Outside of the one dispute, the game was great, neither side having an advantage over their opponents and both teams playing great football, indicating thorough coaching. Bellefonte gained and outplayed their rivals mostly in the first 2 quarters and only ill luck and fumbling prevented a touchdown. Indiana came back strong in the last 2 quarters and very nearly crossed the goal line for the coveted touchdown. Weston's punting and Negley's tackling were outstanding. The lineups:

Academy		Indiana
Symes	RE	McWilliams
Eisenbeis	RT	Blair
Gamble	RG	Hudson
Hess	C	Cannon
Taylor	LG	Shields
Locke	LT	Capt. Ruffner
Beattie	LE	Morrow
Negley	Q	McCartner
Dillon	RH	Smith
Weston	LH	Little
Capt. Smith	F	McCreight

1908 Football Coach Charles E. Hall, a mathematics teacher took a position at Lawrenceville.

Percy O. "Per" Eisenbeis went on to play at Cornell.

1911—Record 7-3

Coach E.C. Weller took the reins at the Bellefonte Academy in 1911; and the Cougars, captained by Ben "Minnie" Taylor opened up with the P.R.R. Team of Tyrone and won by a score of 23-0 before a large crowd. The Blue and Gold put 18 points on the board in the first half and coasted to victory. Forest "Rabbit" Decker had 2 touchdowns; Bill "Dippin" Bloyd 1, and Coffey Dillon had a 20-yard run to pay dirt. Dillon made 3 placekicks after the scores.

Cougar Purcell Beattie scored from 1-yard out with less than a minute to play in the Lock Haven Normal game Oct. 7 at Lock Haven; and Dillon tacked on the point-after for a 6-0 win in a hard-fought contest. Lock Haven failed to record a first down in the second half.

The Academy pushed across touchdowns in the 2nd and 4th quarters for a 12-0 triumph over Indiana Normal. Beattie and W. K. Negley tallied for the Cougars and Dillon booted 2 extra points. At 5:30 p.m. on October 16th, the Academy celebrated the Indiana victory with a large bonfire. A mountain of wood was piled up at the side of the Brockerhoff Hotel on High Street; but city officials decided it was too dangerous to have it at that site, so the heap was moved to the Athletic Field. Two wagons made 2 trips each to carry it all out. Students snake danced around the fire; and pictures of the fire were printed on postal cards.

A large crowd at Hughes Athletic Field on Saturday, October 21, witnessed Bellefonte execute new plays and upend rival Dickinson Seminary 20-5. The attendance was due to notices on the screen at the Scenic Theatre in Petriken Hall. The students were out in force and stretched along the sidelines. Coffey Dillon did most of the damage with touchdown runs of 20 and 11yards, 2 extra points, and a field goal of 20 yards. Dillon kicked off to start the game, and Black of Dickinson received it. The Williamsport lads did much zigzagging across the field, but punted; and Forest Decker returned it for 50 yards and a touchdown. In the 2nd quarter Seminarian Babcock recovered a blocked Bloyd boot in the end zone for 5 points. Ferrel failed at the extra point kick. Dickinson's score was the first against the Academy. Dillon scored the next touchdown after a series of line plunges. The Academy fumbled a punt, but was soon at the opponents' 20-yard line, where Dillon kicked a field goal from a difficult angle. Dillon capped the scoring on an end run. The lineup:

Dickinson		Bellefonte	
Preston	R.E.	Kline	Referee: Weston, Bellefonte.
Connor	R.T.	Seidel	Umpire: Kline, Williamsport.
Lucas	R.G.	Roderick	Field judge: Glessner, Harrisburg.
Babcock	C.	Tiffany	Touchdowns: Decker, Dillon 2,
Groscup-Brown	L.G.	Ben Taylor, Capt.	Babcock. Goals from touchdowns:
Black	L.T.	Chuck Reese	Dillon 2. Goals from field: Dillon.
Strong	L.E.	Bill Bloyd	Time: 2 fifteen and 2 ten minute
Ferrel	Q.	Beattie	quarters.
Prindle	R.H.	Holmes	Sub.—Latshaw for Roderick.
Brumback	L.H.	Coffey Dillon	
Bastian	F.B.	Forest Decker	Cougars: Clay Lindemuth, John

Henderson, Mahaffey, William Rothrock, Jack Hedges, Red Meredith.

The Colgate University football team was in Bellefonte on November 10th, 1911 and practiced at Hughes Field in preparation for a meeting with Penn State College. The team arrived on the 4:45 p.m. train and was met by Mr. James Hughes, who escorted them to the YMCA, where they utilized the Academy's room. The Cougars gave up the field to the Colgate players who practiced for 20 minutes until they were compelled to stop due to darkness.

On Oct. 28, 1911, Forest Decker scored 3 touchdowns on runs of 15 and 30 yards, and a 50-yard return of a Lock Haven fumble in leading the Academy to a 25-0 whitewash of the Normal School at Hughes Field. Bill Bloyd added 2 more scores with a 17-yard pass reception and a 20-yard field goal via a dropkick. Coffey Dillon kicked 2 extra points in the rout. The Bellefonte lineup: Kline & Smith RE; Seidel LT; Roderick & Latshaw RG; Tiffany C; Capt. Taylor LG; Reese LT; Bloyd LE; Beattie Q; Decker RH; Holmes LH; Dillon FB. Time of quarters—15 min. Referee—Bower, Bellefonte; Umpire—Donohue, Lock Haven; Field Judge—Bush, Bellefonte, Head Linesman—Weston, State College.

The next game of 1911 was scheduled with the State College Reserves, but when the Cougars were presented with a chance to play the championship Mercersburg Eleven, the Reserves very kindly released the Academy. Bellefonte received a telegram on Friday, November 3rd, offering the game; and quietly packed up and left on the 4:44 p.m. train for the Saturday, Nov. 4th contest.

Although the game was close in the first half, Bellefonte was out-classed by a stronger Mercersburg Academy team in a 31-0 blowout at Mercersburg. Near the end of the half, Shadt of the Blue Storm blocked a punt and crossed the coveted line. The point-after failed, making the score 5-0. In the 2nd half, Bellefonte was unable to stop the protégés of Coach Frank Sommer. McNulty tallied 2 touchdowns, Turner 2, and Miller tacked on 6 points-after. Decker excelled for the Cougars, making many gains through the heavy opposing line. The Blue and Gold suffered their first loss at the hands of a better-conditioned eleven. The lineups:

Mercersburg		Bellefonte	
Miller	L.E.	Bloyd	Touchdowns: McNulty 2,
Semmens	L.T.	Reese	Turner 2, Shadt 1. Goal
Maxfield-Scott	L.G.	Taylor	from field: Miller. Goals
Conover-Oberly	C.	Gerald Tiffany	from touchdown: Miller 3.
Shadt	R.G.	Roderick-Latshaw	Referee: Col. Wells.
Hetler	R.T.	Seidel	Umpire: Schnavely. Field
Turner-Wangman	R.E.	Kline-Smith	judge: Weaver. Head
Leech-Brawn	Q.	Beattie	linesman: Gilbert.
Hime	L.H.	Holmes	
Soles	R.H.	Dillon	
Legore-Meredith	F.B.	Decker	

Williamsport High was a 31-0 victim of Bellefonte before a large crowd in Bellefonte on Nov. 11. Coffey Dillon scored 2 touchdowns on runs of 10 and 21 yards, Forest Decker hit pay dirt from 8 yards out; and Purcell Beattie was on the receiving end of touchdown passes of 30 and 15 yards in the mis-match. Dillon also kicked a 35-yard field goal and 3 extra points. Coach Hartman's men put up a plucky fight. The Bellefonte lineup: Beattie RE; Seidel & Phillips RT; Roderick RG; Eisenbeis C; Taylor & Bemus LG; C, Reese LT; Smith & Kline LE; J. Reese Q; Dillon LH; Decker RH; Holmes FB. Time of quarters—two 12.5, one 15, and one 10 minutes.

The Cougars put 6 points on the board in the first quarter, and added a field goal in the 4th for a 9-0 victory over the Bucknell Academy. Bellefonte was expecting an easy game, since Bucknell had been swamped by several teams Bellefonte had beaten; but the Bison proved to be a strong opponent.

Academy football alums Wilson, Weston, Hess, Reiter, and Foster were on the 1911 Penn State College team.

Note: For the 1911 season, the field was shortened to100 yards; a touchdown increased from 5 points to 6; and 4 downs were allowed for a team with the ball to gain the required 10 yards.

All the scoring took place in the 3rd quarter as the Blue and Gold were edged by Bloomsburg Normal 6-5, on Saturday, November 25th, 1911, at Bloomsburg. Holmes had a 100-yard kickoff return that set up a 5-yard touchdown run by Forest Decker on the next play. Dillon missed the try at goal. The Normalites scored on a 5-yard run in the 2nd half after a series of Bellefonte penalties; and made the point-after try a successful one. In the 2nd half, Beattie replaced Chuck Reese at quarterback, and Captain Taylor was replaced by Latshaw who filled in admirably for the Academy. Dillon, Decker, Holmes, Bloyd, and Reese played a strong game for Bellefonte; but the muddy condition of the field and many penalties on the Cougars greatly affected the outcome of the contest.

In the final game of the 1911 season, 2500 fans witnessed a good game with Williamsport High, as the Billtown Boys tallied 6 points early in the first quarter and hung on for a 6-0 triumph on Thanksgiving Day. Weiss ripped through the Academy line for big gains and scored. Hullihen kicked the goal.

The lineup:

Williamsport High School		Bellefonte
Henninger	R.E.	Smith-Beattie
Hill	R.T.	Seidel
Todd	R.G.	Roderick
Willis	C.	Tiffany
O'Neil	L.G.	Taylor-Latshaw
Simpson	L.T.	C. Reese
Wycoff	L.E.	Bloyd
Hullihen	Q.	Snyder-Reese
Morris	L.H.B.	Dillon
Davis	R.H.B.	Beattie-Decker
Weiss	F.B.	Holmes

Touchdown—Weiss. Goal from touchdown—Hullihen. Referee—Weston.

Captain "Minnie" Taylor retained his position at guard and put up his usual strong game.

"Deac" Dillon, the Academy's stand-by in all sports, gained his share of ground.

"Rabbit" Decker worked hard in every game and accomplished much toward adding glory to the Academy's name.

Noteworthy is the improvement of Holmes. At first he seemed almost hopeless, but by the end of the season he was considered second to none.

"Chuck" Reese, the Warren recruit, was full of pep and ginger; and was a tower of strength in the line, breaking up many attempts to gain ground by the opponents.

Beattie played his usual game throughout. To anyone who has seen him play this is enough to say concerning his great work.

Bloyd guarded the end opposite Beattie; and "Dippin" was on the job in every game and figured in bringing home the bacon many times. He also did the punting.

The spirit of the scrubs, such as Ellis Balsinger, also deserves special notice. They practiced well for Coach Weller and had a great deal to do with the success of the first team.

Leo Grisbaum, Dale Musser, L. Locke, Schad, and Schaffner were on the Academy squad.

On Saturday, Oct. 14, the third annual football contest between the Third and Second Floors of Old Main was played at Hughes Field in 10 min. periods. Captain Meredith and Jamison played well for the Second Floor; while Chartner, Taylor, and Irwin stood out for the First Floor. The punting of Snyder for the 2nd Floor was a feature of the game won by his team, 6-3.

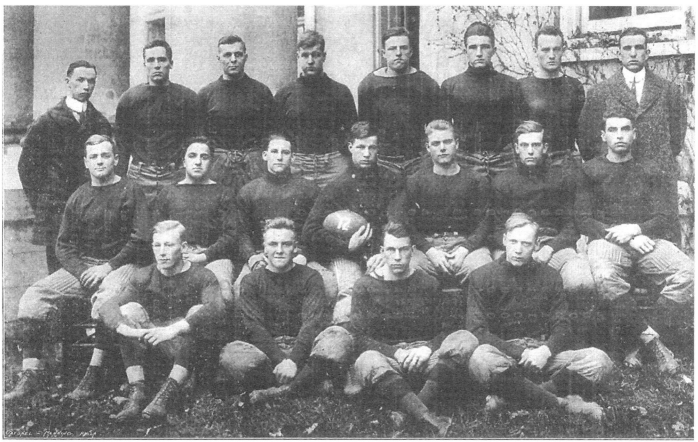

The 1912 Bellefonte Academy 8-1 State Champion Cougars

First row, L-R: Paul E. Smith, Loucks, Schneider, C.A. Luden. **Second row:** Beattie, Carpeneto, P. Jones, Captain Bloyd, Decker, Edwin Beer, Frank Holmes. **Third row:** Mgr. Balsinger, Diehl, "Pud" Seidel, Kuhns, Latshaw, Swain, Carlson, Coach Weller.

Beginning in the 1912 season, a touchdown was worth 6 points, field goal 3, kick conversion 1, and a safety 2. Former players Coffey "Deac"Dillon, Wayne Smith, and Chuck Reese enrolled at Pitt for the fall term; and Bill Bloyd captained the Cougars.

The Academy began the season by defeating Pennsylvania Railroad Y.M.C.A. of Altoona 41-7. Bellefonte scored 27 points in the first half, and added 14 more in the 2nd. Touchdowns were scored by Beer (2); Walter Loucks (2); Purcell Beattie (1); and Frank Holmes (1). Bill Bloyd tacked on 5 extra pt. kicks. Bloyd was from Moundsville, W. VA.
Woolridge stood out for Altoona; but the Railroaders couldn't stop the Cougars.

The next Cougar victim was the Osgood Athletic Club of Altoona by a 49-0 count. Forest Decker had 2 tallies, Walter Loucks 2, Beattie 1 (pass), Seidel 1 (10-yard run after recovering a fumbled punt), and Bloyd 1 (30-yard pass). Bloyd booted 7 extra points. Bellefonte's Seidel broke his shoulder and Osgood's Baker broke his collarbone in the clash.

Bellefonte had a 2:30 p.m. start at Williamsport against Dickinson Seminary and put 26 points on the board in the first 3 quarters. Forest Decker had touchdown runs of 20 and 11 yards, Walter Loucks tallied from 3 yards out, and Bill Bloyd scored on a 20-yard pass. The 4th period belonged to the Seminarians who registered 6 first downs and drove inside the Academy 1-yard line 5 times; but the visitors rose up each time and kept them out of the end zone. A Klein 22-yard field goal was all the home boys could muster; and they fell to the Cougars, 26-3.

All the scoring took place in the 3rd quarter in a hard-fought, close game with Bloomsburg Normal. The Academy amassed 408 yards rushing, with Forest Decker (158), Holmes (88), Walter Loucks (80), Jones (52), and Bloyd (30). Decker had a 15-yard touchdown run, and Loucks had a 60-scamper for a score. Purcell Beattie had the only pass reception of the game for a 25-yard gain. Bill Bloyd kicked 2 extra points.

25

Beattie sprained his ankle in the final period against Bloomsburg and was replaced by Smith. Bellefonte had one turnover the entire game. The lineups:

Bloomsburg—0	Positions	Bellefonte—14	
Thorne (Davis)	Right end	Beattie	Referee—J. Bower,
Smoczynski	Right tackle	Swain	Franklin & Marshall;
Fray	Right guard	Kuhns	Umpire—Hinman,
Croup	Center	Carpeneto	Bucknell; Head
Yurg	Left guard	Latshaw	Linesman—Don
Smith	Left tackle	Carlson	Wallace, Bellefonte;
Walsh	Left end	Smith	Touchdowns—
Williams	Quarterback	Loucks	Decker, Loucks.
Tischler	Right half	Jones	Goals from
Gorham	Left half	Holmes	touchdown—
Miles	Fullback	Decker	Bloyd 2.

1912 Bellefonte Academy State Championship Foot Ball Team
First row, L-R: Mgr. Hadesty, Kann, Glass, Schneider, Heim, Ellis, Luden, Williams, Hunter.
Second row: Beattie, P. Smith, Loucks, Carpeneto, P. Jones, Captain Bill Bloyd, Decker, Ed Beer, Holmes. **Third row:** Mgr. Balsinger, Asst. Mgr. Weaver, W. Irwin, Rogers, Diehl, Dalrymple, Seidel, Kuhns, Chalfont, Latshaw, Creal, Swain, E. Jones, Carlson, Long, Eisenbeis, Coach Weller.

500 freshmen from Penn State College came down to Bellefonte on Saturday, November 2nd at 3 p.m. to watch the clash between the Academy and the freshman team at Hughes Field played in 12-minute quarters. Bellefonte had a 7-0 lead when a dispute arose, and the freshmen walked off the field. Referee Bower and Umpire Hinman promptly forfeited the game to the Cougars, 1-0.

Dick Stead and Harold Hoppley were members of the 1912 Bellefonte Academy squad.

The Academy football team left Bellefonte on Friday, Nov. 8th, 1912 by train; but due to bad connections, did not arrive at Indiana until Saturday morning only half an hour before game time. The field was wet and slippery; but the Normalites had an advantage with their extra long cleats. Carmalt scored in the first quarter, Douglass had a touchdown in the 4th, and Carmalt tacked on 2 extra point kicks. Captain Bill Bloyd injured his knee in the 14-0 loss; and the Cougars were not able to run the ends. Indiana stopped a Bellefonte drive on its 4-yard line. Referee Albert and Umpire McMahon were from Latrobe. The quarters were 12-15 mins.

In a contest at Lewisburg on Saturday, November 16th, the Academy got back into the winning column by defeating the Bucknell Academy, 14-10. Forest Decker scored 2 touchdowns in the 2nd half with end runs and fine broken field running. Sullivan of the Bison booted an 11-yard field goal in the 4th period. The game was played in 10 and 12 minute quarters. Ref. Whittam was from Bucknell and Ump. Church hailed from Bloomsburg Normal.

The Academy left Bellefonte for Wilkes-Barre at noon on Friday for a 3:30 pm. meeting with a strong Wyoming Seminary aggregation on Saturday, November 23rd. 800 fans witnessed an Academy score only 4 minutes into the contest, as Loucks lofted a 30-yard forward pass to Beattie for a touchdown. Beattie booted the extra point for a 7-0 lead. Wyoming took the ensuing kickoff and rushed up the field with Shoulin crossing the goal line. Wyoming failed to kick the goal, making the score 7-6. In the 3rd quarter, Decker had a 60-yard run, which the umpire called back for holding. In the final period, the Seminarians fumbled, and Decker scooped up the ball and ran 40 yards for a touchdown. Beattie added the point-after kick. Wyoming came right back, but had to settle for a 23-yard Evans field goal and a 14-9 loss. Officials: Referee Seeley of Dickinson; Umpire Albert of Lafayette. On Tues. night, Nov. 26, the victory was celebrated by 500 people with a large bonfire.

The final game of the 1912 season was at Steelton against Steelton High and the Academy prevailed, 21-14. Walter Loucks had a 90-yard run for a touchdown in the first quarter, and he and Beer each added a td in the same period for a 21-0 lead. Aided by penalties, Steelton scored in the 3rd quarter on a run and in the 4th period via a 15-yard pass. Bloyd kicked 3 goals after touchdowns. Beer replaced the injured Decker. Carpeneto and Loucks excelled for the Academy. The Cougars claimed to be the top team in Pennsylvania despite the loss to Indiana. The Athletic Banquet was held at the Bush House Feb. 21, 1913.

On Saturday, Nov. 9th, the students of the Main Building and those of the "Frat" House met to decide which had a better football team. The teams were evenly matched, and at the end of the first half, the Gamma Beta Iota House held a 2-0 lead as the result of a safety touchdown. The fray featured more disputes than plays. The players for the Main Building were Holley, Creal, Schmoll, Lines, Chalfont, Renner, Elliott, Kann, Captain Hadesty, Welsenburn, and Hunter. The "Frat" House was represented by Francis, Smith, Doe, H. Eisenbeis, Horne, Heim, McKee, McClure, Bemus, Jones, and Irwin. The Referees were Van Every, Main Building; and Collopy of the "Frat" House. Umpires were Goldsmith of the "Frat" and Dalrymple of the Main Building. The Head Linesman was Andorn and Schaffner was the Time Keeper. Time of qtrs.were 8, 10, 8, 10. The water boy was unknown. The Frat House was at the north corner of East Curtin and North Allegheny Streets.

G.B.I. Frat House

Jim Thorpe, 6' 1", 202 lbs., was an All-American at Carlisle in 1912; and the Indians finished 3rd in the country with a record of 12-1-1 behind Champion Harvard and Penn State. President Dwight Eisenhower played on the Army team that lost to Carlisle 27-6. The other victims of "Pop" Warner's team were: Albright, Lebanon Valley, Dickinson, Villanova, Syracuse, Pittsburgh, Georgetown, Toronto All-Stars, Lehigh, Springfield, and Brown. The lone loss was to Penn, and the tie was with Washington & Jefferson.

Also in 1912, Thorpe won Gold Medals in the Decathlon & Pentathlon at the Olympics in Stockholm, Sweden. A Native American of Sac and Fox lineage, he was declared the greatest athlete of the 20th century out of 15 other athletes in a poll of sports fans conducted by ABC News in 2000, which included Muhammad Ali, Babe Ruth, Jesse Owens, Wayne Gretzky, Jack Nicklaus, and Michael Jordan.

Thorpe

REFINED

MINSTRELSY

BY

THE STUDENTS

OF THE

BELLEFONTE ACADEMY

SECOND ANNUAL APPEARANCE

GARMAN'S OPERA HOUSE, BELLEFONTE, PA.

TUESDAY EVENING, FEB. 23,

1909.

BENEFIT OF NEW ATHLETIC FIELD.

Frame your mind to mirth and merriment, which bars a thousand harms and lengthens life.

New Athletic Field

An 800' by 375' plot was leased from Col. Reynolds by Mr. James Hughes for 5 years with the option to buy. The area was on a high level on East Bishop St., away from the smoke of factories and trains. The old field was sold by Hughes for an automobile factory.

Bill Bloyd, Beattie, and Decker went to the University of Pittsburgh and joined up with former Academy footballers Smith, Dillon, and Chuck Reese.

The Bush House

28

1913 Bellefonte Academy 5-4 Cougars

Sitting in front with striped sleeves: Clarence Hullihen, qb. **First row, L-R:** Richard Jones, hb; Clarence Tobey, e; Ernest Poole, hb; William Long, hb; J. Eisenbrown, g; Joseph Carpeneto, c; Elliott Jones, hb; Edwin Beer, e; Thomas Mangan, qb; Robert Kann, qb; Thomas Thompson, g. **Second row:** Wilson Hayes, e; Paul Smith, e; Leland Stanford, t; Alex Hammond, c; Captain Clifford Carlson, e; Clarence Hachmeister, g; Melvin Locke, t; Philip Guthrie, e. **Third row:** Manager Oscar Weaver; Paul Jones, hb; Tom Casey, t; Edward Stahl, g; Walter Swain, t; Clyde Jones, fb; Jacob Hildebrand, g; Harold Thompson, g; Clarence Leathers, g; Coach E. C. Weller. **Reserves:** Manager Alex Chalfont, Henry Holley, Robert Kann, Edward Fried.

Beer

Mangan

P. Jones

1913 Bellefonte Academy 6-3 Cougars

First row, L-R: Smith, End; Long, Half Back; J. Eisenbrown, Guard; Captain Carlson, End; Carpeneto, Center; E. Jones, Half Back; Beer, End. **Second row:** Casey, Tackle; Stanford, Tackle; Swain, Tackle; C. Jones, Full Back; Hildebrand, Guard; Hammond, Center; Mangan, Quarter Back. **Third row:** Manager Weaver; W. Hayes, End; P. Jones, Left Half Back; Stahl, Guard; Thompson, Guard; Hullihen, Quarter Back; Coach E. C. Weller.

On Sept. 27, Altoona P.R.R. Team got untracked and went to the airways scoring 14 points against the 1913 Cougars in the first half at Bellefonte. Lang had a 25-yard pass reception for a touchdown; and Gearhart tallied on a 20-yard pass. In the 4th quarter, J. Hauffman hit pay dirt from 10 yards out ending Altoona's scoring at 21-0.

Greensburg High's Shields had a touchdown run of 1 yard in the initial quarter, and the 6-0 lead over the Blue and Gold held up the rest of the Oct. 11 game.

Indiana Normal put 6 points on the board in both the 2nd and 4th periods to sink the Academy 12-0 on Oct. 18. Gano had a 10-yard touchdown run and Markle recovered a Bellefonte fumble in the end zone for the 2nd score.

The Academy's first win came at the hands of rival Dickinson Seminary, 33-0 on Oct. 25. Bellefonte's passing game was clicking, as the Cougars rang up 21 points in the first quarter, 6 points in the 3rd, and 6 in the 4th.

On Nov. 1, Bellefonte completely outplayed Bloomsburg Normal; and 14 points in the first half were enough to earn a 14-0 victory.

After a lapse of 6 years, Kiski challenged the Academy to a game, but would not agree to play in Bellefonte, so Tyrone was selected as a neutral field. The game on Saturday, Nov. 8 ended in dispute with Kiski ahead, 5-0; and ended athletic relations between the 2 schools, as well. Kiski won, 1-0 by way of a forfeit. The Pennsylvania Railroad Band of Tyrone played for the 2:30 game. In order to arrive in time, Bellefonte patrons had to leave on the early afternoon train.

Two days after the game with Kiski was scheduled, the Academy football team was strengthened by Long, who enrolled as a student. He was not eligibleto play in that game, but would be in the lineup for the next contest with the Penn State freshmen.

Neutral officials were engaged for the Bellefonte game with the Penn State College freshmen on Saturday afternoon, November 15. Both teams entered the game with a clear understanding that neither was to leave until the final whistle. After a scoreless first quarter on a muddy field at Bellefonte, the Cougars and the Penn State College Frosh each scored touchdowns in the 2nd. The Academy added 7 more points in the 3rd period and 6 in the last quarter for a 19-6 win. The 3 p.m. game attracted the largest crowd of the season, the Penn State team being accompanied by a delegation of several hundred, along with a brass band. The game was hotly contested from start to finish; and the last 10 minutes of play were so late that the field was almost dark and spectators could hardly distinguish the players. Admission was 25 cents.

Wyoming Seminary used a shift play to start the Nov. 22 game which resulted in a long run; but was shut out by the Academy until the 4th period when 7 points were put on the board. Bellefonte's first score came on a forward pass in the initial quarter and the Cougars tacked on 7 more in the 3rd for a 13-7 triumph. The Saturday game began at 2:30.

On Thanksgiving Day, Nov. 27, Bellefonte travelled to Binghampton, New York, for the first time to play a game in that section. The parents of one of the several Binghampton boys at the Academy made the arrangements for the contest. Such a trip necessitated a large guarantee, which was nevertheless put up by Binghampton High School. The Academy threw 3 interceptions near the Binghamton goal line; but 2 Bellefonte touchdowns in the first half sealed a 14-0 win in the regular season ender.

The football team made a trip to Houston, Texas for an exhibition game; but it was cancelled due to rain, and the team found itself stranded without the price of fare home since they lost their share of the gate receipts. A team in Oklahoma decided to test the might of the Bellefonte Academy team, and enough funds were raised to bring the boys back to Centre County.

On Thursday evening, December 18, 1913, at 8:30 p.m., the Bellefonte Academy foot ball dance was held in the Arcade Hall. The interesting innovation marked the winding up of the foot ball season and the opening of the holiday season. On that occasion, Mr. James R. Hughes presented foot ball letters to the Varsity and scrub players who developed under the splendid coaching of E.C. Weller, who led the Academy eleven to a Pennsylvania state prep school championship last season. Any friends of the Academy desiring to attend the dance were asked to apply to George R. McKee, chairman of the committee for tickets.

At the end of the 1913 football season, the elimination of football from West Point athletes was advocated in the annual report of Colonel Townsley, superintendent of the West Point Military Academy. Colonel Townsley stated that 75 % of the men needing the attention of surgeons at West Point last year were injured in football games. This, he asserted, was not adequate compensation for the physical training resulting from participation in the pastime.

Ed "Jake" Stahl—played high school football at Greensburg-Salem, as well as the Bellefonte Academy in the 1913-14 seasons. He went on to play guard and tackle for the University of Pittsburgh from 1915-1918, where he was a 2nd team All-American in 1918. The 1917 team coached by Glenn Scobey "Pop" Warner was undefeated at 10-0; and was dubbed the "Fighting Dentists" since on occasion every position was *filled* by a dental student.

Stahl

Pittsburgh's football *practice* consisted of many *drills*, much to the delight of future dentists Stahl, Kaly Easterly, Skip Gougler, Tank McLaren, and Jock Sutherland.

Jake Stahl was Duquesne University's head football coach in 1920 and 1921 while playing professional football with the Cleveland Tigers and the Dayton Triangles. He officiated high school and college football for 40 years.

A 33-game winning streak by Pitt was snapped by Syracuse in 1919 by a score of 24-3.

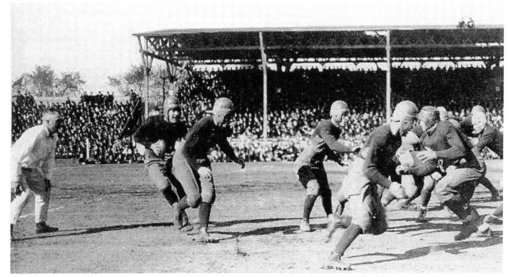

Photo at left:

George Gipp, legendary football player at Notre Dame, carries the ball for the Irish in 1919.

1914 Bellefonte Academy 6-1 Foot Ball Team

On September 3, 1914, Bellefonte Academy Coach E.C. Weller was replaced with Oliver J. Vogel of Butler, PA. The Manager was Chalfont, a Penn State College grad.

Members were: Captain Beer, Scrubby Jones, Casey Jones, Elliott Jones, Fried, Hullihen, Long, Hachmeister, Mangan, Hildebrand, Leathers, , Stanford, Stahl, R. Jones, and Locke.

At right: Cover of Sam Hess's handbook.

The Academy opened up the 1914 season Sept. 26 with the Penn State College Reserves and won, 19-0. Bellefonte put 7 first period points on the board; and tallied 6 in each of the 2nd and 3rd quarters.

Hughes Field on East Bishop Street in Bellefonte was the scene of a 2:15 meeting with Saint Francis Academy Oct. 8. The Cougars rang up scores in all 4 quarters as Monahan had 2 scores and Hullihen had a 90-yard touchdown run in the 25-0 victory. Admission was 25 cents.

Indiana Normal again proved to be a nemesis, giving Bellefonte its only loss of the season to the tune of 13-6 on Oct. 17. Long had a short run of 7 yards for the Cougar score; and Indiana's White (70-yard kickoff return) and Carroll (25-yard pass) tallied for the host Maroon and Grey.

At Bellefonte on Oct. 24 the Carlisle Indian Reserves were no match for the Blue and Gold as the Cougars had numerous long runs and passes which resulted in 33 first half points. The Indians looked lost on defense as the Cougars added 13 points in the 2nd half in the 46-0 rout.

Bellefonte's first team tallied 32 points in the first half against Bloomsburg Normal at Bloomsburg on Oct. 31 and the scrubs tacked on another 13 in the 2nd half for a 45-0 whitewash.

On Nov. 7 the Penn State College Freshman Team gave the Academy a good game; but fell to Bellefonte, 27-13. The Cougars led 14-7 at the half and never trailed at State College.

In the final game of the season, the Renovo Y.M.C.A. was completely outclassed by the Cougars, who scored 40 points in the first half and coasted to a 47-0 victory on Nov. 14.

Two other games—DuBois High at Bellefonte and Duquesne at Pittsburgh were not played.

1915 Bellefonte Academy 6-2 Cougars

Sitting in front: Cheerleader Kelly.

1st row, L-R: Coach Hartman; Shenk, End; Curley, Half Back; Schaffner, Quarter Back; Brennan, Half Back; Smith, Full Back. **2nd row:** Manager Grimm; Poole, End; Hunter, Tackle; Stanford, Guard; Captain J. Lochrie, Tackle; Casey, Guard; Smoczynski, End; Riddle, Guard; Powell, End. **3rd row:** Fried, Tackle; Kelsch, Guard; Fawcett, End; Montgomery, Full Back; Risley, Tackle; Weaver, Centre; Van der Sloot, Tackle; Schonleber, End; Niles, Guard; Samson, Tackle. **Fourth row:** Manuel, Centre; Spear, Quarter Back; Goodling, Half Back; Hasson, Half Back; R. Lochrie, Full Back.

Curley of the Cougars scored touchdowns in the first and 4th quarters and the Academy rolled to a 14-7 win over the Bucknell Reserves. The victory indicated Bellefonte would have a strong team for the 1915 season.

The Academy pushed across a touchdown in the 3rd period and earned a hard-fought 7-0 upset win over the Pitt Freshmen.

Bellefonte led the Carlisle Indian Scrubs 12-6 at the half and a field goal in the 4th quarter was good for a 15-6 victory.

Mansfield Normal was the 4th straight victim of the Academy in a tight, 14-7 game. The Cougars were on Mansfield's 1-foot line when the game ended.

Bellefonte's John Lochrie and Joe Brennan were out with injuries; and the Penn State Freshmen completely outclassed the Blue and Gold gridders. The Frosh put 37 points on the board in the first 3 quarters and coasted to a 37-3 triumph. The Academy avoided a shutout by kicking a 21-yard field goal in the final period.

The Cornell Freshmen pinned the 2nd loss on the 1915 Cougars to the tune of 40-7. All the Big Red points were in the first 3 periods, while the Academy managed crack into the scoring column in the last quarter with 7 points.

The Bellefonte Academy travelled to Loretto to take on Saint Francis College and jumped out to a 13-0 first period lead. Single touchdowns were added in each of the next 3 quarters for a 31-0 victory over the Red Flash.

In the final game of the season for the Academy, the Cougars were victorious over the Penn State College Scrubs, 7-0. The score took place in the 3rd period.

Christian "Mose" Kelsch—born in Pittsburg in 1897, Kelsch was a guard on the 1915 Bellefonte Academy football team. He later played semi-pro football in the Steel City with the Hope Harvey's, the James R. Rooney's, and the Majestic Radio Team as a running back and field goal kicker. Mose was a charter member of the Pittsburgh Pirates (Steelers) n 1933 and kicked field goals at the age of 36. Kelsch may have been the first "specialist" in the National Football League. He died in an automobile accident in 1935.

Kelsch

Quaker Meeting House (left); Headmaster's House (centre); Academy (right) in 1915.

1916—Record 5-3

The Cougars jumped out to an early 7-0 lead over the Lewistown Athletics and tacked on 12 more points in the 3rd period for a 19-0 win.

The 4th quarter was scoreless in the contest between the Academy and the Bucknell Reserves; but Bellefonte racked up 20 points spread over the first 3 periods for its 2nd victory of the season.

The Jersey Shore Ex-Highschoolers were no match for the Academy, as the Blue and Gold triumphed, 24-0.

A large crowd witnessed a heavier Pitt Freshman team topple the Academy, 7-6. Bellefonte got on the board first; but missed on the extra point try. All the scoring took place in the first half.

On November 4, Indiana Normal and the Academy journeyed to Greensburg and played in a drizzling rain. Bellefonte held Indiana Normal to zero first downs and completed 3 of 6 passes for 60 yards; but went down to defeat in a sea of mud. The Indians' Lytle had a 70-yard punt return for a touchdown in the 3rd quarter; and an Indiana safety in the 4th made the final score 9-0.

In a rematch, the Cougars mauled the Lewistown Athletics 51-0.

The Penn State Freshmen exploded for 19 first half points and coasted to a 25-0 victory. The final period was scoreless.

Bellefonte pushed across a touchdown in the 3rd quarter and hung on to defeat Mansfield Normal 7-0 in the final game of the season.

Jay S. "Tiny" McMahon—a 6' 7", 215 lb. tackle and guard for the Bellefonte Academy in the 1916 and 1917 seasons, who refused to wear a headgear when playing football. He lettered at Penn State in 1921&1922 and was a member of the undefeated teams of 1920 and 1921. He was an All-American tackle and captained the Rose Bowl Team of 1923. He earned a degree in Commerce and Finance and received a Distinguished Alumni Award in 1975 due to his invention of the sinter blast furnace that revolutionized America's steel industry.
Tiny died on March 22, 1987, just 2 days before his 90th birthday.

McMahon

35

1917—Record 1-2

President Woodrow Wilson pledged neutrality when World War I began in 1914. However, the Germans were sinking U.S. ships traveling to Britain; and on May 7, 1915, the British ship *Lusitania* was torpedoed without warning. 1,198 of the 1,959 passengers were killed including 128 Americans.

In spite of an apology, the German U-boats continued to sink U.S. merchant ships; and on April 2, 1917 Wilson appeared before Congress and asked for a declaration of war.

Two days after the U.S. Senate voted 82 to 6 to declare war against Germany, the U.S. House of Representatives endorsed the declaration by a vote of 373 to 50; and America formally entered World War I on April 6, 1917.

The 1917 Bellefonte Academy football season was an off-year as no effort was made to recruit new athletes. Many of the prospective football candidates had enlisted in the military service of the United States of America.

Two dozen members of the Academy including the football team and the Milesburg Boys Band made the trip over the seven mountains to take on the Lewistown Athletic Club. The Cougars scored touchdowns in the first 3 quarters in a 19-0 win. On the way home, the group made a wrong turn at Reedsville and ended up in Huntingdon County. Near Pine Grove Mills, the Ford ran into a ditch and hit a fence post. No serious wreck occurred; but the party didn't get home until the wee hours of the morning.

1917 Ford

In a game played at Johnstown, the Indiana Normal squad must have used U-boats to sink the Academy, 106-0. The relentless attack was led by Jones with 5 touchdowns, Millean with 4, and Williams with 3. Redman, Kellogg, Potts, and Dickinson each hit pay dirt; while placekicker Crawford tacked on 10 extra points in one of the most lop-sided games in college history.

The Penn State Freshmen put 46 points on the board in the first 3 periods and coasted to a 46-0 victory over Bellefonte.

The last game of the season was to be a rematch with the Lewistown Athletic Club; but no results could be found.

America's entry into World War I required the mobilization of the country's brightest minds and ablest bodies for military training and leadership. The War Department looked to American Universities to recruit capable men for its military departments. The recruitment effort prompted establishment of 2 prominent military organizations—the Reserve Officers' Training Corp (ROTC) and the Student Army Training Corp (SATC).

The SATC was a way for the colleges to contribute to the war in a greater way. Students were trained to be soldiers while taking part in a collegiate learning atmosphere. A minimum of 100 able-bodied men of military age was required to establish a military unit in a college.

Equipment and uniforms provided by the U.S. War Department were slow in reaching campuses. The students were trained on campus, but it was a slow process. Many colleges were hit by the flu bug resulting in quarantines during the whole period of enlistment.

By May, 1917, 1000 men had withdrawn from the University of Illinois to fight in WWI, leaving 1200 in the campus military department. The following fall, the SATC had grown to 3500.

1918—Record 1-1

William Stitzinger of new Castle left the Academy and enlisted in the Army in 1917; but got sick and was discharged on January 25, 1918.

On May 3, 1918, Academy students were being drilled by an U.S. Army officer who was assigned from State College.

The Bellefonte Academy scored 19 first half points and added another 12 in the 4th quarter to defeat the SATC of Bucknell, 31-0.

The Penn State Freshmen were 6-0 winners over the Cougars.

In the fall of 1918 a pandemic of influenza swept across the world. A few weeks after the academic year began the entire Pitt campus was placed under quarantine and the football schedule was cancelled which included a game between the SATC of Pitt and the Academy. 23,000 were sickened in Pittsburgh and 5000 died. 548,000 Americans died; 20,000 of them servicemen. 20 million were lost world-wide. Of the 2 million who served on Europe's battlefields, 50,000 Americans were killed by war's end on Nov. 11, 1918.

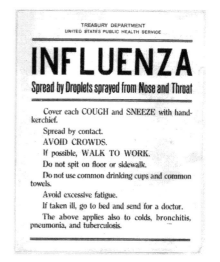

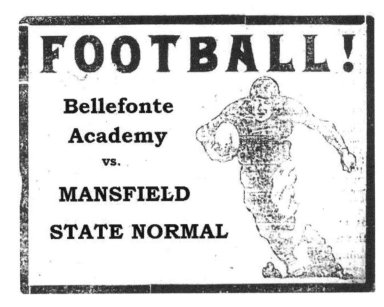

FOOTBALL!

Bellefonte Academy vs. MANSFIELD STATE NORMAL

1919—Record 3-2

The Bellefonte Academy Cougars, with "Red" Fleming as Captain, began the season with a 13-0 victory over an All-Scholastic Team of Altoona. All the scoring took place in the middle 2 quarters.

In a game with the Pitt Freshmen, all Bellefonte could muster was a safety in the 2nd period. The Pittsburgers put 35 points on the scoreboard in the first half and added another 21 in the 2nd half in burying the Academy, 56-2.

The Penn State Freshmen handed the Academy its 2nd loss—this time by a 2-0 margin. A safety in the 2nd quarter accounted for the only points in the contest.

Mansfield Normal became a Bellefonte victim by the score of 34-0. The Cougars rang up 14 points in the first period, 7 in the 2nd, and 13 in the 3rd in the whitewash.

The Cougars jumped out to a 20-0 lead over Dickinson Seminary in the opening period, and upended the Williamsport Methodists by a score of 40-0.

Games were scheduled with the Syracuse Freshmen and the Bucknell Freshmen, but no results could be found.

In 1919, Albion College of Michigan defeated the Detroit Naval Training School by a score of 178-0.

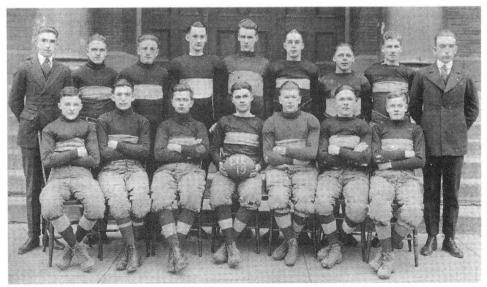

1919 Bellefonte High School Football Team First row—L-R: Phil Johnson, end; Paul Rider, center; Musser Gettig, guard; Walter Fravel, Captain and end; Jay Smith, halfback; Dallas Bullock, tackle; Phil Saylor, guard. **Second row:** Hugh Johnson, Manager; Merle Wetzel, sub back; Bert Tingue, fullback; Jack Decker, quarterback; Gib Waite, tackle; Bill Kline, fullback; Dick Herman, halfback; Fred Herr, guard; Earl K. Stock, coach.

1920—Record 6-3

The Bellefonte Academy football team had a tough schedule but had an exceptional group of strong players:

Captain Buchanan, center; Cronie Carnahan, 210 lbs.; Akin, 198 lbs., played at Mount Union College 2 years previous; Alwine, 240 lb. tackle, handled kickoffs and field goals; "Doc" Hillard, 188 lb. tackle from Indiana Normal; "Dish" Rigby, a strong defensive end at 165 lbs.; Ends Bill Ashbaugh (185 lbs.) and King (175 lbs.), both successful in getting open and catching passes.

Backs: Boyd Pashall (190 lbs.) and Dick Frauenheim (165 lbs.) divided honors in calling signals and running the team; Bob Irwin, 173 lbs., a wonderful line plunger; Charles Fleming, 165 lbs.; McBride, 185 lbs., from Wyoming Seminary; Marsh Johnson, 190 lb. star fullback, due to his line plunging ability, fleet-footedness, and his ability to drive low punts into the opponents' territory.

The home opener was at Hughes Field in Bellefonte at 2:15 p.m. against Altoona High. The Cougars scored in every period en route to a 33-0 shutout. Admission was 25 cents.

The Academy outplayed Wyoming Seminary, having had 2 touchdowns called back due to penalties. Cougar Marshall Johnson scored on a 3-yard run in the 3rd quarter for a 7-0 win.

The contest with the Bucknell Reserves was moved to 10:15 a.m. so as not to interfere with the Penn State-Dartmouth game. The Blue and Gold scored in the first and 3rd periods for a 13-0 victory. The Academy had a Poverty Parade that night with Academy students dressed as hobos and such.

The Carnegie Tech Reserves were the next Bellefonte victim, as the Cougars pushed across touchdowns in the first 3 periods for a 19-0 win. The game began at 2:15 p.m. and 25 cents was the price of admission.

Juniata College fell to the Academy by a score of 14-0 as a result of Cougar counters in the middle 2 periods.

The Penn State Freshmen jumped out to a 21-0 lead at the half; and scored again in the 3rd quarter for a 27-0 win. Charles Fleming, one of the fastest backs to don the blue and gold, did not play and was out until the final game of the season.

Mansfield State Normal took the measure of the Academy, 7-0, having scored a touchdown in the 3rd quarter.

In a rematch with the Penn State Freshmen, Bellefonte played tough, but was defeated 14-7. All the scoring took place in the 3rd period.

Bellefonte got back into the winning column in the last game of the season by thrashing Dickinson Seminary 48-7. The final period was scoreless.

1921 Bellefonte Academy 1-3-3 Cougars

First row, L-R: Prichard, guard; Raschella, fullback; LaBerge, guard; Hillard, tackle; Captain Irwin, quarterback; Dare, end; Byer, center; Kishbaugh, tackle; Van Hee, tackle; McCabe, guard.

Second row: Watkins, Assistant Manager; Schmidt, halfback; Amann, halfback; Linn, quarterback; Quinn, halfback; Lease, guard; Korber, end; Smith, guard; DeWaters, halfback; H. Linn, guard; Lashley, center. **Third row:** Coach Dunbar; Hughes, end; Shuey, tackle; Alexander, end; Sailor, end; Berkes, fullback; C. Smith, end; McCleary, end; Bash, halfback; Rigby, halfback; Waddell, Manager.

The Academy season began with a 0-0 tie with the Bucknell Reserves.

In a 13-0 loss to the Penn State Freshmen, Bellefonte had some success at the State terminals; but the freshmen were strong with their line bucks.

The Cougars had a 13-7 halftime lead; but Greensburg High came on strong in the 2nd half and put 18 points on the board for a 25-13 victory.

Juniata College proved to be no match for Bellefonte, as the Cougars romped to a 64-0 win after scoring 20 points in the first quarter.

The Carnegie Tech Reserves and the Academy battled to a 0-0 tie.

The Academy had a date with the Potomac State School of West Virginia on Armistice Day, November 11th; and the contest ended in a 0-0 deadlock.

In a game with the Pitt Freshmen, the Panthers put 7 points on the scoreboard in each quarter and upended the Cougars, 28-0.

No results for the game scheduled with Wyoming Seminary.

William "Bill" Ashbaugh—Star Center at Washington High School; played End at the Bellefonte Academy in 1920-21 at 185 lbs; was a Fullback-Wingback at the University of Pittsburgh in 1924-25. He was also was a member of the pro Rock Island Independents in 1924 and the Kansas City Cowboys in 1923-25.

Martin Albert "Butch" Kottler—born in Carnegie in 1910, and attended high school at the Bellefonte Academy. Played football at Centre College in Danville, Kentucky and was a charter member of the Pittsburgh Pirates (Steelers) in 1933.

Marty scored the first touchdown in the Steeler franchise history on a 99-yard interception return. The record stood until Super bowl XLIII in 2009 when James Harrison returned an interception 100 yards for a touchdown against Arizona.

Kottler in 1933

Kottler served in the U.S. Army Corp in World War II and the Korean War, attaining the rank of Captain. He left the military in 1953 and had a long career in the auto industry and as an executive at Avis. He died in 1989.

1922 Bellefonte Academy 7-2 Football Team
First row, L-R: Hill, O'Brien, Quinn, Schmidt, Captain Linn, Van Hee, Jennewine, White, McCabe. **Second row:** M. Wilson, Korber, Preece, Breon, Archibald, Labelsky, O'Neil, Coleman, Blackburn, Mates. **Third row:** Manager Tullis, Coach Wilson, Amann, Rockey, Mosko, Van Horn, Buchanan, Assistant Manager Rynd.

1922—Record 7-2

Academy Coach Wilson was greeted by 16 candidates from New England, New York, New Jersey, Pennsylvania, and West Virginia. The husky players worked hard to develop a winning team.

Potomac State School came to Hughes Field for a 3 p.m. meeting with the Academy and went back to Keyser, West Virginia on the short end of a 27-0 score. The largest opening game crowd in Cougar history witnessed a Bellefonte defense that did not allow the visitors to threaten its goal.

The Penn State Freshmen scored a touchdown in the 2nd period for a 6-0 triumph over the Academy. The Blue and Gold protested the loss based on the actions of a prejudiced referee.

The Cougars jumped out to a 33-0 halftime lead and coasted to a 40-0 victory over Mansfield State Normal. The 4th quarter was scoreless.

In a game played in Pittsburgh, the Academy took the measure of the Carnegie Tech Reserves by a score of 13-0. All the points were scored in the 2nd and 4th periods.

The Jersey Shore PRR Shop team seemed bewildered in an 82-0 onslaught by the Bellefonte eleven. The score at halftime was 48-0.

Before the largest crowd ever, the Academy came up short against the Pitt Freshmen, 10-6. The freshmen held a 7-6 lead at intermission; but a 4th quarter field goal by Pitt sealed the fate of the Cougars. Right halfback Hill of Bellefonte injured his leg and his return was unlikely.

The Academy put 6 points on the board in each quarter in a 24-0 victory over St. Francis College of Loretto.

Bellefonte turned a 13-6 halftime lead into a 25-12 victory over the Bucknell Reserves, scoring 12 points in the 3rd period.

Cougar scores in the 2nd and 4th quarters were good enough to defeat the West Virginia Reserves, 12-0.

1923 Bellefonte Academy 7-1 Football Team
Front row, L-R: Guarino, Blackburn, Prichard, Dimeolo, Cutler, O'Neil, Mosko, Conacher, Breon, Beck, Frawley. **Second row:** McAdams, Barbeson, Berkes, Buyny, Shively, McDowell, E. Williams, Captain Welch, Morrow, Cotton, Kutz. **Third row:** H. Williams, Walsh, Hull, Grimm, Lewis, McNally, Rabe, Hansell, Davidson, Wittman, Field, Coach Snavely, Hensen, Soisson, Manager Rynd.

1923—Record 7-1

Carl G. Snavely, who produced strong teams at Kiski, accepted the coaching jobs for all teams at the Academy. He graduated from Lebanon Valley College.

The Academy worked before films shot by a local man at Snavely's request. Only 5 players returned from the 1922 team; but 30 players were out for the 1923 team with an average weight of 180 pounds. Forming the nucleus for the '23 team were Blackburn, O'Neil, Mosko, O'Brien, and Archibald.

Under Snavely, the Cougars had an effective passing game in 1923, completing 25 passes out of 33 attempts with one interception.

The Academy completed 2 passes out of 2 attempts and routed Potts College 58-0. The Cougars had a 40-0 lead at halftime.

Bellefonte pushed across a touchdown in the 4th quarter and downed the Penn Freshmen, 6-0. Snavely's squad was 4 for 6 in the aerial game.

Mosco, Academy tackle, tore a ligament in his right shoulder in an automobile accident on his way to the St. Francis College game. His teammates scored 42 points in the first half and 26 in the 2nd for a 68-0 victory over the Frankies.

The Blue and Gold Cougars scored a touchdown in every period, upending the Bucknell Freshmen, 27-0. O'Neil had a 95 yard run for a score. Teammates Brandiff and McClure were slightly injured; but both were expected to play the following week. Bellefonte complete 3 of 3 passes.

In a game against the Pitt Freshmen, Bellefonte turned a 13-7 first half advantage into a 27-7 win against the Panthers. The Cougars were 5 of 6 in the passing department with an interception. O'Neil had a 60-yard touchdown run.

The 6th game of the 1923 season was another big victory for the Academy at Cumberland, Maryland. The Cougars shut out the Potomac State School by a score of 27-0; and completed 5 passes out of 5. O'Neil had 2 touchdowns, Berkes 1, and Blackburn 1. Blackburn tacked on 3 extra point kicks in the contest which was played before 1500 spectators.

The Carnegie Tech Freshmen were the 7th straight Bellefonte victim in a 40-0 victory. The Academy was 3 of 6 in the air; and O'Neil had 133 yards rushing. The 4th period was scoreless.

The West Virginia Freshmen put 14 points on the board in the first half; and tacked on another 7 in the final period in handing the Academy its only loss. The Cougars completed only 1 pass in 2 attempts in the 21-0 defeat.

Academy players on 1922 College Football Teams: Tiny McMahon (Penn State); Frauenheim and Alwine (Lehigh); Johnson, Ashbaugh, Carnahan, and Atkins (Pitt); McBride (Syracuse); Parshall (Allegheny); Raschella and Kishbaugh (Buckhannon Wesleyan); Davis (West Virginia); Wilson (Virginia); and Jackson (Hamilton University).

John J. "Harp" Vaughan—a single-wing tailback born in Philadelphia in 1903; played his high school football at the Bellefonte Academy; college ball at Indiana Normal of Pennsylvania; and professionally with the Pittsburgh Pirates (Steelers) of the National Football League in 1933 and 1934.

John F. "Jack" McBride—Played at Conshocken H.S., then Bellefonte in 1920-21as a fullback/halfback/quarterback. He went to Syracuse U.; then played pro football with the N.Y. Giants, Providence Steamrollers, and Brooklyn Dodgers.

Luby Dimeolo—Born in Youngstown, Ohio in 1903; played high school football at the Bellefonte Academy. Luby was a captain and guard on the 1929 undefeated Pitt football team. He was an offensive line coach at New York University, and assistant coach at Westminster College of Pennsylvania and Carnegie Tech. Dimeolo was the 2nd head coach of the Pittsburgh Steelers, going 2-10. He was a Navy veteran of World War II and died of a heart attack in 1966 at age 62.

John E. Dreshar—Played on the Bellefonte Academy football team of 1923-24; starred at Carnegie Tech where he was an All-American. Dreshar was a member of the Academy boxing team, earning the nickname "Knockout John". He coached high school football at Tarentum, Pennsylvania, where the stadium is named after him. He later coached at Beaver Falls High School, north of Pittsburgh.

Charles Merrill "Dutch" Waite— Dutch is pictured below as a player at the Bellefonte Academy in 1926. Dutch played 4 years of varsity football at BHS before

enrolling at the Academy where he starred in football and track. He lived at home in Bellefonte while a student at the "School on the Hill".

Charles Merrill Waite, Jr., better known as "Chuck", owns and operates Waite's Body Shop on Zion Road in Bellefonte.

Bellefonte Academy

Bellefonte, Pa.

The 1924 Bellefonte Academy 8-0-1 Cougars—National Prep Champions

1924 Bellefonte Academy Backs. Franklin Hood is on the far right.

Led by freshman Franklin Hood, who completed forward passes that were hurled 65 yards in the air, the Bellefonte Academy with the support of Coach Carl G. Snavely and Headmaster James R. Hughes issued a challenge to play any prep school in the country. The 1924 national champions were sparked by Edwin "Dutch" Hill, "Jimmy" Rooney, and Herman LaMark.

45

The 25 Cougar players, who represented one-fourth of the school enrollment, scored 456 points against none for their 9 opponents. The tie with the Pitt Freshmen was a great feat, inasmuch as the Pitt Varsity was beaten twice by the Frosh in practice.

After beating St. Thomas College 61-0 in the final game of the 1924 season in front of 7500 fans, a Scranton newspaper crowned the Academy the prep school champion of the country, stating "The 456 points is believed to be the greatest score in the country this season by either college, normal, prep or high school. To this honor is added the distinction of holding all opponents scoreless and not having its 25-yard line crossed during the entire season."

Snavely

1924—Record 8-0-1

The season began with a 53-0 win over rival Dickinson Seminary. Hill had several long runs for the Academy and scored 2 touchdowns. The Cougar backs amassed over 300 yards rushing and Franklin Hood, Hartmann, and Jimmy Rooney each had 2 touchdowns. The 2nd team saw a lot of action with the score being 47-0 at the half. Dickinson was held to zero first downs.

With 6000 in attendance, Bellefonte topped the Syracuse Freshmen 28-0. Birney had an 80-yard touchdown run; and Franklin Hood found Green in the end zone at the end of a 19-yard pass.

Rooney scored the first touchdown against the Susquehanna Freshmen. The Selinsgrove Crusaders moved the ball 30 yards via the airways; but a fumble gave the ball to the Blue and Gold Cougars. From that point on, it was all Bellefonte, as Green was on the receiving end of a 50-yard touchdown pass from Hood, and Birney scored from 80 yards out in the 113-0 rout. Harry Burd, who became the Register of Wills of Centre County, played on the Susquehanna squad.

Against the Penn Freshmen, Franklin Hood had 150 yards rushing and tossed 3 touchdown passes—one to Albert Guarino for 81 yards. Whitmore had an 80-yard kickoff return for a score; Rooney hit pay dirt from 1 yard out; and Cunningham recovered a Penn fumble in the end zone for a touchdown in the 39-0 victory.

Bucknell was one of the great teams in the East in 1924, having beaten undefeated Navy and Rutgers on successive Saturdays; and had future Pitt Panthers Jimmy Rooney and Bill Hood on the roster. Bellefonte was scheduled to play the Bison Junior Varsity; but to make the game more interesting, Coach Moran sent 33 players to Bellefonte which included his second string line and backfield—a group that could battle the Bucknell varsity on even terms. Yet, Snavely's team stormed through the big, husky Bison line for 52 points; and could have made it 70 if they had so desired.

10,000 fans witnessed a hard-fought 0-0 deadlock between the Cougars and a strong group of Pitt Panther Freshmen.

Rooney had over 200 yards rushing including a 95-yard run and scored on runs of 25 and 80 yards against the Lafayette Freshmen in a 51-0 win. The Academy's Guarino had a 33-yard touchdown reception, Franklin Hood kicked a 35-yard field goal, and the Cougars scored a safety. Douglass of the 2nd team scored on the last play of the 1924 game. The winners put 31 points on the board in the 3rd quarter.

Albert Guarino scored 2 touchdowns, and Franklin Hood had another on a 70-yard punt return in a 59-0 trouncing of the West Virginia Freshmen.

The Bellefonte Academy capped off the 1924 undefeated season with a 61-0 whitewash of St. Thomas College at Scranton. Scoring touchdowns were Hill (2); Guarino (2); Whitmore (2); Hood (1); Jones (1); and Buyny (1). Whitmore kicked 4 extra points and Hood added 3 more with placekicks. St. Bonaventure College beat the Tommies 10-7; and Bona trounced Niagara College, indicating the strength of Snavely's team.

Conacher

Academy Coach Carl Snavely perfected the single wing trap play: The ball is snapped to the fullback (tailback in the single wing), who executes a spin, fakes a handoff to the left halfback, and then runs inside the defensive left guard who has been trapped by the offensive guard. Downfield blocks by the left end and wingback resulted long yardage.

Snavely supposedly used a shift before Knute Rockne at Notre Dame. Pop Warner and Rockne developed the spinner; but it was Snavely who made it into one of the most potent plays of the single wing formation.

Lionel "Big Train" Conacher—Born in Toronto, Canada in 1900, one of the greatest athletes in Canadian history. He played football at the Bellefonte Academy in 1923-24, then Duquesne University; and his team won professional championships in football (Grey Cup), baseball, and hockey (Stanley Cup). He also played lacrosse, wrestled, and boxed. His passion was football, and was known as the "Jim Thorpe of Canada". However, he was best known as a hockey player. He was elected to the House of Commons in 1949; and from 1955-1994 Conacher was elected to Canadian Halls of Fame in Sports, Football, Lacrosse, and Hockey.

Douds

Forrest McCreery Douds—Forrest "Jap" Douds played football on the Bellefonte Academy's National Championship Team in 1925; and became an All-American at Washington & Jefferson College in 1927-28. In 1928 Grantland Rice named him the greatest lineman in the nation. Douds played pro football with the Providence, Rhode Island Steamrollers, the Detroit Lions, and the Pittsburgh Pirates (Steelers). He was an All-Pro tackle in 1931; and was the first coach of the Pittsburgh Steelers when they entered the National Football League in 1933, recording a 3-6-2 mark. He was born on April 21, 1905 in Rochester, Pennsylvania and died on August 16, 1979 at the age of 74.

The 1924 Academy football team was honored at a banquet on Feb. 5, 1925 at 6:30 p.m. The guest speaker was Tom Davis, former All-American back at Pitt.

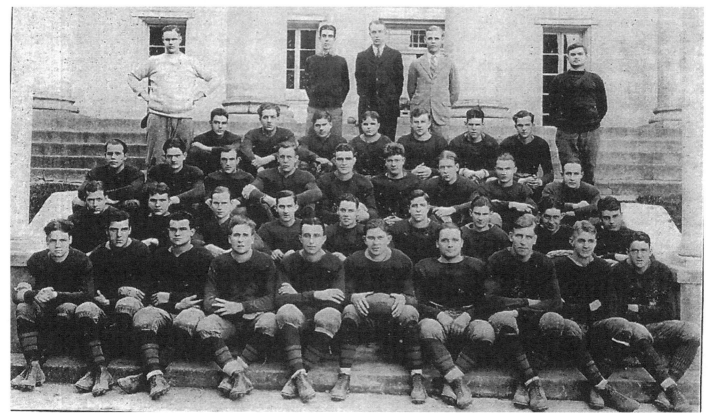

1925 Bellefonte Academy 10-1 Cougars—United States Prep School Champions
First row, L-R: Rankin, sub-end; Sankovic, sub-end; Dreshar, centre; Douds, guard; Yerina, sub-end; Captain Hood, fullback; Kozicki, guard; Schnupp tackle; Bowers, end; McGivern, sub-end. **Second row:** Bossart, sub-quarterback; Brogley, sub-guard; Whitmore, halfback; Marker, sub-quarterback; Thompson, sub-halfback; Dougherty, sub-halfback; Williams, halfback; Hinkle, end; Meckel, sub-guard. **Third row:** Duncan, sub-guard; Hensen, sub-tackle; Gaudet, quarterback; Lockwood, sub-tackle; Mutzel, tackle; Jones, sub-guard; Robbins, sub-end; Scheff, sub-halfback; Iseman, sub-tackle. **Fourth row:** Beachler, sub-end; Pokorny, sub-guard; Ducanis, sub-centre; Lechthaler, sub-halfback; Murphy, sub-fullback; Householder, sub-fullback; ?. **Standing:** Coach Snavely; Cheerleader Beilby; Manager Feit; Assistant Manager Long; Assistant Coach Summer. **Note:** The fullback in the single wing was the tailback.

The Academy jumped out to a 53-0 lead at the half against the Carlisle Army Barracks, and defeated the 1924 Third Corps Area Champs 95-0. Coach Snavely's fast, heavy team held Carlisle to zero first downs; and the strong Bellefonte line allowed Captain Hood, Whitmore, Hinkle, and Thompson to run wild. The 2nd team played the final 2 quarters with Heinie Marker and Josh Williams doing most of the damage. The 3rd team had a date with Lock Haven H. S.

In a very plucky game against California Normal, there was no score going into the 2nd period. California's touchdown pass was ruled illegal because it wasn't 5 yards behind the line of scrimmage.[5] A pass on the very next play carried to the Cougar one-foot line; but the Academy held on downs. The goal line stand fired up the Bellefonte boys, who proceeded to excel on both sides of the ball in the 32-0 victory.

---

[5] Prior to 1933, a forward pass had to be made 5 or more yards behind the line of scrimmage to be legal.

In a game played at Syracuse in the mud and wind in 1925, the field conditions had an adverse effect on Hood's passing. However, the Syracuse Freshmen completed an 11-yard touchdown pass 3 minutes into the contest for a 6-0 lead. Josh Williams broke loose for a 40-yard run; but the play was not used again that afternoon. The muddy field made running and tackling difficult for both teams; but in the last 3 minutes a Hood pass to a wide open Whitmore in the end zone was broken up by Sankovic, thus saving the game for the Orangemen.

On Fri., October 16th, the Bucknell Freshmen came to Bellefonte for a 3 p.m. encounter with the Cougars. Bellefonte wasted no time, putting 21 points on the board in the first quarter and had a 33-0 lead at halftime. Most of the Bison yards came via the air as the Academy 2nd team saw much action. Williams had a 70-yard punt return for a score in the 51-0 rout. Admission was 50 cents.

The next day, October 17th, the Bellefonte Reserves defeated Yeagertown High School 7-0. Thompson caught a 20-yard pass from Marker which carried to the 1-yard line where Thompson took it over for the score.

The Academy football team went to New York and hung a 41-0 defeat on the NYU Freshmen, which surprised the local media. Led by the passing of Hood and the running of Williams and Whitmore, the Cougars led 28-0 at the half. After the game, the Bellefonte players were treated to the Broadway Play *Cinderella*.

Boston, Massachusetts, was the next Academy destination for a game with Dean Academy. Bellefonte dominated the game, as Franklin Hood had 92 passing yards in the 36-7 win; and several newspaper accounts stated that the visitors could have beaten a college team that day. Dean's touchdown was the result of a 92-yard return of a Cougar fumble.

In a game played at Altoona, 2500 fans saw the Academy defeat the Pitt Freshmen 19-0. Pitt, which had several former Academy players on the squad, could only manage 1 first down to Bellefonte's 13. Franklin Hood had 2 touchdowns (6 and 1-yard runs) and Gaudet had a 3-yard run for a score. The leading rushers against the Panthers were Josh Williams and Whitmore.

The Academy travelled to Scranton for a contest with Saint Thomas College; and Coach Snavely decided to start the 2nd team, which scored a touchdown in the first quarter. St. Thomas threatened to score in the same period; but Snavely inserted the first unit which held and promptly put 21 points on the first half scoreboard. In the 3rd quarter, the 2nd team got to start again; and when the protégés of Coach William Moore drove to the Bellefonte 2-yard line, the first team came back in and put out the fire, thus preserving the 28-0 shutout.

The hometown of Franklin Hood in Monaca, Pennsylvania was the site of a meeting with the Beaver Valley College Stars. A huge crowd saw a great performance by Hood, who's running and passing put the Cougars up by 21-0 at the half. Bellefonte coasted to a 34-0 victory.

SHERMAN HIGH SCHOOL
vs.
BELLEFONTE ACADEMY

January 1, 1926   Cashion Field   2 pm

Austin College's Cashion Field in Sherman, Texas was the site of a Texas-Pennsylvania meeting on a Fri. New Year's Day, 1926, between the Sherman High School Bearcats and the Bellefonte Academy Cougars.

Sherman was undefeated and victorious over Oak Cliff of Dallas, Greenville, Terrell, Denison, and Terrill School, the Texas Academy Champions. Bellefonte's only blemish in their 10 game-1925 season was a 6-0 loss to the Syracuse Freshmen. Bellefonte copped the National Prep School Title in 1924.

On Monday, December 28th, at 8:00 a.m., the Sherman High pep squad in uniform, the Sherman High band and Sherman citizens, making up a party of approximately 150 people left the court house square on the first of 3 booster trips planned to cover the county and southern Oklahoma. 20-30 cars were furnished for the trips through the cooperation of P.M. Travis and the Shipp Motor Company.

Pep squads of high schools at Denison, Greenville, Whitewright, Whitesboro, Commerce[6], McKinney, Durant, Leonard, and Gainesville had been wired invitations to attend the game and participate in a huge parade scheduled for 1:00 p.m. on New Year's Day preceding the game.

Posters and handbills were printed to be distributed over north Texas and southern Oklahoma. Daily messages about the game were to be read over the radio through the Fort Worth Star-Telegram station.

The Bellefonte Academy delegation, consisting of Bellefonte representatives, Pittsburgh newspaper reporters, and the football team, arrived in Denison, 10 miles from Sherman on Tuesday, Dec. 29th by Pullman; and were met at 10:10 a.m. by a delegation of more than 200 citizens and Sherman H.S. students who drove the Bellefonte players to Sherman in automobiles.

The Jeffries Brothers, the Rotary Club, the Kiwanis Club, and the Chamber of Commerce, all of Sherman, underwrote a $5000 guarantee[7] to pay the Pennsylvanians to make the trip.

The towns of Sherman in Sherman County and Denison in Grayson County were expected to turn out in great numbers to support the Bear Cats. Bellefonte, because of their sportsmanship and the friends made in Sherman since their arrival, were not without supporters.

On Friday at 11 o'clock, the day of the game, an airplane from Fitch Field east of the city of Sherman, flew over the business district and dropped circulars advertising the game. Several of them were good for a ticket to the afternoon game; and the leaflet stated that the winning team would be given a free airplane ride over North Texas.

A noon parade through Sherman featured the Mayor of Sherman, the Secretary of the Retail Merchants Association, the Superintendent of Sherman Schools, the Headmaster of the Bellefonte Academy, James R. Hughes, and Faculty Manager Charles Hughes.

The football players and honored guests attended a dance at the Elks Club given by the Sans Souci Club, representing the city's younger set, and the Sherman Chamber of Commerce.

The Bellefonte Academy entourage was lodged at the Brinkley Hotel; and was scheduled to leave the next day, Saturday morning, January 2, for a sightseeing tour of Dallas and Fort Worth and then embark for Pennsylvania at 4:10 p.m. on the Sunshine Special for Memphis, Louisville, Cincinnati, and Pittsburgh.

Academy players at a Hughes Field practice.

[6] Mickey Mantle's home town was Commerce, Oklahoma.
[7] Equivalent to $68,000 today.

Probable Lineups

Sherman	Wt.	No.	Pos.	Bellefonte	Wt.	No.
Cole	160	21	LE	Bowers	175	40
Paraduex	170	12	LT	Schnupp	210	44
Reid	165	17	LG	Kozicki	200	45
Belden	163	13	C	Dreshar	185	34
Marshall	163	16	RG	Mutzel	170	39
Keith	168	11	RT	Douds	200	50
Terrell, Captain	168	1	RE	Hinkle	175	37
Moore	145	4	QB	Gaudet	160	6
Welch	187	8	LH	Williams	160	32
Kelleher	165	5	RH	Whitmore	170	33
Caraway	168	7	FB	Hood, Captain	190	1

Substitutes

Cos, LE	154	24		Rankin	155	8
Taylor, RE	138	15		Brogley	175	36
Cunningham, LT	170	19		Marker	149	35
Davis, RT	170	10		Scheff	140	5
Grady, LT	180	25		Meckel	170	38
Hammond, RT	175	18		Dougherty	165	24
Mullinix, RG	230	26		Murphy	185	11
Free, LG	195	20		Yerina	190	42
Shives, RG	143	14				
Ivy, LG	150	25				
Poe, LH	140	3		**Officials**		
Walker, RH	134	15		Berry Holton, Referee; Trinity		
Tackett, FB	153	6		Pete Cawthon, Umpire; Austin College		
Briggs, QB	148	9		Limscomb, Head Linesman; Center		
Noe, C	138	30		Cecil Grigg, Field Judge; Austin		
Sebastian, LE	148	37				

Coaches: Bellefonte Academy—Carl G. Snavely; Sherman High School—Hugh Butler.
Colors: Bellefonte Academy—Blue and Gold; Sherman High School—Red and White.

1925 Modes of Transportation

The final game was in Sherman, Texas, for the national championship; and was played on New Year's Day before 15,000 fans. The contest attracted media attention from all over the country, including Pathe News, which took motion pictures of the game. Radio Station KDKA of Pittsburgh aired the game which pitted the Cougars against the Bear Cats, the champion high school team of the southwest.

Bellefonte rushed for 231 yards; and Hood was sensational—scoring twice and completing 6 of 8 passes for 264 yards and 3 touchdowns in the 48-6 rout.

First Quarter: The Academy received the opening kickoff and punted after a penalty. The Cougars then held on downs and received the punt. With Josh Williams and Whitmore alternating carries, Bellefonte moved to the 10-yard line where Hood scored on a fake pass. Whitmore added the point-after for a 7-0 lead.

Second Quarter: Sherman marched to the Academy 10-yard line; but the defense held and Bellefonte moved to its 32 on a series of line plunges. Hood tossed a 44-yard pass to left end Bowers, which carried to the Bear Cat 24. On the next play Hood connected with a wide open Whitmore for a touchdown. Whitmore tacked on the extra point for a 14-0 lead at the half.

Third Quarter: Sherman received the 2nd half kickoff, but on 4th down left guard Kozicki blocked the punt, and the Academy set up shop on the Bear Cat 20. Quarterback Gaudet and Josh Williams took turns with the pigskin, taking the ball to the 1-yard line where Williams went over the goal line and Whitmore's kick made the score 21-0. Franklin Hood scored his 2nd touchdown on a 50-yard drive which featured his passing and line plunges. Whitmore missed the extra point; but Sherman was offside and the Academy was awarded the point, making the score 28-0. Following the kickoff, Welch of the Bear Cats fumbled on an off tackle play giving Bellefonte possession on the Sherman 40. Line plays and end runs took the ball to the 8-yard line where Hood passed to Whitmore for the touchdown. Whitmore kicked the point-after, putting the Pennsylvania boys up, 35-0.

Fourth Quarter: Sherman went to the air and moved the ball to midfield. The next aerial was intercepted by Bowers, who returned it to the Bear Cat 43. On the first play Hood connected with Whitmore on a 43-yard touchdown pass. The extra point try failed, but Bellefonte led 41-0. Shortly after, the Cougars returned a punt to the Sherman 30, where Hood's pass was caught by substitute Heinie Marker for a score. The same combo accounted for the point-after and a 48-0 bulge. Sherman again went to the air with Welch hitting Kelleher and the 'Cats moved to the Academy 1-yard line where sub quarterback Briggs passed to Captain Terrell for a touchdown. The placekick was blocked, and Bellefonte had a 48-6 victory.

Carl Gray Snavely--Carl Snavely was born on July 31, 1894, in Omaha, Nebraska; but was raised in Pennsylvania and starred in football, basketball, and baseball at Lebanon Valley College, graduating in 1915.

Coach Carl Snavely

From 1915-1926, "The Gray Fox" coached football at a number of high schools and prep schools in Pennsylvania and Ohio; but gained national attention at the Bellefonte Academy (1923-26) where his teams scored 1362 points to the opponents' 71 and won 3 consecutive national titles in 1924-26, catapulting him to the head football job at Bucknell University, succeeding Charley Moran.

At Bucknell from 1927-33, his teams compiled a 42-16-8 record, going undefeated in 1931. He moved to North Carolina University, where his Tar Heels went 15-2-1 in 1934-35. Snavely took over for Gil Dobie at Cornell in 1936; and his teams were 46-26-3 from 1936-44, winning 3 Ivy League Titles, going undefeated in 1939 and finishing 4th in the country. He returned to North Carolina in 1945 and went 59-35-5 from 1945-52, taking his squads to 3 bowl games and winning 2 Southern Conference Championships. He closed out his career at the University of Washington from 1953-58, where his record was 33-18.

After retiring from Washington, he operated a car-wash business in St. Louis.

Snavely was a teacher of the single wing and was one of the first coaches to utilize game films. His overall record as a college coach was 180-96-16; and he was inducted into the National Football Foundation Coaches Hall of Fame in 1965.

He married Bernice Clara Richardson in 1915 and played 2 years of minor league baseball. Their son, Carl Gray, Jr., a Navy pilot, was killed in action in World War II. Snavely died on July 12, 1975 at the age of 82.

Coach Carl Snavely was involved in the classic "5th Down Game" on November 16, 1940, while the head coach at Cornell.

The Big Red went to Memorial Field in Hanover, New Hampshire, with a 6-0 record, riding an 18-game winning streak; while the hometown Dartmouth Indians were 3-4. Leading 3-0 in the 4th quarter, the Indians relinquished to ball to Cornell on their own 6-yard line with less than a minute to play. On the initial down, fullback Mort Landsberg carried for 3 yards. Halfback Walt Scholl then took the ball to the 1; and Landsberg could only gain inches on 3rd down. Cornell was penalized for delay of game, and Referee Red Friesell spotted the ball on the 5-yard line in order to replay 4th down. Quarterback "Pop" Scholl threw an incomplete pass into the end zone on 4th down. Game over? Not so fast!

Head Linesman Joe McKenny signaled first down for Dartmouth, saying the ball should be on the 20. Referee Friesell did not agree and gave the ball to Cornell at the 6-yard line on 4th down, which was actually the 5th down. Quarterback Scholl promptly passed to William Murphy for a touchdown, the extra point was kicked, and Cornell won 7-3.

After looking at the film, Coach Snavely met with Cornell Interim Athletic Director Bob Kane and President Emund Ezra Day, and they agreed to send a telegram to Dartmouth offering to forfeit the game. Dartmouth accepted; and according to NCAA rules, the Indians of Coach Earl "Red" Blaik won, 3-0. Blaik became the head coach at Army the following year.

Arguably the greatest act of sportsmanship in college football history; it also marked the only time that the winner of a game was declared off the field.

The Bellefonte Odd Fellows Band

The band played at the Inauguration of Night Flying at the Bellefonte Air Mail Field on July 1, 1925. Over 10,000 persons attended the event. The Bellefonte Centre County Courthouse is in the background.

Kneeling in front, L-R: Samuel Bryant, Director and Willis Wion, Manager.
First row: Harry "Toney" Garbrick; Nevin Lutz; Woodrow Corman; William Thomas; Ben Fry; Dale Musser; Francis Kozicki; Edward Klinger; Philip Wion; James Martin; Cyrus Hoy. **Back row:** Joel Stover; Ward Stover; Sergeant Steltz; the next 2 unknown; Harry Garbrick; Epley Gentzel; William "Slab" Bryant.

The 1925 Academy football team was welcomed back from Texas by townspeople amidst blaring horns, band music, and red lights. The Odd Fellows Band led a parade from Pennsylvania Depot to the Diamond in Bellefonte where Burgess H.P. Harris delivered a speech. Headmaster James R. Hughes sported a 10-gallon hat.

Academy Accolades:

"Give Bellefonte Academy 11 men and a football and they will perform more tricks than a monkey on a 40-foot pole."—*Dallas Daily News.*

"Bellefonte displayed 'four horsemen' who outrank any school backfield seen in action since the Oak Park High eleven conquered Everett High School."—*Boston Globe.*

On Sunday, December 25th, 1925, the roof of the boiler house at the Academy was destroyed by fire causing several thousand dollars in damage.

1926 Bellefonte Academy 12-1 National Prep Football Champions
First row, L-R: Dougherty, half; Gaudet, quarter; Marker, quarter; Mutzel, guard; Capt. Hood, full; Dreshar, tackle; Schnupp, tackle; Loddy Kozicki, guard; Brogley, sub-guard; Ducanis, centre. **Second row:** Flizack, sub-tackle; Rosenzweig, sub-tackle; Pflaum, end; Hinkle, end; Nemeseck, end; Hook Sample, sub-guard; H. Smith, half; P. Smith, half; Marks, sub-guard; Waite, half. **Third row:** Brubaker, sub-half; Edwards, sub-end; Avington, sub-guard; Graham, sub-end; Andolina, sub-guard; Hedges, sub-half; Williams, half; Osborne, sub-centre; Tom Brown, sub-guard; Hutton, sub-end. **Fourth row:** Porach, sub-end; Richardson, sub-tackle; Beatty, sub-guard; Foster, half. **Fifth row:** Summer, asst. coach; Beilby, Cheer-leader; Iseman, manager; Karle, asst. manager; Snavely, coach.
Regular season—Wins: Gettysburg Freshmen (16-0), All Scholastic Irwin (81-7), Penn State Freshmen (27-6), New York University Freshmen (7-0), Syracuse Freshmen (21-0), Bucknell Reserves (22-0), Erie Prep (42-0), West Virginia Freshmen (67-7). Loss: Pitt Freshmen (14-0).
Playoff wins: Dean Academy, Massachusetts (42-0), Randolph Jr. College, Texas (55-0), Sherman, Texas (21-0), and Tonkawa Jr. College, Oklahoma (73-6).

Charles Merrill "Dutch" Waite (right) played 4 years at
Bellefonte H.S. (1922-25), and was the team captain
in 1924. In his senior season (1925), Dutch played
for both Bellefonte High and the Bellefonte Academy.

1927 U.S.A. Champion

Coach Snavely's veteran team for 1926 opened the season with the Gettysburg Freshman in a steady downpour. Several touchdowns were called back due to penalties, but Bellefonte prevailed by a score of 18-0.

The Academy completely outclassed All-Scholastic Irwin, 81-7. Irwin's touchdown came in the 4th period on a pass. Dutch Waite scored 3 touchdowns in the first 10 minutes, one on a 50-yard interception return.

For the first time since 1922, Bellefonte played the Penn State Freshmen, and won 27-6. Franklin Hood scored 2 touchdowns and was a big force on offense. Penn State's only score came when Miller returned a fumble for a touchdown.

Bellefonte's Josh Williams returned a punt 57 yards to the 10-yard line, zigzagging through the defense. Hood scored on the next play for a 7-0 victory over the New York U. Frosh. The game was filmed and shown in Bellefonte.

The next Academy victim was the Syracuse Freshmen, to the tune of 21-0. Franklin Hood scored early, but left the game with an injury in the first period along with teammates Josh Williams and Kozicki. The winners tacked on 2 more touchdowns in the 4th quarter when a blocked punt was returned for a 5-yard tally by Schnupp, and Gaudet scored from 45 yards out.

An injury-laden Bellefonte squad took on the Bucknell Freshman, and won 28-0. Hood was out, along with 5 regulars. Josh Williams, Paul Smith, Kozicki, and Nemeseck were also hurt.

While the Cougars were defeating Erie Prep 42-0, the second team was trouncing the Bellwood Tigers 51-0. In the Erie game, Wilson had a 60-yard punt return and Dutch Waite was a large factor on offense.

Playing at Morgantown, Bellefonte topped the West Virginia Freshmen, 67-7. Franklin Hood thrilled the large crowd with his passing.

At Lock Haven, the Blue and Gold suffered their first loss of the season at the hands of the Pitt Freshmen, 14-0. All the points were scored in the first half. Despite having 8 starters out, Bellefonte equaled the Panthers in first downs and had 30 fewer rushing yards. Pitt coach Doc Carlson was a former Cougar star.

Williamsport was the scene of a 42-0 Bellefonte trouncing of Dean Academy of Franklin, Massachusetts, prep champions of New England. The Cougars led in first downs 28-5 in the fray. Franklin Hood had a 50-yard interception return to the 2-yard line where Harry Smith scored on the next play. Dougherty scored early from 1-yard out.

The team left Bellefonte on December 17th and arrived in Sherman, Texas, 2 days before a Christmas Day intersectional clash with Randolph Jr. College of Cisco. While training in Sherman, the Cougars played the high school team there and won, 21-0, with mostly 2nd stringers. Franklin Hood, Harry "Oklahoma" Smith, and Whitmore each scored touchdowns; Smith's coming in the opening period. The Sherman game was on a newsreel.

In a semi-final game, Bellefonte routed Randolph College, 56-0. Dougherty scored in the first period on a 1-yard run. Hood kicked the extra point. In the 2nd quarter, Hood threw 2 touchdown passes; one to Paul Smith for 31 yards, and the 2nd to Josh Williams for 48. Harry Smith scored 2 touchdowns in the 3rd period on runs of 10 and 35 yards. In the final quarter, Brimm intercepted a Cougar pass after Hood's 60-yard heave put the Academy in scoring position.

Red Grange

Harry Smith, an Oklahoma native, scored 4 touchdowns in the championship game against the Tonkawa Prep Mavericks of Oklahoma on Jan.1, 1927. Hood stood out with his punting, passing, and punt returns in the 73-6 win. Josh Williams had 2 scores; and Sherman "Heinie" Marker had a 55-yard run, which set up a touchdown. Tonkawa's Gaston picked off a Hood pass early in the 3rd quarter and Stroud turned it into 6 points. The highlight of the drive was a 30-yard pass from halfback McDermed to end Poteet. The game was played in the afternoon in Tulsa, Oklahoma. The Lineups:

Bellefonte—73	Pos.	Tonkawa—6	
Nemeseck	LE	Poteet	**Substitutions**—Bellefonte:
Schnupp	LT	D. Leffler	Flizack for Schnupp; Brown for
Kozicki	LG	F. Michael	Kozicki; Osborne for Ducanis;
Ducanis	C	Bosworth	Sample for Mutzel; Brogley for
Mutzel	RG	Patton, Capt.	Dreshar; Pflaum for Hinkle;
Dreshar	RT	Robison	Gaudet for Marker; Dougherty
Hinkle	RE	C. Michael	for H. Smith; H. Smith for
Marker	Q	Stroud	Dougherty; P. Smith for Williams;
H. Smith	LH	McDermed	Foster for Hood. Tonkawa:
Williams	RH	Gaston	Jones for D. Leffler; K. Leffler
Hood, Capt.	F	Willis	for McDermed; Maxie for Willis.

Bellefonte	13	14	26	20—73	Time of periods—15 min. each.
Tonkawa	0	0	6	0—6	

Scoring—Touchdowns: Hood 3; H. Smith 4; Williams 2; P. Smith, Foster, Stroud.
Points after touchdown: Hood 6 (5 placements, one forward pass); H. Smith (placement).
Missed points after touchdown: Hood (placement); H. Smith (placement); P. Smith (placement); Patton (placement).

Officials: Referee John B. Old, Kansas; Umpire Earl Jones, Arkansas; Head Linesman Lamar Hoover, Baker.

In Oct. of 1926, Red Grange presented the Academy with a silver loving cup honoring the 1924-25 teams. The players watched a newsreel of the NYU game.

1926 Bellefonte Academy Starters and Substitutes
First row, L-R: Gordon Hinkle, End; John Dreshar, Tackle; Louis Mutzel, Guard; Alexander Ducanis, Centre; Walter Kozicki, Guard; Leonard Schnupp, Tackle; Jerry Nemeseck, End.
Second row of 4 backs with hands on knees: Harold "Josh" Williams, Halfback; Ralph Dougherty, Halfback; James Franklin Hood (Captain), Fullback; Albert "Al" Gaudet, Quarterback. **Third row:** Paul Brogley, Sub-Guard; Frank Duncan, Sub-Guard; Hadley Foster, Sub-Halfback; Coach Snavely, Harry Smith, Halfback; Robert Pflaum, End; Frank Flizack, Sub-Guard; Merrill Waite, Sub-Halfback; Sherman Marker, Sub-Quarterback.

The above pic was taken at the Hughes ball field on Bellefonte's E. Bishop St.

The photo at the right is James Franklin Hood, triple-threat tailback of the National Prep Champion Bellefonte Academy Cougars.
Hood accolades:

"The Bellefonte Academy with Hood can play any University eleven in the state of Texas."—*Fort Worth, Texas Star-Telegram.*

"Hood's work by the aerial route justified the ranking given him by foremost critics as the greatest forward passer in the game today."—*The New York Post.*

"It's a darn good thing Bellefonte Academy did not play here on Christmas Day. It would have been a massacre in the first degree. Hood has any man skinned I ever saw play, not barring professional or college."—*Los Angeles Times, California.*

"In Hood you will find one of the greatest passers that ever stepped on a Texas gridiron. He throws the ball with deadly accuracy. All you have to do is to give him the address of an eligible man and he will make the pass."—*Daily American, Breckenridge, Texas.*

"Football as it should be played was the theme selected by the Bellefonte Academy eleven for its appearance on the old athletic field. Headed by Captain Hood, who could make a football do anything but talk, the Bellefonte eleven took pains to show the West Virgina Freshmen gridders what the game was all about."—*Morgantown, West Virginia Post.*

"This writer has seen Brick Miller, Jim Thorpe, and many others of the more prominent pass artists, but we'll take Hood any time. Hood can crash into the line like an express train and with the same damaging effect."—*Anonymous Sportswriter.*

Hood

James Franklin Hood—Franklin Hood was a football star for Monaca High School, the Bellefonte Academy, the University of Pittsburgh, the semi-pro J.P. Rooney's, and the Pittsburgh Pirates (now the Steelers).

The 6', 205 lb. fullback and linebacker's 1922 Monaca team was undefeated; and his 1924-26 Bellefonte Academy teams won 3 consecutive national prep titles, scoring 1,159 points to the opposition's 41. His rushing and scoring ability was complemented by his accurate passing.

Hood enrolled at Pitt in 1927 and received Honorable Mention All-American as a senior. He played 2 years of semi-pro football for the J.P. Rooney's in Pittsburgh and in 1933 played for the Pittsburgh Pirates (now the Steelers).

Hood at Pitt

He could throw a football from goal post to goal post; and received many accolades from the city press.

Franklin Hood died on August 21, 1955 at the age of 52; and Pennsylvania's Beaver County Sports Hall of Fame inducted him posthumously in 1980.

1926 Bellefonte Academy backfield, L-R: Sherman "Heinie" Marker; Harry "Oklahoma" Smith; Charles Merrill "Dutch" Waite; and Hadley Foster.

Gerald Theodore "Snitz" Snyder—Born in Windber in 1905; went to high school at the Bellefonte Academy. Played football and lacrosse at the University of Maryland where he attained 2nd team All-American and 1st team All-Southern as a running back. Played pro football with the New York Giants in 1929; the Staten Island Stapletons in 1930; and was an assistant coach with the pro football Frankfort Legion. He popularized the fake reverse at Maryland.

The Bellefonte Academy Football Team in Action.

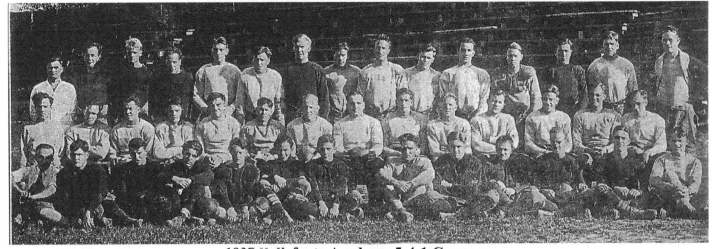

1927 Bellefonte Academy 5-4-1 Cougars

Russell McGee was hired as the new coach for the 1927 season. He played football at Kiski and was a star on Bucknell's 1926 team.

On September 24th, Beckley College of Harrisburg travelled to Bellefonte for a 2:30 date with the Academy. For the first time, wire was put around Hughes Field 10 yards back. On the north side of the field, cars were lined up for people who wanted to watch the game. The visitors, who were thought to have former college players on the squad, were big and strong; but their offensive tactics proved futile against the Blue and Gold Cougars. Paul Smith had a 70-yard touchdown run to put Bellefonte ahead in the first quarter; but shortly after, he suffered a busted blood vessel in his kidney. Harry "Spooks" Temple, formerly of Altoona, also scored a touchdown as the Cougars put 12 points on the board in the 3rd period and 6 in the 4th for a 24-0 victory.

The Bucknell Freshmen jumped out to a 6-0 lead; but Bellefonte scored 18 points in the 3rd quarter and 7 more in the 4th and won, 25-12. Spooks Temple accounted for all his team's points. The Bison tallied again in the 4th period.

The Blue and Gold fell behind the Villanova Freshmen in the first half by a 7-6 count; but scored 7 in the 3rd quarter for a 13-7 win. Nova used Notre Dame's system to the letter.

Franklin Hood, playing for the Pitt Freshmen, scored a touchdown as his team lead at halftime, 7-0. The Academy closed the gap to 7-6 in the 3rd period; but the Panthers tallied again in the final quarter and pinned a 13-6 defeat on the Cougars.

Paul Smith caught a 53-yard pass for a touchdown and Spooks Temple tacked on the point-after for a 7-0 victory over the New York University Freshmen in 1927.

The Penn State Freshmen put 7 points on the board in each of the first 3 quarters and upended the Academy, 21-0. The Cougars walked off the field in the 4th period, thus forfeiting the game.

The Naval Academy Freshmen scored early and took a 7-0 lead; but Bellefonte made it a 7-6 game by halftime when Susce recovered a fumbled punt in the Navy end zone. The Plebes scored again in the 3rd quarter and won, 14-6.

Bellefonte lost its 4th straight game to Wyoming Seminary to the tune of 13-0. After a scoreless first half, the Seminarians put 7 points on the board in the 3rd period and 6 in the 4th.

The Academy battled the Altoona Apprentices to a 0-0 tie.

A foot of snow covered the field in the final game against Erie Prep; but Bellefonte's Paul Smith had 2 touchdowns—the first coming on a 55-yard run and the 2nd on a 69-yard punt return in leading the Cougars to a 13-6 win. An Erie score occurred when Hickey recovered a fumble in the end zone.

Paul Smith was voted the Most Valuable Player of the 1927 football team.

The Academy was invited to play Alhambra High School of California on Christmas Day, but could not accept the offer due to a signed contract with Randolph Junior College of Cisco, Texas for a game on the same day.

The football banquet took place on Feb. 5th, 1928 at the Academy Dining Hall. The guest speaker was E.A. Holbrook, Dean of the School of Miners & Metallurgy at Penn State.

On Friday, Feb. 18th, the Academy football dance took place from 9 p.m. to 2 a.m. with the Joe Bucks Orchestra performing at the State Armory. Admission was $3 a couple.

Above photo: **Franklin Hood dressed in Indian garb.**
Photos below: **Bellefonte Academy snapshots.**

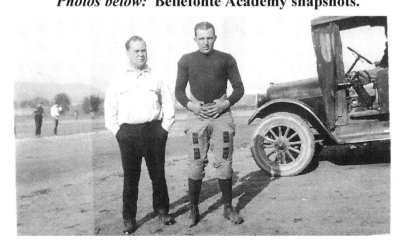

George K. "Lefty" James—born in Lower Allen Twp., Pennsylvania and played high school football at the Bellefonte Academy for Carl Snavely. He played 3 years of varsity football and baseball at Bucknell for Snavely and graduated in 1929. He captained the baseball team as a senior.

Lefty played semi-pro baseball, was a baseball umpire, and followed Snavely to the University of North Carolina and Cornell as an assistant football coach.

James was the head football coach at Cornell from 1947-1960; and utilizing the single wing and T-formation, won 4 unofficial Ivy League titles in 1948, 1949, 1953, and 1954. His 1948 team was 8-1, losing only to Army. In 1951, 35,300 fans saw the Big Red upset then-Rose Bowl champion Michigan, 20-7. His overall record at Cornell was 66-58-2.

James

Lefty James appeared on the Ed Sullivan Show on Dec. 1, 1957.

In 1960-65, James was the head coach of the All-Pennsylvania team which challenged the best high school players from the state of Texas.

In 1979 he was inducted into the Bucknell Athletic Hall of Fame; and in 1981 received the same honor at Cornell.

Is Football a Waste of Time?

In 1926, a cow on the Harnish farm in Bellefonte broke loose and was blindly running toward a deep pit in one corner of a field. Lawrence Harnish, a Bellefonte High School football player, visualizing a steady and monotonous diet of beef for the next month, endeavored to head the bovine away from disaster to no avail. As a last resort, he made a flying tackle and brought the animal down on the edge of the hole. He thus insured a variety in his meals and answered critics who had been bemoaning the time spent by American youth in learning football.

Harnish

Lawrence "Baldy" Harnish was one of six former Bellefonte Academy football players on the 1930 New York University Freshman team which beat the Academy, 27-7. Harnish was a 6', 180 lb. guard for the Violets.

1928 Bellefonte Academy 9-1 Football Team

Front row, L-R: Jacques Croissant, end; Meredith, tackle; Joynt, guard; Captain Temple, full; Barber, centre; Smith, half; Flizack, tackle; Bilotta, guard; Lumley, full; Vavra, tackle; Sample, end. **Second row:** Reider, quarter; Walker, half; Zanarini, end; O'Brien, guard; Demas, tackle; Hardy, end; Isenberg, end; Greenlee, centre; Graham, half; Gramley, guard. **Third row:** Carney, half; Russell, full; Vogel, half; Morgan, end; Rothman, tackle; Leach, half; Sibesta, centre; Ducanis, full; Ballou, half. **Fourth row:** Manager Skinner; Kneebone, tackle; Ochs, centre; Rush, end; Norwood, tackle; Moyer, half; Assistant Coach Summers; Assistant Manager Otto, Coach Bohren.

1928—Record: 9-1

Bohren

Karl W. Bohren was named the football coach at the Bellefonte Academy. He hailed from Reynoldsville, Pennsylvania; played at the University of Georgia and played at Pitt under Coach Pop Warner. Bohren was a Walter Camp All-American selection at halfback in 1923.

In the opening game, the Academy demonstrated it was better than the '26 and '27 teams by trouncing the Donora Athletic Club, 99-0. The Cougars led by 57-0 at the half; and Spooks Temple hit pay dirt 3 times. Coach Bohren only used half of his backfield men in the 3 p.m. contest. Admission was 75 cents.

Bellefonte put 14 points on the scoreboard in the first period and 12 in the 4th in defeating the Villanova Freshmen, 26-0. Several scoring opportunities were lost due to fumbles. Lumley had a 25-yard touchdown run.

The Naval Academy Freshmen were the next Cougar victim in a game played at Annapolis to the tune of 12-0. Lumley scored in the first and 3rd quarters against the Plebes.

Lewisburg was the site of a struggle with the Bucknell Freshmen which was won by Bellefonte, 6-0. The lone touchdown occurred in the 2nd period.

The Blue and Gold won a battle with the West Point Freshmen, 27-6. Bellefonte led 20-6 at halftime and scored again in the 4th quarter.

The Academy outplayed the New York University Freshmen; but 2 fourth quarter Violet interceptions were turned into touchdowns which led to the demise of Bellefonte by a 13-0 count.

The Cougars jumped out to a 14-0 lead against Wyoming Seminary and tacked on 21 more for a 35-0 victory. Harry "Spooks" Temple had 4 touchdowns and Reider added 1, giving the Seminarians their worst beating in years.

The game with the Washington & Jefferson Freshmen see-sawed back and forth after a 7-7 first half deadlock. Temple scored on a 5-yard run and Reider caught a 10-yard touchdown heave. Washington's safety man intercepted a Cougar aerial in the 4th period and raced 40 yards to the end zone. W & J missed the extra point resulting in a 14-13 Bellefonte win.

The Academy turned a 7-6 halftime lead against Beckley College of Harrisburg into a 21-6 victory by putting 14 points on the 3rd quarter scoreboard. Temple had 2 touchdowns and several long runs, totaling 80 yards rushing.

On February 10th, the Academy football banquet was held at the Brockerhoff Hotel in Bellefonte. The guest speaker was Gibby Welch, former Cougar and captain of the 1927 Pitt Panthers, who entertained 200 people. Russ Stime, former All-American tackle at Washington & Jefferson was in attendance.

The Johnny Bucks Orchestra of State College provided the music for the football dance at Hecla Park on February 27th.

1928 State Championship Game

Harry Temple

On December 8, 1928, Bellefonte Academy won the Pennsylvania State Prep School Title at Franklin Field in Philadelphia by beating Perkiomen School 14-0 before 3000 fans.

Bellefonte had won all of its games except for a 13-0 loss to the New York University Freshmen. Headmaster John R. Hughes and his brother E. L. Hughes of Alhambra tried to arrange a game between the Academy and Alhambra High, winners of the West Coast League and C.I. F. Champs for Christmas Day in the L.A. Coliseum. The provisions that the C.I.F. would sanction the game and make the usual guarantees were not met, so the trip to California never materialized.

Perkiomen started quickly, driving down the field and making 5 first downs with L. Hatton and Morris lugging the leather; but Bellefonte braced on the 16-yard line and took the ball back when a forward pass was short of the 10-yard line.

Captain Harry "Spooks" Temple, a 185 lb. Fullback from Altoona, became "Scoops" Temple late in the opening period when Fullback Mitchell of Perkiomen, attempting a double pass play, fumbled the ball; and Temple scooped it up and raced 37 yards to pay dirt. Hardy's placekick was good; and Bellefonte took a 7-0 lead.

The lighter Perkiomen team held off the Centre County boys in the 2nd and 3rd quarters; but in the final period Temple and Lamarick, who was substituting for Walker, made several long gains. Leach went off tackle for the final 5 yards; and his placekick was good for a 14-0 victory for the Academy. The Lineups:

Bellefonte—14		Perkiomen—0	
Croissant	LE	Isett	Substitutions: Bellefonte—
Vera	LT	Foresman	Zanarini for Croissant;
Bilotta	LG	Stoner	Flizack for Vera;
Barber	C	F. Hatton	Leach for Minkle;
Joynt	RG	Hill	Vogel for Graham;
Meredith	RT	Suydam	Lamarick for Walker;
Hardy	RE	McCarthy	Kline for Joynt.
Graham	Q	Whittock	Perkiomen—
Walker	LH	L. Hatton	Walter for Hill.
Minkle	RH	Morris	
Temple	F	Mitchell	Bellefonte....7 0 0 7—14
			Perkiomen...0 0 0 0—0

Dutch Hill

Referee—Wilmer Crowell, Swarthmore; Umpire—Charles J. McCarthy, Germantown Academy; Field Judge—Charles G. Eckles, Washington & Jefferson; Head Linesman—Palmer, Colby. Time of periods—15 minutes.

The New York University Varsity Football Team scored 456 points and won the 1928 Eastern Collegiate Championship, led by All-American Edwin "Dutch" Hill. He played high school football, basketball, and baseball in Ohio at Burgettstown from 1917-21 and Massillon in 1922 where he was an All-State fullback. The triple-threat tailback played football, basketball, and baseball for the Bellefonte Academy in 1924-25. He was accidently shot to death in May of 1929 during a friendly scuffle with a New York policeman while participating in a college prank.

The Inter-sectional Board of Football Coaches

GLENN S. WARNER
KNUTE ROCKNE
TAD JONES

December 22nd, 1928

Dear Mr. Hill:-

We want to congratulate you on your splendid showing and performance during the football season recently ended.

It was indeed a pleasure for us to name you among our Honorable Mentions for 1928.

With best wishes,

THE INTER-SECTIONAL BOARD OF FOOTBALL COACHES

Glenn S. Warner

Knute Rockne

Tad Jones

Edwin "Dutch" Hill of New York University, formerly of the 1924 Bellefonte Academy team, received Honorable Mention from the Inter-Sectional Board of Football Coaches in 1928:

Glenn Scobey "Pop" Warner—Head Coach at Georgia (1895-96); Cornell (1897-98, 1904-06); Carlisle Indian Industrial School (1899-03, 1907-14); University of Pittsburgh (1915-23); Stanford (1924-32); Temple University (1933-38). College record: 319-106-32. National Champions @ Pitt—1915, 1916, 1918. National Champions @ Stanford—1926. Elected to College Football Hall of Fame as a coach in 1951.

Knute Kenneth Rockne—All American @ Notre Dame in 1913; stunned a highly regarded Army team 35-13 in 1913 with accurate downfield passes. Played pro football with Akron Indians in 1914 and Massillon Tigers in 1915. Assistant coach @ Notre Dame—1914-17; South Bend J. F. C.'s in 1916-17; Head Coach @ Notre Dame 1918-1930. College record: 105-12-5. Four National Titles @ Notre Dame (1919, 1924, 1929, 1930); 5 undefeated seasons without a tie. Elected to College Football Hall of Fame in 1951.

Thomas Albert Dwight "Tad" Jones—All-American Quarterback @ Yale University in 1906 and 1907—undefeated both years. Head Coach @ Syracuse University (1909-10); Yale University (1916-17, 1920-27). College record: 69-24-6. Elected to College Football Hall of Fame as a coach in 1958.

1929 Bellefonte Academy 8-1 Cougars

First row, L-R: Shoits Croissant, Russ Meredith, Johnny Joynt, Spooks Temple, Tom Barber, Paul Smith, Frank Flizack, Frank Bilotta, Lumley, Ernie Vera, Hook Sample. **Second row:** Pail Reider, Ray Walker, Zen Zanarini, Abby O'Brien, Tiny Demas, Mike Hardy, Art Isenberg, Greenly, Barney Graham, Red Gramley. **Third row:** Pete Carney, Russ Russell, Nip Vogel, Red Morgan, Benny Rothman, Sam Leach, Sebastian, Ducanis, Bellow, ?. **Fourth row:** Mgr. Skinner, Kneebone, Ochs, Rush, Norwood, Moe Moyer, Coach Bohren, Asst. Mgr. Morgan Otto, Mgr. Jackey Summers.

Wins: Goodwill Fire Company of DuBois (62-6), Villanova Freshmen (20-0), Navy Freshmen (20-0), Bucknell Reserves (46-0), Penn Freshmen (44-0), Bingville Independents (48-0), New York University Freshmen (7-0), and Western Maryland Freshmen (13-0). The only loss was to the West Point Freshmen (13-7). Coach Karl W. Bohren had enough players for 3 teams.

In the opener with DuBois at 2:30 p.m. the 3 Bellefonte teams saw action and looked strong in the 62-6 rout. Touchdowns: Harry Temple (2); Bill Abee (2), Barney Graham (1), and Bill Nevel (1). Stepp stepped up and scored for the Goodwill Fire Company on a 20-yard return of a blocked punt. The cost of admission for the contest was 75 cents.

The Academy put touchdowns on the board in the 1st, 2nd, and 4th quarters and shut out the Villanova Freshmen, 20-0. Spooks Temple scored one touchdown.

Aided by several former college players, Army edged the Academy, 13-7. The 3 scores came in rapid succession: A long pass by the Cadets put the ball on the Academy's 4-yard line; and the next play resulted in a score. On the ensuing kickoff, Bellefonte drove for a touchdown in 6 plays and Temple scored the tying tally. Army took the kickoff and marched to the Academy 25; and aided by a penalty, the Black Knights threw a touchdown pass for the victory.

In the 1934 Rose Bowl, the Columbia Lions with a 7-1 record defeated the Stanford Indians who were 8-1-1, by a score of 7-0. Bellefonte Academy alums William Nevel (#24) and Mike Demshar (#54) played for the NYC college.

Annapolis was the scene of a 20-0 win for Bellefonte. After a lack-luster start, the Cougars racked up 13 first downs and scored 20 points in the 4th period. Navy moved the sticks 4 times. Abee scored on runs of 12 and 3 yards; and Matesic had a 30-yard tally.

The Academy scored at will in topping the Bucknell Freshmen, 46-0, which included an 80-yard kickoff return by Harry Temple.

The next day the Bellefonte Reserves lost to the Bellwood Legion, 7-6. The Reserves scored early; but later in the game, Legion quarterback Carr drove over the goal line and Freedman booted the winning point-after. The Legion coach was Charles Fleming, a former Academy football star.

Harry "Spooks" Temple starred for Bellefonte in the 44-0 trouncing of Penn. The Quakers threatened the Academy goal several times, but the defense held.

A large crowd at DuBois witnessed a 48-0 trouncing of the Bingville Firemen by the Academy which included a large delegation from Punxsutawney. The Punxy High School football team was to play on the same field on November 11th. DuBois, 2 teams strong, did not get within 60 yards of the Bellefonte goal; and the Cougar offense put 14 points on the board in the first quarter. Barney Graham scored on a 25-yard run around right end, and Bill Abee hit pay dirt. Mike Hardy tacked on 2 points with placekicks.

Bellefonte fielded 4 teams against the Bingville Firemen; and exploded for 20 points in the 2nd period, as touchdown passes were caught by Stevens and Ed Matesic and Nip Vogel made one goal out of 2 placements. Abee scored again and Hardy made good on the extra point for a 34-0 Bellefonte lead at the half.

In the 3rd quarter, Spooks Temple had a 50-yard punt return for a touchdown and Bill Nevel completed the touchdown parade in the 4th period. Hardy added 2 more points with placekicks to make the final score 48-0. The Lineups:

DuBois—0	Pos.	Bellefonte—48	
Ord	LE	Hardy	**Substitutes:** DuBois—Boob Jones,
Gallup	LT	Meredith	Murphy, Balavace, Johnston,
Sobczak	LG	Hundertmark	Kineder, Stepp. Bellefonte—
Rokoski	C	Joynt	Sullivan, Harnish, Hughes, Ed
Radish	RG	Dreshar	Zanarini, Mensch, Martak, Roberts,
Poco	RT	Marchi	Vogel, Rosenzweig, Manfrieda,
Chambers	RE	Stevens	Davis, Heydrich, Temple, Park,
McNally	QB	Abee	Zaremba, Bartley, G. Zanarini.
Sampson	LH	Matesic	
Suplizio	RH	Graham	Officials: Referee Herb Stein,
Maybee	FB	Ducanis	W & J; Umpire Alderfer,

Bellefonte	14	20	7	7—48	Swarthmore; Linesman Woodring,
DuBois	0	0	0	0—0	Bucknell. Time of qrtrs.—12 min.

The Academy beat the New York University Freshmen 7-0, as Ed Matesic rushed for 71 yards and Harry Temple scored from 1 yard out in the victory over the Violets. The Bellefonte boys were treated to a football game at Yankee Stadium between NYU and Missouri.

The Western Maryland game was played on a frozen field, with spitting snow and a wind chill of zero degrees; consequently, very few fans witnessed the 13-0 Bellefonte victory. The contest was highlighted by 2 goal line stands—Western Maryland stopped the Cougars inside its

Matesic

5-yard line; and the Academy forced the Maryland boys to run out of downs on its 6-inch line. In the passing department, Bellefonte's Barney Graham was 2 for 2 for 115 yards and 2 touchdowns. Abee caught one for 65 yards and Mike Hardy's reception went for 50 yards.

John Joynt of Wilkinsburg received the 1929 Academy MVP pin for football.

Pitt, Carnegie Tech, NYU, and West Virginia urged their recruits to attend the Bellefonte Academy before matriculating at their respective colleges.

A semi-formal Academy football dance was held on February 8th at Hecla Park from 9 p.m. to 2 a.m. Music was provided by the Varsity of Penn State Orchestra.

The Cougar athletic banquet was held on Feb. 21st in the Academy dining hall.

Ed Matesic—A football player at the Bellefonte Academy in 1929-1930 (pic above), a halfback at the University of Pittsburgh and a player with the Philadelphia Eagles in 1934-1935 (pic below). In 1936 he signed with the Pittsburgh Steelers and set a single

season passing record, completing 64 of 138 heaves for 850 yards in leading the Steelers to a 2nd-place finish in the NFL East.

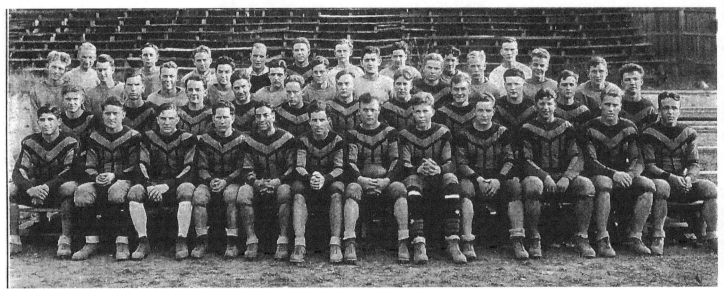

1930 Bellefonte Academy 1-6-1 Cougars

Coach Bohren resigned and took a similar position at Hobart College in Maine. The new coach for the Blue and Gold was Sylvester V. Pauxtis of Dickinson College, a mathematics teacher.

The Academy fought hard in a 7-0 loss to the Duquesne Freshmen; but couldn't punch the ball over the Dukes' goal line.

A large crowd witnessed Bellefonte get its first and only win against the Western Maryland Freshmen, 19-13. The score at the half was deadlocked at 6-6; but the Cougars pushed across a touchdown in the 3rd period, added another in the final quarter, and held Maryland to a single score in the 4th period.

The Bucknell Reserves' defense rushed the Bellefonte passer hard and threw the Cougar runners for losses in a 7-0 shutout. The Bison scored in the 4th quarter on a 22-yard pass and tacked on a successful kick in defeating the Blue and Gold.

The Penn Freshmen took the measure of the Academy, 6-0.

The Cougars avoided another loss as they fought hard to tie the Carnegie Tech Freshmen, 0-0.

Bellefonte's next opponent, the New York University Freshmen, came into the game with a 6-1 record; their only loss coming at the hands of Dean Academy of Boston, Massachusetts. Spooks Temple, one of 6 former Cougars on the Violet roster, scored 3 touchdowns in defeating his Alma Mater, 27-7. The other grads were William Abee, Lawrence Harnish, John Joynt, Basilio Marchi, and Peter Zaremba.

In their first meeting with the Temple Freshmen, the Cougars played their best game of the season; but fell to the Owls, 13-0. Zukus caught a 45-yard pass for a touchdown, and Pileonis was at the end of a 10-yard aerial for the 2nd score.

Dickinson Seminary put touchdowns on the board in the first 3 periods in downing the Academy 19-0. Fred Meyers scored on a 16-yard pass, and Rollie Meyers tallied on a 10-yard toss. Downs intercepted a Bellefonte pass and returned it 58 yards for a touchdown.

New York University Freshmen Football Squad

No.	Name	Wt.	Ht.	Position	High School
2	William Abee	195	5.11	Back	Harding High School
4	Anthony Borrelli	160	5.07	Back	Cliffside Park H. S.
5	Harold Brown	195	6.00	Tackle	Boys' High School
7	Rudolph Cohen	180	5.11	End	Boys' High School
10	Val Connolly	175	5.11	End	Medford High School
12	Eldon Dungey	175	5.11	Back	Oneida High School
14	Cecil Fine	155	5.07	Back	New Utrecht H. S.
15	Cliff Flowers	175	6.00	End	Roosevelt H. S.
16	Sol Fuchs	180	6.00	Back	Richmond Hill H. S.
17	Nathan Goldstien	170	6.00	Guard	Monticello H. S.
18	Nathan Grossman	185	6.01	Back	James Madison H. S.
19	Lawrence Harnish	180	6.00	Guard	Bellefonte High
20	Orrin Hertz	175	6.01	Tackle	Free Academy
22	Abraham Itzkowitz	200	6.02	Centre	James Madison H. S.
23	John Joynt	175	5.08	Centre	Wilkinsburg H. S.
25	Anthony Julian	140	5.03	Back	Stuyvesant H. S.
26	John Kohler	180	6.00	Tackle	Parkersburg H. S.
28	Joseph Laub	175	5.10	Back	Boys' High School
30	Joseph Lefft	180	6.02	End	Boys' High School
31	Wade Mallard	180	5.10	Guard	Richmond Hill H. S.
34	Basilio Marchi	190	6.01	Guard	Parkersburg H. S.
36	Charles Rose	190	6.00	Tackle	Staunton Military Acad.
37	Maurice Sirkin	125	5.08	Back	Crosby High School
38	Leon Smelstor	175	5.10	Back	Norwood High School
39	Frank Tavano	145	5.06½	Back	Ossining High School
40	Harry Temple	185	5.11	Back	Altoona High School
41	Paul Troshkin	185	5.09	Guard	Evander Childs H. S.
42	John White	165	5.10	Back	Naugatuck High School
44	Maynard White	170	6.00	End	Haverhill High School
45	Peter Zaremba	195	6.03	Tackle	Harding High School
47	Vincent DeLeo	130	5.04	Back	James Madison H. S.
	Samual Shamas	175	5.10	End	New Utrecht H. S.

Freshmen Coach—Arthur H. Roberts, N. Y. U. '29

Freshmen Manager—John Weigert, '31

RECORD

19	St. John's Prep	9
0	Dean Academy	6
52	Eastman B. C.	0
27	Bellefonte Academy	7
19	Mackenzie School	0
6	Rutgers Freshmen	0
6	Vermont Academy	0

— BELLEFONTE ACADEMY. BOYS

Harry "Spooks" Temple, Johnny Joynt, and Lawrence "Baldy" Harnish starred for the 1930 New York University Freshmen. Against St. John's Prep, Temple had touchdown runs of 6 & 36 yards; and Harnish had a fumble recovery. In the loss to Dean Academy, Temple consistently gained 6-8 yards on each carry.

The Academy Athletic Banquet was held on February 15th at 6:30 p.m.

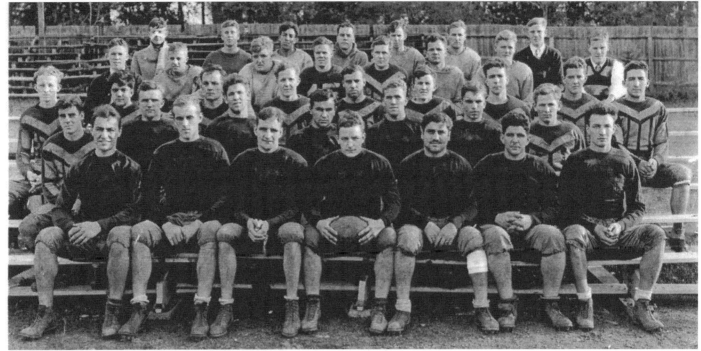

1931 Bellefonte Academy 1-4-4 Cougars

Win: Penn State Freshmen (6-0). **Ties:** Duquesne Freshmen (0-0), Keystone Academy (0-0), and Wyoming Seminary (6-6), New York University Freshmen (6-6). **Losses**: West Virginia Freshmen (26-0), Dean Academy of Massachusetts (7-0), and Western Maryland Freshmen (7-0), and Bucknell Freshmen (13-0). No score for a second game with Wyoming Seminary. Coach William Gutteron. The 36 players were from NY, OH, PA, NJ, and WVA.

In the tie with Duquesne, Bellefonte stopped the Dukes twice in scoring range; and the Pittsburgh school was on the yard and a half-line when the game ended. There were only 2 penalties in the contest.

Against the Keystone Academy, Bellefonte had a touchdown called back due to a penalty in a 0-0 tie. Neither team had a successful aerial attack.

The Cougars scored early; but Wyoming Seminary, located near Wilkes-Barre, scored the tying touchdown with time running out in the 4th quarter.

The West Virginia Freshmen handed the Academy a 26-0 defeat.

Dean Academy put 7 on the board in the 2nd period and hung on for a 7-0 win.

After a scoreless first half; Wyoming Seminary scored a touchdown in the 3rd quarter and kicked the point-after in defeating the Academy, 7-0.

New York University's Rosen hit pay dirt in the 2nd period, and Bellefonte's Donald matched that fete in the 3rd quarter for a 6-6 tie with the Violets.

The Bucknell Freshman defeated the Academy, 13-0.

Sam Confer, formerly of Bellefonte High, crossed the goal line of the Penn State Freshmen in the 2nd period; and Bellefonte topped the Lions, 6-0.

1930 Academy coach Sylvester V. Pauxtis failed to meet all requirements of coach and instructor of 2nd year algebra; so he was replaced with William Gutteron in 1931. The new coach hailed from Quanter, California; and was named physical director, and coach of the football, boxing, and baseball teams. Gutteron was an alumnus of Nevada University and was picked by "Buck" Shaw as an All-American tackle. He coached at Santiago among other schools; and in 1935 took an assistant football coaching job at Muhlenberg University.

Sam Confer, pictured at the right, captained the 1928 Bellefonte High School football team; dropped out of school and did not play on the 1929 squad. He enrolled in the Academy and performed well for the 1931 and 1932 Cougars.

1932—Record 2-4-1

Sam Confer scored touchdowns in the 2nd and 3rd quarters against the Altoona Apprentices; and the Academy rung up a 12-0 opening win.

Bellefonte took a 7-0 lead in the first period in a contest with Cook Academy with a touchdown by Confer; but Cook made it a 7-6 game at halftime. A safety in the 3rd quarter was the difference in an 8-7 Cougar loss.

A game with Lock Haven Central was played in a sea of mud; but the Havenites managed to score in the final period for a 6-0 victory over Bellefonte. Lasich crossed the goal line from the Cougar 3-yard line.

The Penn State Freshmen made it 3 losses in a row for the Academy by a score of 14-0.

The Blue and Gold Cougars battled the Bucknell Freshmen to a tie.

The Bellefonte Governors took on the Bellefonte Academy, and came up short by a score of 7-0. Sam Confer scored the only touchdown.

Dickinson Seminary tallied 6 points in each of the middle 2 quarters and upended the Academy, 12-0.

William Gutteron, University of Nevada, was a mathematics teacher as well as football coach and athletic director.

The annual athletic banquet was held on Saturday, Feb. 6, 1932.

The annual football assembly was held Friday evening, Feb. 12, 1932.

Circa 1931, the Bellefonte Academy had 41 players on college teams, 4 of whom captained their respective elevens.

Bellefonte Academy Football Coaches and Records

Name	Year(s)	W	L	T		
?	1890	0	1	0	complete	
?	1891	2	0	0	complete	
?	1892	0	1	0	incomplete	
?	1893	2	1	0	complete	
?	1894	1	1	0	incomplete	
?	1895	2	2	0	incomplete	
?	1896	3	3	1	complete	
?	1897	4	1	1	complete	
?	1898	2	1	2	complete	
?	1899	1	3	2	incomplete	
?	1900	3	3	2	incomplete	
?	1901	4	3	1	complete	
?	1902	2	0	2	incomplete	
Sharp	1903	4	2	0	incomplete	
James R. Hughes	1904	4	3	1	complete	
?	1905	3	4	1	complete	
Walker	1906	6	3	0	complete	
?	1907	2	4	5	complete	
Charles E. Hall	1908	10	2	0	incomplete	
Evans	1909	5	2	1	incomplete	
I.C. Kimble	1910	7	0	2	complete	PA State Champs
E.C. Weller	1911	7	3	0	complete	
Weller	1912	8	1	0	complete	PA State Champs
Weller	1913	5	4	0	complete	
Oliver J. Vogel	1914	6	1	0	complete	
Hartman	1915	6	2	0	incomplete	
?	1916	5	3	0	incomplete	
?	1917	2	4	0	incomplete	
?	1918	1	4	0	incomplete	
?	1919	3	2	0	incomplete	
?	1920	6	3	0	complete	
Donald C. Dunbar	1921	1	3	3	incomplete	
Wilson	1922	7	2	0	complete	
Carl Snavely	1923	7	1	0	incomplete	
Snavely	1924	8	0	1	complete	Natl. Prep Champs
Snavely	1925	10	1	0	complete	Natl. Prep Champs
Snavely	1926	12	1	0	complete	Natl. Prep Champs
Russell Magee	1927	5	4	1	complete	
Karl W. Bohren	1928	9	1	0	complete	PA State Champs
Bohren	1929	8	1	0	incomplete	
Sylvester V. Pauxtis	1930	1	6	1	incomplete	
William Gutteron	1931	1	4	4	incomplete	
Gutteron	1932	2	4	1	incomplete	

Coaches in Bellefonte Academy History

Coach	Years	
Sharp	1903	
James R. Hughes	1904	
Walker	1906	
Charles E. Hall	1908	Left for Lawrenceville.
Evans	1909	Left for Cleveland, Ohio
Kimble	1910	
E.C. Weller	1911-13	
Oliver J. Vogel	1914	
Hartman	1915	
Donald C. Dunbar	1921	
Wilson	1922	
Carl Snavely	1923-26	Left for Bucknell University
Russell Magee	1927	
Karl W. Bohren	1928-29	Left for Hobart College
Sylvester V. Pauxtis	1930	
William Gutteron	1931-32	Left for Muhlenberg University

Longest Touchdown Runs

Player	Year	Opponent	Yards
1. Ron Hoy	1901	State College Reserves	95
2. Valen O'Neil	1923	Bucknell Freshmen	95
3. Jimmy Rooney	1924	Lafayette Freshmen	95
4. Clarence Hullihen	1914	Saint Francis Academy	90
5. Walter Loucks	1912	Steelton High	85
6. Ed Keichline	1902	Philipsburg High	80
7. Ed Roelof	1904	Altoona High	80
8. Birney	1924	Syracuse Freshmen	80
9. Jimmy Rooney	1924	Lafayette Freshmen	80
10. Paul Smith	1927	Beckley College	70
11. Miller	1899	Penn State Scrubs	65
12. Harry Symes	1910	Tyrone P.R.R. Y.M.C.A.	65
13. Paul Cruse	1893	Philipsburg	65
14. Walter Loucks	1912	Bloomsburg Normal	60
15. Valen O'Neil	1923	Pitt Freshmen	60
16. Paul Smith	1927	Erie Prep	55

Most Yards Rushing—Game Individual

Player	Year	Opponent	Yards
Jimmy Rooney	1924	Lafayette Freshmen	212
Forest Decker	1912	Bloomsburg Normal	158
Valen O'Neil	1923	Carnegie Tech Freshmen	133
Dutch Waite	1926	Bucknell Reserves	121
Ed Keichline	1902	Philipsburg	120
John Weaver	1903	Lock Haven Normal	117

Most Yards Passing—Game Individual

Player	Year	Opponent	Yards	Touchdowns
Franklin Hood	1927	Sherman High-Texas	6/8-264	4
Franklin Hood	1927	Randolph College	6/6-213	
Franklin Hood	1924	Penn Freshmen	150	3
John Graham	1929	Western Maryland Freshmen	2/2-115	

Longest Touchdown Receptions

Player	Year	Opponent	Yards
1. Albert Guarino	1924	Penn Freshmen	81
2. Conway Abee	1929	Western Maryland Freshmen	65
3. Paul Smith	1929	New York U. Freshmen	53
4. John Green	1924	Susquehanna Freshmen	50
5. Dutch Waite	1926	All-Scholastic Irwin	50
6. Mike Hardy	1929	Western Maryland Freshmen	50
7. Josh Williams	1927 (Jan.)	Randolph College	48
8. Wilmer Whitmore	1926	Sherman High-Texas	43
9. Richard Weston	1909	Bucknell Reserves	40

Longest Kick-off Returns for Touchdown

Player	Year	Opponent	Yards
Coffey Dillon	1910	Tyrone Y.M.C.A.	100
Ralph Cummings	1897	Lock Haven Normal	85
Heinle	1902	Philipsburg High	85
Wilmer Whitmore	1924	Penn Freshmen	80
Spooks Temple	1929	Bucknell Reserves	80

Longest Punt Returns

Player	Year	Opponent	Yards
Franklin Hood	1924	West Virginia Freshmen	70
Josh Williams	1925	Bucknell Freshmen	70
Paul Smith	1927	Erie Prep	69
Forest Decker	1911	Dickinson Seminary	50

Record Crowds To Watch Academy Football Teams

B-A Team	Opponent	Attend.
1. 1924	Penn Freshmen	25,000
2. 1924	Pitt Freshmen (at Greensburg)	10,000
3. 1925	at Sherman, Texas	10,000
4. 1924	at Saint Thomas	7,500
5. 1924	at Syracuse Freshmen	6,000
6. 1925	Pitt Freshmen (at Altoona)	1,500-2,000

Most Touchdowns-Game Player

Player	Year	Opponent	TD's
Coffey Dillon	1908	Altoona High	5
Coffey Dillon	1909	Bucknell Reserves	4
Harry Smith	1927	Randolph College	4
Harry Smith	1927	Tonkawa College, OK	4
Harry Temple	1927	Bucknell Freshmen	4
Harry Temple	1928	Wyoming Seminary	4

Most Touchdowns-Season Individual

Academy Player	Year	TD's
Coffey Dillon	1908	20
Harry Temple	1928	11
Harry Smith	1926	10
Coffey Dillon	1909	8
Forest Decker	1912	8
Josh Williams	1926	8
Forest Decker	1911	7
Franklin Hood	1926	7
T Purcel Beattie	1911	6
Rooney	1924	6
Albert Guarino	1924	6
Dutch Waite	1924	6

Records by Decade

1890-1899: 17-14-6
1900-1909: 43-26-13
1910-1919: 49-19-2
1920-1929: 73-17-5
1930-1932: 4-14-6

Overall Record: 186-90-32

Most Touchdowns-Career

Academy Player	TD's
Coffey Dillon	36
Harry Temple	21
Franklin Hood	16
Forest Decker	15
T Purcel Beattie	10
Harry Smith	10
Wayne Smith	9
Walter Loucks	8
Whitmore	8
Joe Twitmyer	7
Guy Smith	7
Josh Williams	7
Weston	7
Bill Bloyd	6
Albert Guarino	6
Rooney	6
Dutch Waite	6

Longest Field Goal

Player	Year	Opponent	Yards
Coffey Dillon	1911	Williamsport High	35
Franklin Hood	1924	Lafayette Freshmen	35
Coffey Dillon	1908	Philipsburg	30
Coffey Dillon	1910	Indiana Normal	25
Wayne Smith	1908	Altoona High	23
Wright	1908	Philipsburg	22
Coffey Dillon	1910	Lock Haven Normal	20
Coffey Dillon	1911	Dickinson Seminary	20
Bill Bloyd	1911	Lock Haven Normal	20

Most Field Goals-Season

Player	Year	FG's
Oakley Pantall	1906	2
Coffey Dillon	1910	2

Most Field Goals-Career

Player	FG's
Coffey Dillon	5
Oakley Pantall	2

Most PATS-Game

Player	Year	Opponent	PAT's
Coffey Dillon	1909	Bucknell Reserves	7
Bill Bloyd	1912	Osgood Athletic Club	7
Whitmore	1925	Sherman High, TX	6
Carson	1901	Lock Haven Normal	5
Clyde Oberlin	1908	Altoona High	4
Coffey Dillon	1909	Osgood Athletic Club	4
Coffey Dillon	1910	Tyrone YMCA	4
Franklin Hood	1924	Saint Thomas College	4

Most PATS-Season

Player	Year	PAT's
Bill Bloyd	1912	19
Coffey Dillon	1908	14
Coffey Dillon	1909	14
Coffey Dillon	1911	12

Most PATS-Career

Player	PAT's
Coffey Dillon	45
Bill Bloyd	23
Franklin Hood	15

Offensive Team Records

Most Yards Rushing-Game

BA Team	Opponent	Yards
1912	Bloomsburg Normal	408
1924	Lafayette Freshmen	351
1924	Dickinson Seminary	321
1904	Altoona High	297
1927	Randolph College, TX	266
1904	Altoona High	240
1926	Sherman High, TX	231

Most Yards Offense-Game

BA Team	Opponent	Yards
1926	Sherman High, TX	495
1927	Randolph College, TX	479
1912	Bloomsburg Normal	433
1924	Lafayette Freshmen	351
1924	Dickinson Seminary	321
1904	Altoona High	297

Most First Downs-Game

BA Team	Opponent	1st Downs
1926	Dean Academy	26
1925	Pitt Freshmen	13

Most Points-Game Player

Player	Year	Opponent	Points
Coffey Dillon	1909	Bucknell Reserves	27-4tds, 7pats
Coffey Dillon	1908	Altoona High	25-5tds
Harry Temple	1927	Bucknell Freshmen	25-4tds, 1pat
Harry Smith	1927	Tonkawa, OK	24-4tds
Harry Smith	1927	Randolph College	24-4tds
Whitmore	1925	Sherman High, TX	18-3tds
Dutch Waite	1926	All Scholastic Irwin	18-3tds

Most Points-Season Player

Player	Year	Points
Coffey Dillon	1908	114
Harry Temple	1928	66
Harry Smith	1926	60
Franklin Hood	1926	50

Most Points-Career

Player	Points
Coffey Dillon	241
Harry Temple	126
Franklin Hood	108
Josh Williams	66
Harry Smith	60

Most Points-Game Team

BA Team	Opponent	Score
1924	Susquehanna Freshmen	113-0
1928	Donora Athletic Club	99-0
1925	Carlisle Army Barracks	95-0
1922	Jersey Shore PRR Shopteam	82-0
1926	All Scholastic Irwin	81-7

Most Points Season-Team

BA Team	Points
1926	493
1924	458
1925	431
1929	267
1928	254

Fewest Points Season-Team (6+ games)

BA Team	Points
1930	19
1932	19
1907	32
1903	36
1905	41

Defensive Records

Fewest Yards Rushing-Game

BA Team	Opponent	Yards
1908	Altoona High	-23

Fewest Yards Offense-Game

BA Team	Opponent	Yards
1908	Altoona High	-23

Longest Fumble Return-for td

Player	Year	Opponent	Yards
Forest Decker	1911	Lock Haven Normal	50
Forest Decker	1912	Wyoming Seminary	40
Coffey Dillon	1908	Penn State	40
Orbison	1893	Philipsburg	31
Harry Temple	1928	Perkiomen	27
Wayne Smith	1908	Punxsutawney	23

Fewest First Downs-Game

BA Team	Opponent	First Downs
1923	Dickinson Seminary	0
1924	Carlisle Army Barracks	0
1925	Pitt Freshmen	1
1926	Randolph College	2

Most Points Given Up-Game

BA Team	Opponent	Score
1917	Indiana Normal	106-0
1919	Pitt Freshmen	56-2
1916	Penn State Freshmen	46-0
1894	Williamsport High	40-0
1915	Cornell Freshmen	40-7

Fewest Points Season-Team (6+games)

BA Team	Points
1924	0 (9 games)
1903	10
1925	13
1910	14
1909	15

Most Points Season-Team (6+games)

BA Team	Points
1917	152
1915	90
1927	86
1907	84
1921	66

Opponent Records

Longest Touchdown Run

Player	Year	Team	Yards
Andy Farabaugh	1899	Altoona High	50
Reuban Mull	1897	Philipsburg	40
Wheeland	1899	Potts College	25
Bastian	1906	Lock Haven Normal	25
Lytle	1907	Kiskementas	21
Andy Farabaugh	1898	Altoona High	17

Longest Touchdown Pass

Player	Year	Team	Yards
Zukus	1930	Temple Freshmen	45
	1929	West Point Freshmen	25

Longest Field Goal

Player	Year	Team	Yards
Nichols	1910	Bucknell Reserves	40
Kelley	1899	Altoona High	35*
Hodgson	1910	Dickinson Seminary	30
Fleming	1910	Lock Haven Normal	25

*drop kick

Longest Fumble Return-for td

Player	Year	Team	Yards
	1925	Dean Academy	92
	1897	Philipsburg	80
Barnes	1893	Philipsburg	30
Smith	1907	Kiskementas	30

National Prep School Champions: 1924, 1925, 1926.

Pennsylvania Prep School Champions: 1910, 1912, 1928.

Chapter 2: Bellefonte Academy Baseball 1890-1932
1890

Shortly after the 1890 major league baseball season ended the first week in October, John Montgomery Ward, a major leaguer born in Bellefonte, who played for the Academy and Penn State, brought his professional team to Bellefonte. The Brooklyn Ward's Wonders of the Players League beat a picked nine, 5-3, before a large crowd that included students from Penn State College, who had been given a half-day holiday to watch the game.

Ward went to Bellefonte in the off-season to hunt and work his dogs.

Ward

1893

Milesburg	0 0 0 0 1 1 0 0 0—2	WP: Houck
Academy	0 0 3 0 0 1 0 0 x—4	LP: Boggs

On July 4, 1893, a game of baseball was played in the afternoon at Centre Hall between the Academy and State College in which State College was victorious, 6-4.

1894

In the first game played at Hunter's Park, Lock Haven Normal defeated the Academy, 14-3.

1896

The Academy baseball team had a record of 2-2, scored 42 runs and allowed 37.

1897

The Cougars scored 65 runs to their opponents' 43 and finished at 3-2.

1898

The Academy went 12-0. Some of the games:

State College Town Team	1 0 1 0 0 0 3—5	WP: McIntyre
Bellefonte Academy	4 7 0 0 6 1 x—18	Date: May 19

Milesburg	0 3 0 0 2 0 2—7	WP: McIntyre
Academy	4 6 6 0 1 3 x—20	Date: May 26. Academy stole 15 bases.

Academy—7		WP: McIntyre
Resolute Athletic Club—6		Academy stole 8 bases.

Academy	5 1 11 0 5 0 0—22	WP: McIntyre—13 strikeouts.
Business Men	1 2 0 0 0 0 0—3	Academy stole 14 bases.

Player	Hits	HR	Runs	SB	2B	3B
John Henderson	7	0	7		1	1
Cummings	15	0	11			
J. Curtin	12	0	10		2	2
Maurice Otto	9	0	9		1	1
McIntyre	11	2	11		2	0
Potter	7	0	9			
Miller	6	0	5			
Gephart	12	0	6		1	0
Crowell	9	0	10		1	0
Brew	4	0	4			
Green	1					

McIntyre went 8-0 with 48 SO's, 19 BB's , 1 WP, and 5 HB. Green was 1-0.

1899

The Academy was outplayed by a strong Lock Haven Normal team in a 21-10 loss. Bellefonte beat the Has Beens, 17-16; the stats follow:

Player	Hits	Runs	HR's	SB	2B	3B
Gephart	3	3			1	1
John Henderson	2	3				
Cummings	2	3			1	
Miller	2	1			1	
Saylor	1	2				
Van Tassill	2	1	1			
Mac Curtin		2				
Crowell		1				
Keichline	1	1				

Saylor was the winning pitcher against the Has Beens.

1900

Bellefonte Academy	6	7 2 0 2 0 2—19						
State College Preps	1	0 4 4 1 4 6—20	LP: J. Curtin					

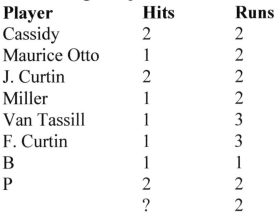

Player	Hits	Runs
Cassidy	2	2
Maurice Otto	1	2
J. Curtin	2	2
Miller	1	2
Van Tassill	1	3
F. Curtin	1	3
B	1	1
P	2	2
?		2

John Henderson--catcher

Note: Mike "King" Kelly, pictured above, played for Albert Spaulding's Chicago White Stockings. One of Spaulding's private detectives, circa 1885, reported to the owner that Kelly was spotted at 3 a.m.-- way past curfew—drinking lemonade in a Chicago bar. Kelly, called on the line, was mightily offended at what he considered a damned lie. It was straight whiskey he'd been drinking, he told Spaulding. "I never drank lemonade at that hour in my life."

1902

In a game at Glass Works Meadow, Bellefonte beat the State College Preps 14-1.

Bellefonte Academy	3 0 0 1 3 0 1 2 0 1 0—11
Lock Haven Normal	2 1 0 0 0 2 0 5 0 1 1—12

Lock Haven Normal	1 0 0 0 0 0 1 10 0—12
Bellefonte Academy	4 0 0 0 2 0 0 2 5—13

Cy Young

Academy second baseman Keichline got hurt.

1902—cont.

Player	Hits	Runs
Ferguson	6	4
J. Mahaffey	10	7
McCandless	8	8
G. McGee	16	12
Keichline	5	3
D. Mahaffey	4	4
Crider	4	5
J. McGee	9	9
J. Kerr	7	6
Cromer	2	2

Pitcher J. McGee was 1-1.

Pitcher G. McGee was 3-0, with 9 SO's & 3 BB's.

"Doc" McCandless became a star catcher at Washington & Jefferson College.

1903

Bellefonte Academy	0 0 0 2 0 0 2 2 0—6		
Susquehanna University	0 0 0 0 0 0 0 0 4—4		

Player	Hits	Hrs.	Runs
Ferguson	1		5
Harry Otto	2		2
McClafferty	5	1	5
Louder	3		3
McCandless	1		3
Thomas	2		3
Elliot Van de Vanter	2		1
McIntosh	2		1
Keichline	1		0

Pitcher McClafferty: 3 Wins, 1 Loss. SO's—24; BB's—4

Pitcher Harry Otto: 1 Win.

1904

Snow Shoe	0 0 0 3 1 0 0 0 0—4
Bellefonte Academy	2 4 1 2 0 2 0 3 x—14

A large crowd witnessed a 7-1 Bellefonte Athletic Club victory over the Academy.

The Academy played its home games at the Glassworks Meadow Field, on the road to Coleville, from 1904-1909.

Photo at right: **1904 Bellefonte Academy Baseball Team.**

Bobby Burns and William Louder were members of the squad.

1904—cont.

Player	Hits	Runs
Ferguson	2	1
Lauder	1	1
Henry	3	3
Bob Burns	2	1
Gutellius		2
Leathers	1	1
Roeluf	2	2
Pleck	2	1

Edward Kinsella

1905

Academy lineup: Harry Otto, catcher; Gutelius, 1st base; Broughton, 2nd base; Bamman, 3rd base; Rouselli, shortstop; Mellors, left field; Beddali, center field; Wetrick, right field.

Juniata College	1	0	2	0	2	0	0—5
Bellefonte Academy	1	0	0	9	5	4	x—19

Player	Hits	Runs	2b	3b	SB
Harry Otto	5	5	1		
Rouselli	4	5			
Jacobs	4	6		1	
Broughton	3	3			
Homan	3	3			
Gutellius	3	3			
Beddali	5	5			
Mellors	1				
Bamman	4	3	1		
Joe Twitmire	3	3			
Wetrick	2				

Photo at right: 1905 Bellefonte Academy Baseball Team.

Mortimer Miller and John Jacobs played for the Academy in 1905.

88

John Montgomery Ward

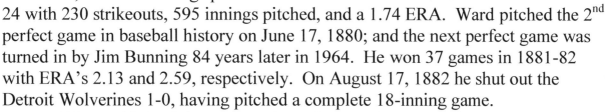

John Ward was a major league pitcher, shortstop, and manager, born on Blanchard Street in Bellefonte, PA, on March 3, 1860. He grew up in nearby Renovo and attended the Bellefonte Academy in the early 1870's. At age 13, the 5'9", 165 lb. Ward enrolled at Penn State College; and played on Penn State's first baseball team in 1875 at the age of 15.

Pitching for the Providence Grays, he went 22-13 with a 1.51 ERA; and in 1879, at age 19, was 47-19 with 239 strikeouts and a 2.15 ERA, with 587 innings pitched. In 1880 his record was 39-24 with 230 strikeouts, 595 innings pitched, and a 1.74 ERA. Ward pitched the 2nd perfect game in baseball history on June 17, 1880; and the next perfect game was turned in by Jim Bunning 84 years later in 1964. He won 37 games in 1881-82 with ERA's 2.13 and 2.59, respectively. On August 17, 1882 he shut out the Detroit Wolverines 1-0, having pitched a complete 18-inning game.

In 1883 Ward joined the New York Gothams (Giants in 1885); but an arm injury in 1884 forced him to teach himself to throw left-handed so he could play centerfield. He managed the team for the last 16 games. With a recuperated arm, he played shortstop in 1885; and graduated from Columbia Law School. He was a leader in forming the first sports labor union, *The Brotherhood of Professional Base Ball Players*.

Monte married actress Helen Dauvray, an avid baseball fan, in 1887; and the following year the Giants won the National League Pennant as well as a playoff series against the Saint Louis Browns of the American Association for the "Dauvray Cup", a trophy symbolic of major league baseball supremacy.

Over the winter, Ward was sold to the Washington Nationals for a record price of $12,000; but he insisted on a large portion of the money go to himself, causing the Nationals to nix the deal.

In 1889 he hit .299 for the Giants, who won a 2nd straight "World Series"; after which he created a Players' League and became a player/manager for the Brooklyn squad. Initially the new league drew about 50% of the National League players; but it eventually folded and Ward returned to the Giants for the 1892-94 seasons.

Monte Ward retired from baseball at the age of 34 with a career .275 average, 2,104 hits, and 540 stolen bases. He is the only man in history to win over 100 games as a pitcher and collect over 2000 hits.

He promptly entered the legal profession, representing baseball players against the league; and later turned to golf, winning several championships in the New York area. He died at age 65 in 1925 after a bout with pneumonia.

Ward is the only Penn Stater in the Hall of Fame, having been elected in 1964.

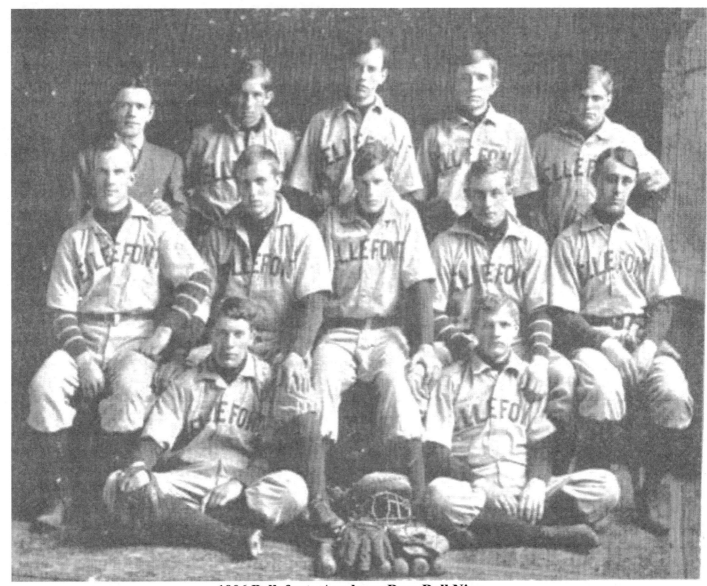

1906 Bellefonte Academy Base Ball Nine
First row, L-R: John Mitchell, Milford DuBarry. **Second row:** Harry Otto, Joseph Mosser, Captain Hallie Jacobs, Harry Driver, Charles Stoehr. **Third row:** Mgr. Jones, Frank Seyler, George Row, Edward Riddle, Oakley Pantall.

1906

Williamsport High School	0 0 2 0 0 0 0 0 0—2	
Bellefonte Academy	0 0 2 2 0 1 0 0 x—5	

WP: Hallie Jacobs; 5 SO's; 2 BB's. 200 spectators.

Bellefonte Academy 4, Dickinson Seminary 2.
WP: Hallie Jacobs; 14 SO's.

Player	Hits	Runs
Oakley Pantall	2	1
Riddle	1	1
Harry Otto	1	1
Hallie Jacobs	1	1

Joe Dunn

1907 Bellefonte Academy Base Ball Nine
First row, L-R: David Renton, Fred Moore. **Second row:** Paul Whetstone, McCardle Rollins, Captain "Toby" Fullerton, Louden, Oberlin. **Third row:** Francis Thompkins, Raymond Lingle, Shenk, John Mitchell, W. Grubb, Manager McCaslin.

1907

22 candidates came out for baseball, indicating a strong team in 1907. Manager McCaslin secured games with Lock Haven Normal, Juniata College, Kiski, Williamsport High, and Penn State Reserves. More dates were being pursued.

In a sloppy game with Kiski at State College, the Academy committed 7 errors and Kiski had 2 miscues. 600 people witnessed a 4-3 Bellefonte loss.

Player	Hits	Hrs	Runs	SB	2B	3B
C. Fullerton	1				1	
Lingle			1			
Rollins	2		1			1
Steele	1		1			

The Academy had a total of 100 students; 12 of which were from Wheeling, West Virginia, who called themselves the "Wheeling Club".

Toby Fullerton pitched for the Academy.

91

Sleppy, W.E. Carroll—A 3-year athlete at the Bellefonte Academy; played end on the football team, pitched for the baseball team, and was a member of the track team. From Allegheny H.S. in Pittsburg, he lost a 2-week battle with typhoid pneumonia, and died at the Bellefonte Hospital on January 30, 1910 at the age of 19. He had been elected captain for the 1910 baseball season.

Sterling, Hugh—A catcher on the Bellefonte Academy baseball team; he joined the Pittsburg Filipinos in the United States League in 1912. The team was named for Manager Deacon Phillippe, a former player for the Pittsburg Pirates.

1908   Capt. Wagner

In an opening game win over the Bucknell Reserves, R. Meyer and Mullen starred for the Academy. James Redding of Snow Shoe was a pitcher.

On June 18th, Coach Arthur Sloop and the Academy Athletic Association selected the following managers: Football—Arthur Abrams; Basketball—Merrill Wals; Baseball—William Crooks; Track—Harold Stevens.

1909 Bellefonte Academy Champion Baseball Team
First row, L-R: Rollins, Bolton, Wilson, Capt. Wagner, Sleppy, McCandless, Condo. **Second row:** Coach Hall, Mgr. Crooks, Jamison, Smith, Hugh Sterling, Craig, Asst. Mgr. Reish, Dillon, Mgr. Entrekin. The Academy won all the games played on its eastern trip.

Joseph Woods and Willard Boyd were members of the 1909 team. On April 22nd, the Academy beat Princeton Prep 3-2. Mullen was the winning pitcher; loser was White. Craig, Smith, and Sleppy had hits.

1909

In a 3-1 loss to the Bellefonte Ball Club, the Academy's Bolton started on the mound, but had to leave due to wildness. He was replaced by Carroll Sleppy, who was the losing pitcher. Kline was the winning pitcher for the Bellefonte Club

The Academy played Indiana Normal at 3:35 p.m. at the New Athletic Field on E. Bishop St. and won, 8-3.

McCandless

Bellefonte Academy	1	1	0	2	0	0	0	0	0—4
Bucknell Reserves	0	0	0	0	0	0	0	1	0—1

Player	Hits	Runs
Wilson	1	
McCandless	3	2
Rollins	6	2
Wayne Smith	5	3
Archy Condo	3	0
Sprague	1	0
Carroll Sleppy	6	3
Hugh Sterling	6	2
Coffey Dillon	4	3
John M. Wagner	5	4
Craig	3	5
Frank Jamison	3	2
Laderer	1	1
Rathmeyer	1	1
Elsey	2	1
Mullen	2	0

Pitchers:

Carroll Sleppy—Record 4-1; SO's—20; BB's—1;HB—1; Shutouts—2.

Bolton—Record 4-0; SO's—3; BB's—1.

Mullen—Record 1-0.

Coach Evans

After winning the series with the Bellefonte town team, the Academy Baseball Team continued with scheduled games.

Lock Haven Normal was defeated by a 3-2 score. A game was arranged with Juniata College for May 22nd, but it was rained out. The team left for Indiana on May 23rd, stopping at Altoona for the night and going on to Indiana the next day where they lost by a 6-4 score. On Saturday of the same week, the team went to Bloomsburg and was defeated by 10-5. On the return trip, due to time-table mix-ups, the boys spent 4 hours in Northumberland before reaching Lock Haven by train the evening of May 31st. Bellefonte won the game with Lock Haven Normal 7-1. Sleppy performed well for the Academy, which has a .667 winning percentage.

The Bellefonte Academy Second team defeated the Milesburg team in a highly exciting game by the score of 17-10. The good work of the second team indicated there is good material for a future varsity squad.

1910

Player	Hits	Hr.	Runs	SB	2B	3B
Coffey Dillon	6	2	8		1	1
George Cheers	4		2			
Beattie	8		6	1	1	
Negley	4		4	1		
Hugh Sterling	8		4	2	2	
Frank Jamison	5		6		3	
Wayne Smith	7		4		1	1
Archy Condo	10		8	1		
Louden	2		1			
Twitmire		3		2		
Bassett	8					
Sprague		1		1		
Harry Symes	3					

Pitching:
Cheers—Record 5-0;
SO—1; BB—1.

Harry Symes—
Record 4-0; SO's—24;
BB's—6; Shutouts—2.

Capt. Condo

Twitmire—Record 1-1
SO's—13; BB's—1

On Saturday, September 23rd, 1910, the new men beat the old men in an annual baseball contest. The battery for the new men was Beattie and Symes; for the old men, Basset and Robison made up the battery. The lineup for the old men: Irwin, 1b; Miller, 2b; Negley, ss; Jamison, 3b; Gray, Yocum, and Reiter in the outfield. The new men lined up with: E.E. Eisenbeis, 1b; Myers, 2b; Smith, ss; Meredith, 3b; Stead, rf; Reese, cf; Dunsmore, lf. The game was called in the 7th inning due to rain; and the new men won 7-1.

Hits: new 7, old 4. Errors: new 2, old 3. Strikeouts: Beattie 3, Reese 2. Symes 5, Bassett 4.

The umpire was "Dutch" Otto.

On a cold spring 1910 Saturday afternoon in Bellefonte, the Cougars took on Indiana Normal at the complex on East Bishop Street and won, 6-1. Indiana was able to put men on base, but the Academy defense allowed only a run in the 4th inning. The Blue and Gold came back with 2 in the 5th, added 3 in the 6th, and tacked on an insurance run in the 8th. The spectators that came to watch the game were compelled to wear overcoats, indicating public interest in Academy baseball. The visitors remained in Bellefonte Saturday night and left Sabbath morning on the 9:05 a.m. train back to Indiana. The lineups:

Bellefonte 6	R	H	O	A	E		Indiana 1	R	H	O	A	E
Bassett, 2b	0	2	3	1	0		Martin, 3b	0	0	1	3	0
Sterling, 1b	0	1	9	0	1		Ruffner, 1b	0	3	14	0	0
Condo, lf	1	1	3	0	0		Johns, 2b	0	1	2	3	0
Smith, rf	1	1	0	0	0		Brickley, ss	0	0	0	2	2
Dillon, cf	2	1	3	0	0		Rodkey, lf	0	1	0	0	0
Beattie, c	1	1	7	6	0		McCreight, rf	0	0	1	0	0
Jamison, 3b	0	0	0	2	0		Crotley, cf	0	1	0	0	0
Negley, ss	1	1	1	1	2		Hart, c	0	1	5	2	0
Cheers, p	0	1	1	4	1		Blase, p	0	0	1	4	0
Totals	6	9	27	14	5		Totals	1	7	24	14	0

Indiana	0	0	0	1	0	0	0	0	0—1
Bellefonte	0	0	0	0	2	3	0	1	x—6

1910 Bellefonte Pennsylvania Champion Base Ball Nine

Front row, L-R: Cheers, Beattie, Jamison, Bassett. **Second row:** Louden, Sterling, Dillon, Captain Condo, Symes, Sprague. **Third row:** Manager "Skinny" Boyd, Gray, Irwin, Smith, Miller, Negley, Coach Evans. Absent: Foster Doane.

The season was from April 1st to June 4th.

Academy 7	Bellefonte Athletic Club 2		Academy 17	Carnegie Tech Pittsburg 1
Academy 4	University of Vermont 2		Academy 4	Penn State Varsity 10
Academy 8	Bucknell Academy 3		Academy 1	Altoona P.R.R. 0
Academy 6	Alliance of State College 5		Academy 4	Juniata College 1
Academy 1	Lock Haven Normal 0		Academy 3	Bloomsburg Normal 0
Academy 6	Indiana Normal 1		Academy 2	Altoona P.R.R. 3
Academy 12	Juniata College 1		Academy 1	Bloomsburg Normal 12
Academy 0	Bloomsburg Normal 4		Academy 5	Bucknell Academy 0
Academy 1	Lock Haven Normal 1			

Manager Willard J. Boyd; Asst. Manager Ivan Mahoney; Captain Archibald Condo.

Bellefonte had its best record ever at 12-4-1; scored 82 runs and gave up 45.

Archy Condo replaced Carroll Sleppy as captain. Sleppy had passed away. Evans coached the team and W.J. "Skinny" Boyd was the manager.

Negley was hit in the eye by a thrown ball in the game with Bloomsburg Normal and knocked unconscious.

Hugh Sterling went on to catch for the Pittsburgh Club of the newly formed U.S. League.

The remarkable record of the 1910 Academy Nine gave them an unquestioned title to the Secondary School Championship of Pennsylvania. Gold baseball medals were presented to each Academy player for their excellent work.

Archy Condo is now playing for Swarthmore and Paul McCandless is suiting up at Washington & Jefferson.

1911

Coach Evans left the Academy for a position at a large school in Cleveland, Ohio.
New **Coach I.C. Kimble** is pictured at the left.
T. Purcell Beattie, pictured at the right, was the baseball captain for the 1911 season.
Mgr. Ralph "Count" Yocum; Asst. Mgr. D.B. Piper.
Returning players: Beattie, Smith, Symes, Bassett, Irwin, Negley, Jamison, and Dillon.
New men: Myers, Bloyd, Wilson, Watson, and Wallace.
Watson, Kline, and Symes are working in the box, and Wallace will catch them.

1500 fans were on hand for the season's opener on April 1st with Penn State, which the Academy lost, 3-1. State lineup: Bubb, rf; Kelly, 2b; Workman, cf; Eberlein, 1b; Haddow, 3b; Craig, ss; Carlson, lf; Young, c; Whitney, p; Minich,p. Bellefonte lineup: Bassett, 2b; Negley, ss; Bloyd, lf; Dillon, cf; Smith, rf; Doc Irwin, 1b; Jamison, 3b; Beattie, c; Symes, p.

	Runs	Hits	Put-outs	Assists	Errors
Penn State	3	5 (Eberlein 3; Kelly, Young 1)	21	11	2
Bellefonte	1	6 (Smith 2; Bassett, Negley, Jamison, Symes 1)	18	8	4

Due to the cold weather, only 7 innings were played.

With the game tied at 7 in the 8th inning, Red Smith hit a home run to win the game over Juniata College, 8-7.

The Academy played the Penn State College Reserves at Hughes Field at 3 p.m. and lost, 7-4.

Forsythe, a professional player, pitched for Lock Haven Normal in a 4-2 win over Bellefonte Academy.

Other wins: Beaver Club, 15-0 & 14-10; Lock Haven Normal, 5-1; Bloomsburg Normal, 9-2; Williamsport High, 11-2; Bucknell Academy, 10-2; Juniata College, 14-12. Bellefonte was defeated by Susquehanna, 4-1.

Player	Hits	Hrs	Runs	SB	2B	3B	
James Bassett	7	0	1	0	0	0	**Pitching:**
Negley	6	1	8				Harry Symes—
Wayne Smith	9	2	11	0	4	1	Record 4-2;
Frank Jamison	6		3		1		SO's—21; BB's—4.
Harry Symes	4		2		2		
Coffey Dillon	9	0	6		2	1	Watson—Record 2-0;
T. Purcell Beattie	7		7		1		SO's—17
Bill Bloyd	7		4		2		

Kline—Record 1-0; SO's—2

The Athletic Banquet was held on Saturday evening, March 2, 1912 at the Brockerhoff House. Guests included Rev. George R. Hawes, D.D. William P. Humes, Col. Hugh S. Taylor, Burgess John J. Bower, and Principal Emeritus James Potter Hughes.
John Van Pelt played on the 1911 team.

1911 Bellefonte Academy Baseball

T. Purcell "Cocky" Beattie, of Wheeling, West Virginia was elected to lead the Varsity nine by a unanimous vote by the letter men of last year's team.

J.A. "Doc" Irwin was the first baseman. Arbenz was a member of the squad.

Bellefonte 14, Beaver Club 10

The Academy nine travelled to State College and played a return game with the Beaver Club on April 22nd, 1911. Rain fell throughout the contest and the pitchers resorted to fast balls. Bellefonte's Watson pitched both Beaver Club games.

Bellefonte	AB	R	H	PO	A	E	Beaver Club	AB	R	H	PO	A	E
Bassett 2	5	0	1	0	0	0	Gillband 3	5	3	4	1	0	1
Negley s	3	3	0	0	0	0	Atkinson c	4	1	1	5	2	0
Dillon m	4	3	3	0	0	0	Kline 2	4	1	2	0	3	0
Beattie c	2	2	1	8	3	0	Snyder s	3	0	0	1	1	2
Smith r	4	2	0	0	0	0	Crumrine 1	3	1	0	8	0	2
Symes 3	5	2	3	0	0	1	Garver m	3	2	1	1	1	0
Irwin 1	2	1	1	6	0	2	Fulton l	2	1	1	0	0	0
Bloyd l	4	1	2	0	0	0	Johnstonbaug r	3	1	3	0	0	0
Watson p	3	0	0	3	1	0	Weaver p	3	0	0	1	5	0
Totals	32	14	11	21	5	3		33	10	11	21	12	6

Struck out—Weaver 2, Watson 9. Two base hits—Irwin, Symes, Atkinson.

Bellefonte Academy	1	5	0	2	0	5	1—14
Beaver Club	1	0	0	1	2	0	6—10

FERGUSON, BOSTON NAT'L

Bellefonte 5, Lock Haven 1

On Friday, April 28th, Bellefonte defeated Lock Haven Normal 5 to 1 in one of the fastest games ever played on the Normal's field. Harry A. "Libby" Symes pitched and had Central State at his mercy. Normal's Ritter was strong at first, but the Academy bats came alive, highlighted by Smith's 8th inning home run. James E. Bassett was the second baseman.

Bellefonte	AB	R	H	PO	A	E	Central State	AB	R	H	PO	A	E
Beattie c	3	1	2	10	1	0	Metley c	4	1	1	11	3	0
Negley s	3	0	0	1	2	1	Anderson l	4	0	0	0	0	0
Irwin 1	4	0	1	8	2	0	Benson 2	3	0	0	3	0	0
Dillon m	4	0	1	2	1	0	J. Ritter 1	4	0	1	12	0	0
Smith r	2	2	2	0	0	0	Sherman m	4	0	0	0	0	0
Bassett 2	3	1	2	1	0	0	Maloney r	3	0	2	0	0	0
Jamison 3	4	0	0	2	1	0	Hunter s	3	0	0	0	0	0
Bloyd l	2	1	0	0	0	0	Henninger 3	3	0	1	1	1	1
Symes p	2	0	0	2	4	0	H. Ritter p	3	0	0	0	7	1
Totals	27	5	8	27	11	1		31	1	5	27	11	1

Home runs—Smith. Two base hits—Dillon, Irwin. Struck out—Symes 11; Ritter 11. Base on balls—Symes 1; Ritter 3.

Bellefonte 8, Juniata College 7

On May 2, 1911, in a game marked by much wrangling over decisions and very cold weather, Bellefonte defeated Juniata College, 8-7. The game was called in the 8th inning to permit the Academy squad to catch a train home. Although this was agreed upon prior to the game, the local papers accused Bellefonte of quitting as soon as they had one run to the good. Red Smith had 2 doubles and a game- winning home run; while Dippin Bloyd chipped in with 2 doubles and a single. Pitcher Watson started for the Academy but was replaced in the 4th inning by Symes.

DELAHANTY, l f
St. Louis National League Ball Club "CARDINALS"
by H. H. Bregstone, St. Louis.

Bellefonte	AB	R	H	PO	A	E		Juniata	AB	R	H	PO	A	E
Beattie c	3	1	0	5	2	0		Bilger c	4	2	2	8	2	0
Negley s	3	1	0	1	2	0		Emmert l	3	2	1	1	0	0
Irwin 1	3	1	0	10	0	0		Wardlow 1	2	1	1	8	0	0
Dillon m	4	1	2	1	0	0		Omo s	4	1	2	2	3	0
Smith r	4	3	3	0	0	0		Schuss m	4	0	1	2	0	2
Bassett 2	4	0	1	3	1	0		Nickel 2	4	0	0	0	0	0
Jamison 3	4	1	1	3	1	0		Ream r	4	0	0	2	1	1
Bloyd l	4	0	3	1	0	0		Putt 3	3	1	0	0	2	0
Symes p	2	0	0	0	2	0		Stairs p	2	0	0	1	0	0
Watson p	2	0	0	0	2	0								
Totals	33	8	10	24	10	1			30	7	7	24	8	3

Home runs—Omo, Smith. Two base hits—Smith 2; Dillon; Bassett;
Bloyd 2; Bilger 2; Wardlow. Struck out—Symes 4; Watson 1; Stairs 7.

Bellefonte	0	1	3	1	1	1	0	1	x—8
Juniata	2	0	0	3	0	0	2	0	x—7

Bellefonte 9, Bloomsburg 2

On Friday afternoon, May 5th, 1911, the Academy defeated a strong Bloomsburg Normal nine by the score of 9-2. The game was played at Hughes Field and the nice weather accounted for the large crowd. Sheets Watson, the Academy's new heaver, scattered 5 hits while striking out 8 against one of Bellefonte's oldest rivals. Negley and Bloyd each had 3 hits, while Jamison, Bloyd and Dillon each had 2 singles. Smith starred with the stick for Bloomsburg.

Bellefonte Academy	AB	R	H	PO	A	E		Bloomsburg Normal	AB	R	H	PO	A	E	
Beattie c	1	1	1	10	2	0		Keiser lf	4	1	2	2	0	0	
Negley ss	5	2	3	0	4	1		Smith 1b	3	0	2	0	0	0	Two base hits—
Irwin 1b	5	0	3	10	0	0		Lubach 2	3	0	0	2	0	0	Bloyd 2; Smith.
Dillon cf	5	0	2	1	0	0		Sheridan c	3	0	1	3	0	0	Three base hit--
Smith rf	4	1	1	2	0	5		Fausel 3	3	0	0	3	2	0	Smith.
Bassett 2	4	1	1	2	1	1		Clemmens ss	4	0	0	0	4	2	Struck out by
Jamison 3	4	2	2	1	1	0		Creasy rf	4	0	0	0	0	0	Watson—8;
Bloyd lf	3	2	2	0	0	0		Engelhart cf	4	0	0	5	2	1	by Pace—4.
Watson p	4	0	9	1	3	1		Pace p	4	1	0	0	1	0	Umpire—Curtin
Totals	35	9	15	27	11	8			32	2	5	24	9	3	

Lock Haven Normal 4, Bellefonte Academy 2

For the first time this year, on Sat., May 13, 1911, the Academy nine went down to defeat on their own grounds. Aided by several Bellefonte errors and a few bunched hits, the visitors scored 4 runs in the 7th inning. Lock Haven used a pitcher who had pitched several games for Harrisburg in the Tri-State League. Bellefonte tallied their 2 runs in the 4th inning and seemed a likely winner until the 7th. Symes pitched well for the home team despite the errors by his team.

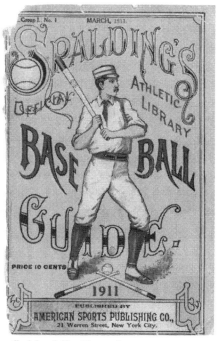

Lock Haven Normal	R	H	O	A	E
Metley c	1	2	15	2	1
Benson 2b	0	1	2	1	0
Ritter 1b	0	0	6	0	0
Anderson lf	0	1	1	0	0
W. Ritter 3b	0	0	1	0	0
Henninger 3b	0	0	1	0	0
Sherman cf	0	0	1	0	0
Maloney rf	1	0	1	0	0
Hunter ss	1	1	0	1	0
Forsythe p	1	1	0	0	0
Totals	4	6	27	4	1

Bellefonte Academy	R	H	O	A	E
Beattie c	0	1	10	2	0
Negley ss	0	0	5	3	2
Irwin 1b	1	0	8	0	0
Dillon cf	0	0	0	0	0
Smith rf	1	0	1	0	0
Bloyd lf	0	0	2	0	0
Jamison 3b	0	1	0	1	1
Bassett 2b	0	0	0	1	0
Symes p	0	0	1	4	0
	2	2	27	11	3

Lock Haven Normal   0 0 0 0 0 0 4 0 0—4
Bellefonte Academy   0 0 0 2 0 0 0 0 0—2

Umpire—Donovan. 3-base hit—Forsythe. 2-base hit—Jamison.

Bellefonte Academy 10, Bucknell 2

Bellefonte won its 7th victory by defeating Bucknell Academy 10-2 in a one-sided game on Saturday, May 20th. Kline pitched for the Blue and Gold, allowing only 3 hits. Negley was outstanding in the field while Captain Beattie and Eisenbeis excelled at the plate.

Bellefonte	R	H	P	A	E
Beattie 2b	2	3	0	1	0
Negley ss	1	1	2	2	1
Irwin 1b	0	1	13	0	0
Dillon m	2	1	2	0	0
Smith r	2	1	0	0	0
Eisenbeis l	1	3	0	0	0
Jamison 3b	0	1	0	3	0
Wallace c	1	1	10	3	0
Kline p	1	0	0	4	0
Totals	10	12	27	13	1

Bucknell	R	H	P	A	E
Lonen 1b	0	0	10	0	1
Miller ss	1	0	2	2	0
Fahringer 3	0	2	3	4	1
Bucher lf	0	0	3	0	0
Grover r	0	1	0	0	0
Clark c	1	0	3	0	0
Davis 2	0	0	1	0	0
Hause m	0	0	1	0	0
Harter p	0	0	1	2	0
	2	3	24	5	2

Bellefonte   4 0 1 1 1 0 1 2 0—10
Bucknell   0 1 0 0 0 0 0 0 1—2

Two base hits—Jamison, Grover, Beattie, Eisenbeis 2,
Three base hits—Dillon, Fahringer.
Strikouts—Kline 2; Harter 3.

Penn State Reserves 7, Bellefonte Academy 4

Bellefonte lost its 3rd game of the season to the State Reserves, a team composed of reserved men on the State Varsity squad, on Friday, May 19th. The game began beneath a threatening sky and in the 6th inning the rain fell in torrents, necessitating calling the game. Until that point the game was fast and close; but in the 5th inning errors by the Academy and a few opportune hits gave the visitors 6 runs, only 3 of which were earned. Bellefonte scored 3 earned runs; but the remaining one came on an error. Symes and P. Murphy pitched excellent ball, keeping the hits scattered and both finished strong despite the extreme heat of the afternoon. The lineups:

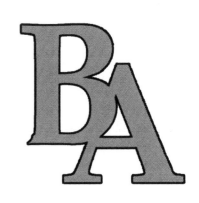

Bellefonte	R	H	PO	A	E		State	R	H	PO	A	E
Beattie c	1	0	6	3	0		Barrett cf	1	1	4	0	1
Negley ss	0	0	2	0	0		Butz ss	1	2	0	2	0
Irwin 1b	0	2	5	0	0		McKlom rf	1	0	0	0	0
Dillon cf	0	0	1	0	0		Turner 2b	1	1	1	3	0
Smith rf	1	1	2	0	0		Prolette lf	1	0	1	0	0
Jamison 3b	0	0	1	0	1		Hartz 1b	0	0	5	1	0
Wallace 2b	0	0	1	1	1		Murphy 3b	1	0	1	0	0
Eisenbeis lf	1	1	0	0	0		Graham c	1	2	5	0	0
Symes p	1	1	0	3	0		P. Murphy p	0	0	1	0	0
Totals	4	5	18	7	2			7	6	18	0	1

Bellefonte	0	1	1	0	2	0	—4	
State Reserves	0	1	0	0	6	0	—7	

Two base hit—Butz. Three base hits—Eisenbeis, Symes.
Struck outs—Symes 6; Murphy 5. Umpires—Kimble, Bellefonte; Weaver, State.

Second Team Scores

By fast and consistent playing the Reserve Squad of the Academy have annexed 2 of the 3 games they have played this year. With Kline in the box* and good support behind him, they succeeded in defeating their close rivals, Bellefonte High School and also State College High, but went down to inglorious defeat before the Lock Haven scrubs on May 13th by the score of 6-4. The many errors were the cause of this defeat as no fault could be found in Kline's pitching.

On Saturday morning, March 25, 1911, the second and third floors of the main dormitory clashed in a game of baseball, the latter team winning by the score of 22-4. The second floor's poor showing was due to the lack of a good pitcher and of their poor stick work. The feature of the game was the pitching of Weekley for the third floor, who held his opponents down to 5 scattered hits.

								H	E
2nd floor	0	0	2	0	0	0	2—4	5	4
3rd floor	1	1	0	0	15	5	x--22	11	2

Batteries: 2nd floor—Stead, Smith, Elliott, and Heathcote.
3rd floor—Weekley and Taylor.

*Note: In the early days of baseball, there was no mound and pitching plate. The pitcher delivered the ball underhand from a 6 ft. by 8 ft. rectangle, which was called the "box"

1912 Season—March 30-June 1.

Academy 11	State College High School 1	Academy 13	Bloomsburg Normal 10
Academy 1	Penn State Varsity 3	Academy 15	Beaver Club of State College 0
Academy 14	Beaver Club of State College 10	Academy 5	Lock Haven Normal 1
Academy 8	Juniata College 7	Academy 9	Bloomsburg Normal 2
Academy 11	Williamsport High School 2	Academy 2	Lock Haven Normal 4
Academy 4	State Reserves 7 (unfinished)	Academy 10	Bucknell Academy 2
Academy 14	Juniata College 12	Academy 1	Susquehanna University 4
Academy 15	Bucknell Academy 5	Academy 2	Susquehanna University 1
Academy 2	Bloomsburg Normal 1	Academy 6	Indiana Normal 0
Academy 18	U. of Pittsburgh 7	Academy 0	Duquesne U. 4

Manager Ralph "Count" Yocum; Asst. Manager Dwight Piper; Captain Purcell Beattie.

John Maioli of the Academy team was hit in the head by a batted ball. Reserves Myers, Stead, Eisenbeis, McKee, and Taylor tried out for the varsity team.

Player	Hits	Hrs	Runs	SB	2B	3B	
T. Purcell Beattie	7	0	7	1	1	1	**Pitching:**
Bill Bloyd	12	2	9	0	0	0	Harry Symes—
Coffey Dillon	10	2	7	2	1	0	Record 3-1; SO's—45;
Myers	2	0	2				BB's—4; HB—1;
Francis	6	0	1				WP—1; Shutout—1.
Frank Jamison*	6	0	7	1	2	0	
Forest Decker	2	0	4	1			Forest Decker—
Arbenz	3	0	6	1			Record 2-1; SO's—19;
Negley	5	0	2	2	1	0	BB's—11; WP—3.
Harry Symes**	7		9				

*Captain for 1912.   **Joined the United States Baseball League.

Frank "Jamie" Jamison was from Moundsville, West Virginia.

The eastern trip during Easter vacation included games with prominent eastern schools.

Symes was winning pitcher against Indiana Normal on May 23rd and Pitt on May 24th in relief of Smith. Decker was the losing pitcher against Duquesne on May 25th. The game with E.

Liberty of Pittsburgh was cancelled.

On Wednesday, June 11, 1910, a wonderful and sensational game occurred between the Academy Champions and the Chinese 9 of the University of Hawaii, which Bellefonte won, 4 to 1.

Since leaving San Francisco, the Chinese won about 60 out of 70 games on their tour.

1913 Bellefonte Academy Baseball Nine
First row, L-R: Carlson, ss; Kennedy, p; Elliott, 2b; Captain Symes, p; Frank Jamison, 3b; Beattie, c; Beer, 1b. **Second row:** Coach Weller; Negley, rf; Bloyd, cf; Decker, lf; Smith, p; Mgr. Skip Hadesty.

Since the warm weather had set in, the fellows who had been anxiously awaiting such weather were practicing daily. Under the supervision of Coach Weller, squads went daily to the field and light batting and field work were practiced. The diamond was too wet to play upon; but with nice weather and no rain the fellows began working hard to prepare for the hard schedule Manager Hadesty arranged.

Returning from last year's team was the battery of Beattie and Symes, which had won many games. Francis, Decker, Bloyd, and Jamison were expected to provide good material about which to build a fast team.

New candidates were: Elliott, Carlson, Kann, Lines, Eisenbeis, Beer, Jones, Heim, Weisenburn, Polansky, Eisaman, Ellis, Soles, Palmer, Holley, Beddal.

Games were being arranged with teams the likes of the University of Pittsburgh, Dickinson College, Bloomsburg Normal, Indiana Normal, Westinghouse of Pittsburgh, Juniata College, and State College High School.

Harry "Libby" Symes, having returned to the Academy after Easter vacation, was elected captain of the Academy baseball team. A great player, Symes was best known for his ability to heave the pill.[8]

---

[8] Symes was an outstanding pitcher.

Bellefonte Academy 16, State College High School 1.

On an April Friday afternoon in 1913, the Academy defeated the State College High School baseball team by the score of 16-1. Jamison (2 singles,4 runs), Beattie (single, 2 runs, 3 stolen bases), and Smith (5 shut-out innings, scored a run) played well for Bellefonte; and Smith struck out 5 and walked 1 in 5 innings. He was relieved by Kennedy. Beer, Elliott, and Carlson played good defense at first, second, and third base respectively. Bloyd, Decker, and Symes handled their outfield positions well. McClure and Smith were the only Academy players without a hit. Hits: Symes 2, Bloyd 2, Decker 2, Elliott 2, Beer 2, Carlson 1, Kennedy 1, Francis 1.

State College High School	0 0 0	0 0 0	1 0	0—1
Bellefonte Academy	5 4 2	0 2 3	0 0	x—16

E.C. Weller coached the baseball team. Frank Seyler was on the squad.

Harry Symes signed with Pittsburgh of the Federal League and Wayne "Red" Smith signed with the Conemaugh team.

Player	Hits	Hrs	Runs	SB	2B	3B		
T. Purcell Beattie	8	0	8	3	0	0		
Harry Symes	2	0	2	1	1	0	**Pitching:**	
Frank Jamison	8	0	5				Harry Symes—	
Elliott	7	0	7	0	2		Record 4-0; SO's—21;	
Forest Decker	9	0	7	1	1	1	BB's—5; HB—3	
Negley	4	0	1					
Doc Carlson	4	0	2				Kennedy—Record 2-0.	
Bill Bloyd	9	0	5	1	1			
Kennedy	3	0	2					
Beer	2	0	1					
Francis	1		1					

On May 10th, Bellefonte topped Lyceum of Altoona 8-6 in very cold weather.

The team left Bellefonte Thursday morning, May 22nd for its western trip and returned Sunday on the 8:25 train. The Academy beat Indiana Normal 4-2; the game with Westinghouse of Pittsburgh was cancelled; and the game with the University of Pittsburgh was rained out.

The Base Ball Nine for Season of 1914

L-R: Henry Shenk, Manager; Danny Francis, leftfield; Mangan, third base; Hammond, leftfield; Carlson, short stop; C. Jones, first base; Kennedy, pitcher; Captain Elliott, second base; Montgomery, pitcher; Pott, catcher; Steiniger, centerfield; Snyder, pitcher; Hullihen, rightfield; P. Jones, catcher; Weller, coach.

Other players: Frank Jamison, third base; Henry Holley, left field; Fred Palmer, pitcher; Victor Polansky, centre field.

The first game of the season at the field on East Bishop Street was against the Altoona Collegians.

The Academy lost to Bloomsburg Normal on an overthrow.

Bellefonte topped the Chinese University of Hawaii 13-6 before a crowd of 1500.

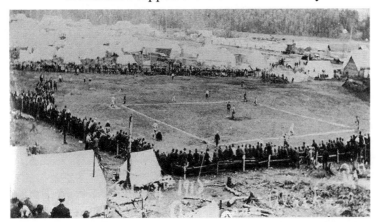

1915

Vogel coached the baseball team with Miksch as manager.

Baseball Players: Manager Carl Miksch; Captain Clarence Hullihen, rf; Casey Jones, 1b; Thomas Mangan, 3b; John Pott, c; George Dreese, cf; Henry Leasure, p; Joseph Harrick, p; Gordon Callender, p; J.R. Stephens, 3b; Allum Grimm, 1b; James Curley, ss; John Powell, 2b.

Baseball game in Anchorage, Alaska in July of 1915

Bellefonte Academy Varsity Baseball Team of 1916
First row, L-R: Riddle, pitcher; Myers, center field; Dahlin, pitcher; Smith, catcher; Curley, short stop; Smoczynski, right field; Manuel, third base. **Second row:** Hartman, coach; Grimm, left field; Goodling, pitcher; Kelly, second base; Kelsch, first base; Josephson, first base; Moffitt, manager.

1918

Mrs. Fulton of Scranton made new uniforms for the Academy baseball team.

On Friday afternoon, May 14th, Bellefonte Academy and Buffalo, New York High School played 12 innings of close and exciting play at Hughes Field in Bellefonte, ending in a 6-5 victory for the home team.

The First Catcher's Mask

The first catcher's mask was used by James Alexander Tyng in 1877 in a Harvard game with the Lynn Live Oaks. It was invented by Fred W. Thayer, a 1978 Harvard grad, who got his idea from the mask used in fencing. It was made by a tinsmith in Cambridge and tried out in a gymnasium in the winter of 1877. The first time it was used in a game, the opponents claimed an "unfair" advantage.

In 1878 the mask sold for $3 and was manufactured by A.G. Spaulding and Brothers Company. Sales took off in 1879 with the elimination of the one bounce rule—catchers were then required to catch a 2-strike foul tip in order to record an out.

Thayer (L) & Tyng (R)

Prior to using a mouthpiece in the 1860's, catchers would put tightly wound rubber bands around their teeth to protect them from getting knocked out.

Buffalo, New York High School vs. the Bellefonte Academy, May 14, 1918 at Hughes Field.

1919

1920

The Academy played Susquehanna Freshmen in the first game of the season at Hughes Field in Bellefonte at 3:30 p.m.

1921

A Baseball Tragedy

In 1889, a young boy named Edgar S. Howard was returning from his day's chores when he joined a sandlot game already in progress. We don't know exactly what he was doing, but he must have been clearing a field of stumps or destroying a beaver dam.

He dug in at the plate, waiting on the pitch. When it came it hit him near the hip. An explosion followed and the whole fleshy portion of his right arm was blown away. The boy had been given a dynamite cap, and he put it in his pocket and forgot all about it when he began playing ball. He was carried to his father's house, but was not expected to survive long.

106

The Baseball Team—Season of 1922
First row, L-R: Schmidt, Chase, Ash, Captain Rigby, Frauenheim, Fleming, McCleary.
Second row: Coach Hamberger, McCabe, Raschella, Irwin, Anderson, Holter, Manager
Greenwald. The pitchers were Jones and Ash.

This team was the only one that defeated the strong Pitt Freshmen Team in the
1922 season. It also defeated such teams as the Bucknell Reserves, Dickinson
Seminary, and Stroudsburg Normal.

1922 Fraternity Baseball Game. Ohio Stadium being constructed in the background.

1923 Bellefonte Academy Base Ball Nine

First row, L-R: Arras, pitcher; Diffenbach, left field; O'Neil, third base; Schmidt, catcher; Berkes, short stop; McCabe, right field. **Second row:** Manager Boyd; Fisher, pitcher; Breene, right field; Coleman, second base; Archibald, center field; O'Brien, first base; Blackburn, second base; Assistant Manager Wilson.

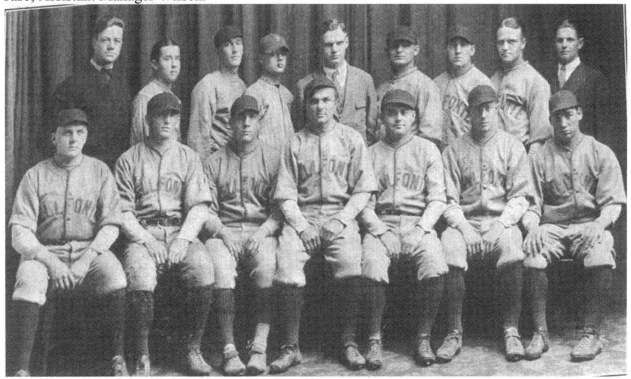

The 1924 Victorious Base Ball Nine

First row, L-R: Blackburn, 3b; Cutler, 1b; E. Williams, c; Buyny, ss; Walsh, c; Grimm, p; Dimeolo, cf. **Second row:** Kutz, rf; Jones, p; Sub. Shively, cf; Sub. Rugh, 2b; Coach Snavely; Guarino, lf; Captain O'Neil, 2b; Wittman, p; Manager S. Wilson.

This nine won eight of 9 scheduled games, defeating Dickinson Seminary twice, Bloomsburg Normal twice, Bucknell Reserves, Pitt Freshmen, Syracuse University Freshmen, and Franklin and Marshall Academy. They were defeated by the Penn Freshmen.

1925

Edwin Hill of the Academy hit a homer over the Montgomery & Co. sign in left field against the Bellefonte Baseball Club. He was the first player to accomplish that feat.

George James, leading run scorer, hitter and base stealer, broke his leg stealing 2nd base versus Saint Vincent College.

Sam Harshbarger was the starting pitcher vs. the Carnegie Tech Freshmen.

Franklin Hood hit a home run vs. St. Vincent College in a 10-7 win.

In a 6-2 win over Lock Haven High, Albert Guarino hit a home run and Whitmore injured his ankle.

The 1925 baseball team of Coach Carl Snavely was undefeated.

Franklin Hood   **Franklin Hood and Edwin "Dutch" Hill**

Base Ball Squad—Season of 1926

First row, L-R: Snavely, coach; Gaudet, short stop; Gettings, pitcher; Captain Marker, second base; Scheff, left field; Rankin, third base. **Second row:** Hood, catcher; Williams, center field; Douds, right field; Forsythe, pitcher; Schnupp, right field; Raught, sub-catcher; Ducanis, left field; Anderson, manager.

In the first game of the 1926 season, the Academy defeated Indiana Normal by the score of 16-3. Jap Douds had 3 homeruns.

Bellefonte beat the Bucknell Freshmen 3-1. Gettings was the winning pitcher.

Indiana Normal was an 11-3 Academy victim with Forsythe getting the win.

Against Rockview, Franklin Hood had 2 homeruns in an 11-3 victory.

The 1926 baseball team of Coach Carl Snavely lost only one game.

1927

With Carl Snavely as the coach, the Academy won 8-1 over the Juniata YMCA in the first game of the season at 2:20 p.m. Admission was 50 cents.

Down 2-1 to the Bucknell Freshmen, Bellefonte scored 2 runs in the bottom of the 8th inning to win 3-2.

The Academy topped Mars Semi-Pro 2-1. Josh Williams broke his ankle sliding into second base.

Bellefonte's Rosenzweig struck out the first 9 batters without even a foul tip as the Academy beat the Penn State freshmen, 15-4. The 1927 team won 9 out of 11 games.

Bellefonte Academy Base Ball Squad, 1928
First row, L-R: Pflaum, short stop; Temple, first base; Quigley, pitcher; Ducanis, right field; Layer, third base; Sample, center field; P. Smith, left field; Theil, first base. **Second row:** Marker, second base; Susce, catcher; Croissant, left field; Mitchell, assistant manager; Vavra, pitcher; W. Jones, right field; Andolina, catcher; Lipski, third base.

1928

In the first game of the year, the Academy played the Juniata YMCA.

Bellefonte lost 6-2 to Wyoming Seminary. Wyoming won 8 of its 10 games for the season.

1929

The Academy bombed the Navy Freshmen pitcher, who lasted only one inning for a 16-8 victory.

In what was supposed to be the toughest game of the season, heavy hitting and speedy running resulted in a 9-0 Bellefonte win over Wyoming Seminary.

Note: From 1872-1921, the Bellefonte Academy Baseball Team was 95-60.

The Bellefonte Academy Baseball Squad—Season of 1930

1930

The Academy defeated Pitt Junior College 8-6. Heydrick was the winning pitcher with 8 strikeouts. Bellefonte's Hundertmark had 3 hits, Demslar and Rosenzweig were the top hitters. Pitt's Bryson had 2 homeruns in the 2:30 game. Admission was 50 cents.

Bellefonte scored 5 runs in the 8th inning to top Dickinson Seminary 6-4. Shortstop Bartley was the leading hitter for the Academy; and Dickinson's pitcher Stokes had 13 strikeouts.

Heydrick pitched the Academy to a 6-4 triumph over Bethlehem Steel of Pittsburgh. The game was at Hughes Field and began at 2 p.m.

1931

1932

The first game was with Altoona High on April 23rd at 2:30 p.m. Admission was 25 cents.

At right: Babe Ruth in the 1932 World Series.

Bayard Heston Sharpe

Bayard "Bud" Sharpe was born on August 6, 1881 in West Chester, PA. He graduated from West Chester High in 1899, where he played football, basketball, and baseball.

In 1899 he enrolled at Penn State College where he captained the 1901 baseball team and played first base. He led the team in hitting in 1902 and played on the basketball squad. He graduated from Penn State in 1903 with a degree in electrical engineering.

Penn State offered him a job teaching math, but he chose to play semi-pro baseball with the Brandywine Club. In the fall of 1903 he took a position as math instructor at the Bellefonte Academy.

In 1904 Bayard went back to West Chester, took a position with Sharpless Separator Works, and continued to play baseball for Brandywine. He signed with the Boston Nationals in 1904, married Bertha Elizabeth Thorp on October 5, and took a job teaching electricity at Penn State College.

He made his major league debut on April 14, 1905; but was fired for urging some of his teammates to jump to the Tri-State League. In 56 games with Boston, he was unimpressive, hitting .182 with a fielding average of .904 at first base.

Sharpe received an offer to play for Coatsville of the Tri-State League, but signed with the Scranton Miners of the New York State League in Dec. of 1905. He hit .295, with a fielding pct. of .990 in leading the Miners to a pennant. In the off-season he worked as an electrical engineer at power plants in Pennsylvania.

In 1907 he signed with Newark of the Eastern League and stayed through 1909. Having been hit in the head with a pitch, he struggled at the plate. In the winter he stayed in the New York area, teaching electricity at Pratt Institute in Brooklyn, where he was a player/coach. In 1908 he hit .270 with a .989 fielding average.

The fall of 1909 found him at Georgia Military Academy in Milledgeville, Georgia where he coached baseball. He was drafted by the Pittsburgh Pirates for the 1910 season; and reported for camp despite a case of malaria contracted in Georgia. After 4 games with the Pirates, he was traded to the Boston Nationals where he hit .239 with a .987 fielding average. He lost playing time in July due to an attack of malaria; and played in his last major league game on Sept. 4th, 1910.

In 1911 Sharpe played with Buffalo of the Eastern League where he captained the team, had a batting average of .281, stole 26 bases, and fielded at a .992 rate. However, he became ill, and went back to Georgia where he resumed his managerial duties.

He was a player/manager for Oakland of the Pacific Coast League in 1912 where he hit .300 and led the Oaks to a first place finish. In September he was confined at home with a severe attack of pleurisy; and died on June 1, 1916 from tuberculosis at the age of 34.

Bellefonte Academy Baseball

Year	Runs scored	Runs allowed	Wins	Losses	Ties	
1890						incomplete
1891						incomplete
1892	14	21	0	3		incomplete
1893	42	59	4	4		incomplete
1894	31	39	2	2		incomplete
1895						incomplete
1896	42	37	2	2		complete
1897	65	43	3	2		complete
1898	90	33	7	0		incomplete
1899	35	53	1	3		incomplete
1900	63	67	1	4		incomplete
1901	30	33	1	3		incomplete
1902	68	30	4	1		incomplete
1903	48	48	3	4		incomplete
1904	78	51	5	4		incomplete
1905	77	40	5	2		incomplete
1906	69	42	5	2	1	incomplete
1907	49	43	4	4		incomplete
1908	9	25	2	4		incomplete
1909	55	32	10	3		incomplete
1910	82	45	12	4	1	complete
1911	114	61	11	4		incomplete
1912	76	47	7	3	1	incomplete
1913	81	41	10	2		incomplete
1914	48	70	4	10		incomplete
1915	87	72	7	5		incomplete
1916	27	39	2	3		incomplete
1917	14	16	3	3		incomplete
1918	27	57	4	4		incomplete
1919	25	42	3	3		incomplete
1920	18	23	2	3		incomplete
1921	54	44	6	4		incomplete
1922	53	25	4	2		incomplete
1923	13	33	0	5		incomplete
1924	76	32	7	1		incomplete
1925	53	22	5	0		incomplete
1926	58	23	6	1		incomplete
1927	58	28	7	1		incomplete
1928						incomplete
1929						incomplete
1930						incomplete
1931						incomplete
1932						incomplete

Chapt. 3: Academy Basketball
1902-1931

The Armory at the corner of Lamb and Spring Streets in Bellefonte was constructed in 1894 by Colonel W. Fred Reynolds, and was the early home of the Academy cagers; and later became a practice facility. The team began play in 1902 and attained a 2-0 record, scoring 31 points and giving up 24. A railroad track ran alongside the Armory on Lamb Street; and when used as a dormitory, it was known as the Track House.

Bellefonte Armory

In **1903,** the Basketball Manager was Erle Leathers.

The **1903** Academy season consisted of a 3-game schedule—a series with the Bellefonte Athletic Club. The Cougars collected 48 points and allowed 44.

The first game was played on Saturday, February 18, before a large and enthusiastic crowd. The Academy was ahead at halftime; but the young men from town rallied and won the game 16-9.

Game 2 was played on Thursday, March 19th. Ed Keichline and Frank Newbaker of the Athletic Club were out with injuries; and the Academy won the hotly contested game, 19-11.

The rubber match was played on Wednesday, April 8th. With a 20-17 victory, the Academy earned bragging rights in Bellefonte for the year.

Bellefonte Academy team roster: William Louder, Guard; McCafferty, Centre; McCandless, Guard; McIntosh, Forward; Taylor, Forward; Thomas, Guard.

Bellefonte Athletic Club roster: Curtin, Guard; Gephart, Guard; Keichline, Forward; Lane, Guard; Newbaker, Centre; Quigley, Forward; Yearick, Guard.

1904

The first game of the season was played at the Armory; and the Academy fell to Williamsport High by the score of 28-20. Admission was 25 cents.

Boundaries became lines; prior to that the boundaries were the walls.

Above: **The 1904 Bellefonte Academy Basket Ball Team.**

1905
The Academy played Williamsport High at the
Bellefonte YMCA on High Street (above). The cost
was 25 cents per person. The YMCA became the
home court of the Cougars.

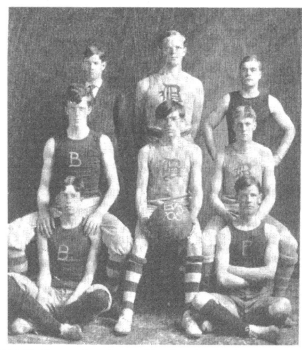

1905 Bellefonte Academy Basket Ball Team.

1906
At left: **1906 Bellefonte Academy Basket Ball
Team.**
First row, L-R: Mitchell, Captain DuBarry, Renton.
Second row: Stoehr, Creighton, Acheson.

1907 Bellefonte Academy Basket Ball Team.
1ˢᵗ row, L-R: Colestock, Irwin, Captain Dunsmore, Oberlin, Myers. **2ⁿᵈ row:** Heiner,
Fullerton, Lingle, Mitchell, McCaslin.
     In one of the most exciting games of the 1907 season, Bellefonte netted a 24-19 win over the
Tyrone YMCA. Tyrone had defeated Altoona the week before, 39-1.
     John Dunsmore scored 30 points in a 58-10 win over Lock Haven High.
1907 Player (Points): John Dunsmore (76); Colestock (20); Clyde Oberlin (14); Mitchell (14);
Lingle (13); Irwin (13); Clyde Fullerton (6); Renton (6); Myers (6); Shields (4); Heiner (2).

1908

Clarence Bolton was the basketball manager.

In a 54-16 win over the Big 5 of Tyrone, Captain Heiner sat out with a hand injury; but Lingle, a former Academy player, replaced him and played well.

Bellefonte defeated the Cascadeli Club of Cornell University by a score of 44-23. Laderer, Meyers, and Clyde Oberlin starred for the Academy. Markle led the Cornell Club.

1908-09 Bellefonte Academy Basket Ball Championship Team
First row, L-R: Dillon*, David Succop*, Captain McCandless*, H. F.Wright*, Gilbert Meyers*. **Second row:** Coach Hall, Sleppy*, Whitey Wilson*, Eisenbeis, Manager Hummel.

*Letter winners

117

1909

On March 14, a banquet was held at the Brockerhoff Hotel for the Academy Championship football team and the Star basketball team.

Merrill Waltz was the basketball manager.

In 1901, players were permitted to bounce the ball once. In 1909, continuous dribbling and shots off dribbles were allowed. A goal from the field became 2 points in 1896.

Harry Wright, Doc McCandless, Coffey Dillon, Meyers, and Ted Shields were the nucleus of the basketball team. Al Wilson was a sub.

In a 53-33 loss to the Tyrone YMCA, McCandless got injured and the team seemed to go flat after he was taken out of action.

McCandless

One of the largest crowds of the season witnessed a 57-18 victory over Dickinson Seminary.

Captain "Doc" McCandless was the leading scorer for the 1909 season with 85 points.

Bellefonte Academy Basketball Team of 1909-10
Record: 8-4
First row, L-R: Dillon, Foster, Captain Meyers, Bauer, Sprague. **Second row:** Colestock, Brenneman, Yocum, Negley. **Third row:** Assistant Manager Kenneth Chambers, Eisenbeis, Foster Doane, Smith, Weston, Manager Lee, Coach Evans. Missing: Tom McBride.

First three games of 1909:

Academy 85		Juniata 14	Academy 58		Clearfield 10
Wright	F	Reynolds	Meyers	F	Chase
Meyers-Wilson	F	Houser	Wright-Succop	F	Johnson
Shields-Eisenbeis	C	Bricker	Shields-Eisenbeis	C	Stage
Dillon-Succop	G	Beigle	Dillon-Sterling	G	Mitchell
McCandless, Capt.	G	Kuck	McCandless	G	Patterson

Field goals: Wright 9, Meyers 3, Shields 5, Dillon 3, McCandless 17. Points from field: Houser 3, Bricker 2, Reynolds 7. Foul goals: McCandless 11, Reynolds 2.
Referee—Barnes, Y.M.C.A.
Timer—Entrekin, Academy.
Scorer—Mugele, Academy.

Field goals: Meyers 2, Wright 9, Shields 3, Dillon 5, McCandless 8, Succop 1, Eisenbeis 1. Points: Chase 2, Johnson 2, Mitchell 1, Patterson 2, Stage 3.
Referee—Barnes, Y.M.C.A.
Timer—Entrekin, Academy.
Scorer—Malotte, Y.M.C.A.

Academy 57		Dickinson 18
Meyers-Wilson	F	Anderson
Wright-Succop	F	DelCarte
Shields-Eisenbeis	C	Humbers
Dillon-Sterling	G	Hodson
McCandless	G	Beckley

Field goals: Meyers 5, Wright 5, Shields 1, Dillon 7, McCandless 7, Wilson 2, Anderson 2, DelCarte 1, Humbers 3, Beckley 1. Foul goals: McCandless 3, Anderson 3. DelCarte 1.
Referee—Dr. Platts, Bellefonte.
Timer—Entrekin. Scorer—Malotte, Y.M.C.A.

In a second game with Dickinson Seminary at Williamsport in March, Wright and Dillon were put off the floor for roughness in the first 2 minutes of play. McCandless made 12 of 13 foul shots, but the Academy lost 40-20.

Also in March, Bellefonte topped the Collegians of Pittsburg 32-29. Toby Fullerton, who pitched for the 1907 Academy baseball team, played for the Collegians.

Scores of other games: Bellefonte Academy 13, Williamsport High School 24.
Bellefonte Academy 41, Clearfield High School 36.

On Friday evening, January 14th, 1910, the Bellefonte Academy had a game scheduled with a strong Altoona team at home, but the Railroaders never showed up.

On Saturday, January 15th, 1910, the Bellefonte Academy defeated a Wyoming Seminary team 27-22 that had lost to Penn State College. The Wyoming team remained over the night and returned home on an early train the next morning. The lineups:

Academy	Pos.	Wyoming
Meyers	F	Dick
Bauer	F	Maier
McBride	C	Probst
Weston	G	Beach
Eisenbeis-Sleppy	G	Cross

Goals from the field—Bauer 5, McBride 3, Weston 2, Maier 3, Cross 3, Dick 2.
Foul Goals—Meyers 7, Dick 6.
Time of halves—20 minutes.
Referee—Dr. Platts.

1910 Player (Points): Weston (47); Bauer (47); Gilbert Meyers (18); Coffey Dillon (14); McBride (6); P.O. Eisenbeis (6); Negley (6).

Academy 36 Juniata College 47
Academy 27 Wyoming Seminary 22
Academy 26 Pittsburg Collegians 45
Academy 30 Dickinson Seminary 28
Academy 47 Clearfield High School 34
Academy 45 Dickinson Seminary 23
Academy 47 Clearfield High School 34
Academy 13 Bucknell Academy 45
Academy 40 Bucknell Academy 33
Academy 27 Lock Haven Y.M.C.A. 24

Manager George Lee
Asst. Mgr. Kenneth Chambers
Capt. Gilbert Meyers (at right).

Academy 69 Lock Haven Y.M.C.A. 13

Gilbert B. "Stuffy" Meyers played for Pitt against the Academy the following season.

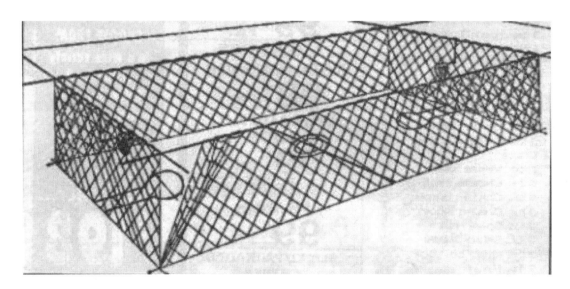

Basket Ball was formerly played in a cage, hence the reference "Cagers".

Note: Early basketball games were primarily played with 9 players on each side; the reason being Dr. Naismith, creator of the game, had 18 students show up for his class. In 1897, five players became the mandatory team size.

Dr. James Naismith invented basketball in late 1891 while teaching at the International YMCA Training School (now Springfield College) in Springfield, Massachusetts. Born in Canada, he became a United States citizen in 1925.

THE PADUCAH EVENING SUN

BASKETBALL MAY BECOME POPULAR

Many Local Teams May Organize League Here.

Picked Champion Team May Uphold Honors of City Against Outside Players.

ENTHUSIASTS HAVE PLANS.

120

1910-11 Bellefonte Academy Basketball Team

First row, L-R: Coach Kimble, Captain Eisenbeis, Manager Fiske. **Second row:** Dillon, Jack Brenneman, Wilson, Weston, Sam Colestock. Mgr. Evert L. Fisk. Asst. Mgr. Hugh J. "Spider"Bubb.

The outlook for the 1911-12 basketball was promising, as 20 candidates responded to Captain Brenneman's call to practice on December 6, 1911. Brenneman and Dillon were the only returning starters. Gustave Chartner, Taylor, Reese, J. Locke, and E. Eisenbeis from last year's reserves made strong bids for varsity letters. C. Reese, Decker, Koch, Hadesty, and B. Bair showed up well. Coach Weller was looking forward to the following schedule from Dec.10-March 25:

Tyrone Big Five, Academy Alumni of Penn State College, Williamsport Dickinson Seminary, Bloomsburg Normal, Clearfield High School, @Bloomsburg Normal, @Clearfield High School, @DuBois High School, Williamsport, @Williamsport Dickinson Seminary, @Williamsport High School, State Forestry School of Mt. Alto, DuBois High School, Open, Bucknell Academy, Open, Open, Open, Open.

Academy vs. Bucknell Lineups

Bellefonte	Field Goals	Foul Goals	Bucknell	Field Goals	Foul Goals
Wilson,f	3	8*	Sowen, f	1	5*
Brenneman, sub f	5	0	Schaffner, f	3	0
Colestock, f	0	0	Crouse, c	0	0
Reese, sub f	0	0	Sharpe, g	0	0
Weston, c	6	0	Hause, g	1	0
Dillon, g	5	0			
Eisenbeis,g	5	0			
Totals	24	8—56		5	5—15

Referee—Wallace.   Time: 20 minute halves.   Scorekeeper—Reiter

Construction at the Bellefonte YMCA was completed in January of 1911. The balcony was extended to 3 sides of the gymnasium and could comfortably sit 300 people.

*Until 1924, any player could shoot the foul shots rather than the player who was fouled.

GAMES PLAYED 1910-11 Season. Record 9-3

Bellefonte...................... 44	Susquehanna.....................18
Bellefonte.......................79	Clearfield........................13
Bellefonte.......................26	Pittsburg Collegians.............46
Bellefonte.......................30	Bucknell Academy..............35
Bellefonte.......................83	Acad. Alum. of State...........26
Bellefonte.......................38	Clearfield High School.........40
Bellefonte.......................62	Williamsport High School......31
Bellefonte.......................69	Dickinson Seminary............18
Bellefonte.......................56	Bucknell Academy..............15
Bellefonte.......................37	Williamsport High School......35
Bellefonte.......................100	Bucknell Univ. Reserves.......21
Bellefonte.......................79	Penn State Freshmen............22
700	320

The last 2 games, with Susquehanna and Dickinson Seminary, were cancelled due to illness at those schools.

In 1911, player fouls for disqualification increased from 2 to 4. In 1945, the number was increased to 5.

On Thursday, January 19th, the basketball five travelled to Lewisburg and met defeat on Bucknell's floor 35-30. Due to a much larger floor and listless play, the Academy trailed 26-6 at the half. Adjustments were made and Bellefonte scored 24 points to the Bison 9 but ran out of time. Brenneman came off the bench and played well. The lineups:

Bellefonte Academy 30		Bucknell 35	
Colestock	Forward	Fulmer	
Wilson	Forward	Sowen	Goals from the field:
Weston	Center	Crouse	Fulmer 10.
Dillon	Guard	Hause	Sowen 5.
Capt. Eisenbeis	Guard	Sharpe	

On Friday night, January 27th, 1911, the Academy team defeated the Academy Alumni from Penn State College by the score of 83-25. The home team was in great form and play was rough, but there was no ill feeling as the players were all old friends. At the end of the first half, Capt. Eisenbeis retired from the game; and Brenneman added 6 points in his stead. The lineups:

Bellefonte 83		Alumni 25	
Colestock	Forward	Meyers	Substitutions: Miller for
Wilson	Forward	Foster	Shields, Tasker for Foster,
Weston	Center	Aikens	Brenneman for Eisenbeis.
Dillon	Guard	Wilson	Field Goals: Colestock,
Capt. Eisenbeis	Guard	Shields	Wilson 10, Weston, Dillon,
			Brenneman 3, Meyers 3,

Tasker 2, Foster 2, Wilson, Aikens, Shields. Foul goals: Wilson 5, Meyers 5. Time of halves—20 minutes. Referee—Keichline of Bellefonte. Time keepers—Kimble and Entrekin of State. Scorer—Reiter.

On Friday afternoon, February 3rd, 1911, the Big Five of the track house and the Old Main team again matched strength on the basketball floor. The Big Five was without the services of Libby Symes and Yocum. The Old Main team was intact except for Hemperly, whose place was filled by McKee, a new student at the Academy. "Gus" Robinson and Hallenbach from town filled the positions that were vacant on the Big Five team. The lineups:

Big Five 104		Old Main 50	
Reese	Forward	Bloyd	Substitutes—Winslow for McKee.
Irwin	Forward	Chambers	Referee—Prof. Sabine of Bellefonte.
Hallenbach	Center	Chartner	Field Goals—Reese 25,
Robinson	Guard	McKee	Eisenbeis 11, Irwin 6, Robinson 3,
E. Eisenbeis	Guard	Locke	Hallenbach 3, Bloyd 9, Chambers 4,
			Chartner 4, McKee 2, Locke 3.

Foul goals—Reese 10, Chartner 5, Locke 1.

On Friday evening, February 10, 1911, the Bellefonte Academy five defeated the fast Williamsport High School team by 62-31 in a Central League game at Bellefonte. The first half was played on even terms, but in the second half, the Cougar center and forwards completely outclassed the boys from Billtown. The game was marked by roughness; and Brenneman filled in nicely for an absent Sammy Colestock. The lineups:

Bellefonte Academy		Williamsport H.S.	
Wilson	Forward	Sloatman	Field Goals—Wilson 8, Brenneman
Brenneman	Forward	Norris	10, Weston 4, Dillon 4, Eisenbeis 2,
Weston	Center	Weiss	Sloatman 4, Norris 5, Weiss 1.
Dillon	Guard	Pott	Foul Goals—Wilson 4, Pott 7.
Capt. Eisenbeis	Guard	Meade	Referee—Wallace. Timekeeper—
			Kimble. Scorekeeper—Rose.

Time of halves—20 minutes.

On Friday night, February 17th, 1911, at the Y.M.C.A. gymnasium, the Academy won another victory on the basketball floor, defeating the Dickinson Seminary team by the score of 69-18. The game was rough, and Dillon was tossed from the game. Wilson filled in for Dillon, while Brenneman filled Wilson's forward position. Bellefonte scored almost at will. The lineups:

Bellefonte		Dickinson	
Wilson-Brenneman	Forward	Hodson	Goals—Hodson 3, Numbers, Banks
Colestock	Forward	Numbers	2, Simmons, Hutchinson 2, Wilson
Weston	Center	Banks	4, Colestock 6, Weston 8, Dillon 4,
Dillon-Wilson	Guard	Simmons	Eisenbeis 3, Brenneman 4. Fouls—
Eisenbeis	Guard	Hutchinson	Wilson 11. Referee—Wallace,
			Bellefonte. Time—20 min. halves.

At the Y.M.C.A. gymnasium on Tuesday night, February 21st, 1911, Bellefonte atoned for an earlier loss of 35-30 at Lewisburg by defeating Bucknell Academy by the score of 56-15. After a slow start the Cougars began to click near the end of the first half and their good work continued into the second half in a game as rough as any this season. The lineups:

Bellefonte		Bucknell	
Wilson-Brenneman	Forward	Sowen	Field Goals—Wilson 3, Weston 6,
Colestock-Reese	Forward	Schaffner	Dillon 5, Brenneman 5, Eisenbeis 5,
Weston	Center	Crouse	Sowen, Schaffner 3, Hause. Foul
Dillon	Guard	Sharpe	Goals—Wilson 8, Sowen 5. Referee
Capt. Eisenbeis	Guard	Hause	Wallace. Time—20 min. quarters. Scorekeeper—Reiter.

On Friday night, March 10th, 1911, Bellefonte Academy and the fast Bucknell Reserve squad clashed arms on the basketball floor with the result that the Academy came off victorious by the score of 100-31. The Reserves had the advantage of size and weight, but were completely bewildered by the fast work of the home team. Wilson had the honor of making the last goal, raising the score to 100. The Lineups:

Bellefonte		Bucknell Reserves	
Wilson	Forward	Goodwin	Goals—Wilson 12, Brenneman 14,
Brenneman	Forward	Bell	Weston 8, Dillon 5, Eisenbeis 6,
Weston	Center	Dunkle	Colestock 2, Goodwin 3, Richards 4,
Dillon	Guard	Richards	Bell 3. Referee—Wallace,
Eisenbeis	Guard	Loewall	Bellefonte. Timekeeper—Kimble. Time of halves—20 minutes.

On Saturday night, March 18th, 1911, the Academy five closed their basketball season by defeating the Penn State College Freshmen team by the score of 79-22. One of the largest crowds of the season turned out at the Bellefonte Y.M.C.A. and witnessed a close game at first, but the Academy quickly put the game on ice. The lineups:

Bellefonte		State Frosh	
Wilson	Forward	Meyers	Substitutes: Colestock for Eisenbeis,
Brenneman	Forward	Hollman	Cummings for Meyers. Goals—
Weston	Center	Craig	Brenneman 12, Colestock 2, Wilson
Dillon	Guard	Miller	11, Weston 5, Dillon 2, Eisenbeis 2,
Eisenbeis	Guard	Louney	Meyers 3, Hollman 2, Craig 1, Louney 1, Miller 1. Foul Goals— Wilson 1, Meyers 3, Hollman 1, Louney 2.

Howard Neeley, 1911 graduate of the Bellefonte Academy, was the manager of the Academy Alumni Basketball Team of Pennsylvania State College.

1911-12 Basketball Season

About 20 candidates responded to Captain Brenneman's call to practice on Wednesday, December 6th, and out of the material present, the authorities were expected to pick a team which would bring home many scalps for the year.

Of last year's varsity, Captain Brenneman and Coffey Dillon were the only ones back. Those two, however formed a good start for the team and the remaining positions were filled with good men in a very short time. Practice was held at the Y.M.C.A. gymnasium.

Chartner, Taylor, Reese, J. Locke and E. Eisenbeis, of last year's reserves were out again and were expected to make strong bids for varsity berths. The new men were C. Reese, Decker, Koch, Hadesty, B. Bair, and several others.

The Cougars were coached by Weller; and defeated Juniata Y.M.C.A. by a score of 44-34.

GAMES PLAYED 1911-12 Season

Academy	44	Susquehanna University	18
Academy	79	Clearfield High School	13
Academy	26	Pittsburgh Collegians	46
Academy	30	Bucknell Academy	35
Academy	83	Academy Alumni of State	26
Academy	38	Clearfield High School	40
Academy	62	Williamsport High School	31
Academy	69	Dickinson Seminary	18
Academy	56	Bucknell Academy	15
Academy	37	Williamsport High School	35
Academy	100	Bucknell Reserves	21
Academy	79	Penn State Freshmen	22

The season began on December 20th and ended on March 15th.

On March 15th, 1913, the Academy five travelled to Pittsburgh and finished their schedule for the season by playing the University of Pittsburgh and the Pittsburgh Athletic Association fives in 10 minute quarters. H. Campbell and McDowell played well for Pittsburgh in the 44-23 win, while Chuck Reese and Dillon starred for Bellefonte. In a 42-27 loss to the P.A.A. the next evening, Brenneman and Reese led the way with 19 and 6 points, respectively.

The 1911-12 Academy team travelled to Bloomsburg on January 27th and lost to the Normal School 31-21 in 2 periods of 20 minutes each. The lineups:

Bloomsburg		Bellefonte	
Mosteller	G	Chartner—Koch	Field goals—Davis 5, Wagonseller
Thorne	G	Beattie	2, Smorkzinck 2, Thorne 3, J. Reese
Smorkzinck	C	Hadesty—C. Reese	3, Chartner 1, Beattie 1, Koch 2.
Wagonseller	F	J. Reese	Referee—McCan. Foul goals—
Davis	F	Brenneman	Davis 7, Brenneman 1, J. Reese 6.

The Academy 5 travelled to Clearfield on February 3rd and played the high school team to a 35-35 tie. Very few fouls were called. At the close of the game a dispute arose over the score; and although Bellefonte wished to play an extra period, it was decided to let it go as a tie.

Clearfield		Bellefonte	
Aiger	F	Brenneman	Time of periods—20 minutes.
Shapiro	F	Reese, J.	Goals—Aiger 3, Shapiro 4. Row 2,
Row	C	Reese, C.	Fulton 1, Troxell 2. Stewart 3,
Troxell	G	Koch	Brenneman 3, Reese, J. 1, Reese, C.
Stewart	G	Beattie	2, Koch 6, Beattie 3. Fouls—
Fulton	G		Shapiro 2, Stewart 1, Brenneman 5.

The Cougars came back strong after the loss to Bloomsburg and the Clearfield tie and topped Williamsport High 54-34 on Friday night, February 9th, 1912. The addition of football players Coffey Dillon and Bill Bloyd made a huge difference.

Williamsport		Bellefonte	
Morris	F	Brenneman	Goals—Brenneman 7, Bloyd 11,
Fluck	F	Bloyd	Reese 2, Dillon 3, Koch 2, Morris 6,
Weiss	C	Reese	Fluck 5, Weiss 3, Sloatman 1.
Sloatman	G	Dillon	Fouls—Brenneman 4, Sloatman 4.
Meade	G	Koch	Referee—Wallace. Time of periods:
			20 minutes. Scorers: Bubb & Davis.

On Saturday, February 10th, the Academy 5, along with Coach Weller, Mr. James (Hughes) and manager Bubb went to Williamsport to play Dickinson Seminary and brought home the bacon to the tune of 32-21 in a 40-min. clash.

Dickinson		Bellefonte	
Alderfer	F	Brenneman	Goals—Brenneman 2, Bloyd 2,
Simpson	F	Bloyd	Reese 1, Dillon 2, Koch 2, Alderfer
Banks—Babcock	C	Reese	2, Simpson 2, Prindle 2, Banks 1.
Shannon	G	Dillon	Fouls—Brenneman 8, Simpson 5.
Babcock—Prindle	G	Koch	

Season of 1911-12—Cont.

On February 16th, Bellefonte Academy played Williamsport High at Williamsport and was defeated by the score of 30-27. At the eleventh hour, the 2 expert referees who were hired could not get to Williamsport. A substitute was found but toward the end of the 2nd half his decisions became so unbearable that a hurried call was sent to the secretary of the Y.M.C.A., Mr. Fleming, who officiated the remaining part of the game.

Williamsport		Bellefonte	
Morris	F	Brenneman	Goals—Brenneman 3, Bloyd 6,
Fluck	F	Bloyd	Reese 1, Dillon 1, Koch 1, Morris 3,
Weiss	C	Reese	Fluck 5, Weiss 4, Sloatman 1.
Sloatman	G	Koch	Fouls—Brenneman 3, Fluck 4.
Meade	G	Dillon	Referee—Fleming. Periods: 20 min.

On Saturday, February 17th, the basket ball team representing the Mt. Alto School of Forestry came to Bellefonte and played the Academy on the Y.M.C.A. floor. 52 fouls were called in the hard-fought contest; and Captain Jack Brenneman caged 24 of 31 foul shots in the 36-30 victory.

Bellefonte		Mt. Alto	
Brenneman	F	Ryan	Goals—Bloyd 2, Reese 4, Ryan 4,
Bloyd	F	Golden	Golden 5. Fouls—Brenneman 24,
Reese	C	Sheeber	Sheeber 5, Golden 2, Ryan 5.
Koch—Beattie	G	Houtz	Referee—Wallace. Umpire—Davis.
Dillon	G	Mustin	Time of periods—20 minutes.

In a rough, fast, and interesting game at Bellefonte, the Academy defeated the Juniata Y.M.C.A. team by the score of 44-34. A fight broke out between big Chuck Reese and Juniata guard Holmburg. Both men were ejected.

Bellefonte		Juniata Y.M.C.A.	
Brenneman-J. Reese	F	Bennett—Leathers	Field goals—Bloyd 6, Brenneman 6,
Bloyd	F	Brenner	C. Reese 2, Koch 1, Dillon 6,
C. Reese-Brenneman	C	Rappie	Bennett 6, Brenner 3, Rappie 8,
Koch	G	Harris	Harris 1. Fouls—Brenneman 4,
Dillon	G	Holmburg-Bennett	Bennett 8. Referee—Wallace.
			Timer—Beattie.

Scorer—Bubb

Harold "Nig" Hoppler was on the 1912 basketball squad.

127

On Saturday, December 14, 1912, the Main building basketball team defeated a strong Frat House all-star five.

During the first half the game was fast and furious and the scoring ended with the Main Building 3 points ahead. During the 2nd half the Main Building succeeded in running up the greater number of points and the game ended with the score of 36-27 in favor of the Main Building.

The Frat House team was minus 2 or more of their best players; but nevertheless they made the Main Building aggregation travel some.

The lineups and score:

FIRST HALF			SEC. HALF			FIRST HALF			SEC. HALF		
Frat House	G	F		G	F	**Main Bldg.**	G	F		G	F
Collopy—C	3	0	Collopy— C	0	1	Swain—C	0	1	Swain—C	0	1
Jones—F	0	0	Beer—G	0	0	Carlson—F	1	0	Carlson—F	0	0
Heim—F	3	0	Carpeneto—G	2	0	Smith—F	2	0	Smith—F	6	0
Beer—G	0	0	Jones—F	2	0	Beattie—G	2	0	Elliott—G	4	0
Carpeneto—G	2	0	Heim—F	1	0	Decker—G	2	0	Decker—G	0	0
End of half—16			End of half—11			End of half—15			End of half—21		
Total score—27						Total score—36					

Referee—Don Wallace

The first game of the 1911-12 season was played with the Tyrone Big Five and resulted in an Academy victory, 36-24.

The Pittsburgh Collegians, on their way to Penn State College, passed through Bellefonte and asked for a game with the Academy. The Y.M.C.A. was unavailable that evening; but rather than disappoint the Collegians, a game was arranged for the afternoon of January 13, 1912, which was won by the visitors, 37-27.

Scoring Record of 1911-12 Basketball Team (Goals-Fouls-Total points)
Brenneman (57-119-233), C. Reese (28-1-58); Bloyd (57-0-114); Dillon (34-0-68); Koch (25-0-50); Beattie (13-0-26); Decker (1-0-2); Chartner (2-0-4); J. Reese (11-6-28); Hadesty (2-0-4); Weaver (3-0-6).
Lettermen: Captain Brenneman, Bloyd, J. Reese, C. Reese, Dillon, Koch, Beattie, Chartner, Mgr. Bubb. **Reserves:** Hadesty, Smith, Decker, Hoppler, Mgr. Shaffner.

1912-13 Basketball Schedule
Manager Schaffner has arranged the following schedule for the Academy basketball team:

January 14—Juniata College, home | February 1—DuBois, home
18—Renovo, home | 7—St. Francis College, abroad
24—Pittsburgh Univ., abroad | 8—St. Francis College, home
25—Westinghouse A.C., abroad | 14—Open
31—Dickinson Seminary, home | 15—Open

Bellefonte Academy Basket Ball Team of 1912-13
First row, L-R: Carpeneto, guard; Kennedy, centre and forward; Captain Loucks, forward; Heim, guard; Elliott, forward. **Second row:** Manager Schaffner; Swain, centre; Carlson, centre & guard; Coach Weller.

1912-13 Player (Points): Doc Carlson (136); Walter Loucks (124); James (68); Smith (30). Coach Paul Jones.

On Friday evening, February 21, 1913, the Bellefonte Academy topped the University of Pittsburgh Freshmen at Bellefonte by the score of 35-30. Chuck Reese, a 1912 grad of the Academy, played for Pitt.

In 1913 there was an outbreak of Scarlet Fever at Pennsylvania State College.

The June reception was held at the Armory instead of the Academy Bldg.

NEW SERIES 17

4 **$875** **STUDEBAKER** **$1085** 6
The Great Value of the Year.

Buying a car is merely a matter of getting the biggest value, the most satisfactory car for the price you pay. Every man who owns or operates a farm knows from long experience the QUALITY that the name Studebaker insures. And the unexcelled manufacturing facilities, the GREAT financial resources, the long manufacturing experience and the largely increased volume that the remarkable popularity of the new cars has produced has made possible many refinements

And a Reduction in Price to $875 and $1085 (f o. b. Detroit) that makes this new SERIES 17 Studebaker FOUR and SIX the great value of the year. See them before you decide on any car. Handsome catalogue on request.

GEORGE A. BEEZER

BELLEFONTE, - - - - - - - PENNA.

DuBois High School 49, Bellefonte Academy 23.

On Friday, January 17th, 1913, the Academy five journeyed to DuBois where they met the fast team of that place. DuBois was expecting a very fast game as shown by accounts in their papers and worked all the harder at their practices, and they were certainly in fine shape when the Academy began the game at 8:30.

Not for an excuse but in a way of explanation the Academy boys were handicapped by a slightly larger floor, a low ceiling and being forced to play different rules from their own during the first half.

There was a large crowd who witnessed the game and cheered the high school boys to victory. The first few minutes of play started in whirlwind fashion as DuBois had caged their baskets before Bellefonte saw the ball. Settling down from that, the Academy played a consistent but unlucky game as many of their chances for goals were spoiled by the low ceiling. At the end of the first half, DuBois had a 29-3 lead over the visitors.

The second half began in better style as the Academy had a different and also a better goal. Both sides scored the same number of points in the second twenty minutes of play. For DuBois, Blakeslee and Craig played an exceptional game while Loucks, Jones, Carpeneto, and Carlson played well for Bellefonte.

The team as a whole received fine treatment and all the members were guests at a class dance after the game. The box score:

ACADEMY	GOALS	FOULS	TOTAL	GOALS	FOULS	TOTAL
Smith, F						
Jones, F	1		2	1		2
Swain, C						
Carlson, G		1	1	2	2	6
Carpeneto, G				3		6
Loucks, F				3		6

Total first half score—3
Total second half score—20
Total score—23

DUBOIS	GOALS	FOULS	TOTAL	GOALS	FOULS	TOTAL
Blakeslee, F	3	5	11	1	4	6
Craig, F	5		10	5		10
Platt, C	3		6	1		2
Harbridge, G	1		2			
Bausert, G						
Swisher, G				1		2

Total first half score—29
Total second half score—20
Total score—49

Summary—Field goals: Blakeslee 4, Craig 10, Platt 4, Harbridge 1, Swisher 1, Loucks 3, Jones 3, Carlson 2, Carpeneto 3. Foul goals: Blakeslee 9, Carlson 3. Fouls called on DuBois—3; on Academy 15. Referee Herbert Weaver. Scorers and Timers—Mike Guilling, W.J. Schaffner. Time of halves: 20 minutes.

1912-13 Basket Ball Summary

Manager Schaffner, who had hard luck with his schedule, gave the following summary:
Seven games were canceled limiting the number of games to 12. Had all games scheduled taken place, the greatest number of games in the basket ball history of the Academy would have been played. Bellefonte ended the season with an 8-4 record.

Bellefonte	35	Juniata	28	
Bellefonte	23	DuBois	49	Loucks had 62 baskets in 11 games; and
Bellefonte	23	Pitt University	28	23 baskets in one game.
Bellefonte	21	Westinghouse A.C.	39	Jones had 34 baskets in 8 games.
Bellefonte	41	Dickinson Seminary	18	Carlson had 38 baskets in 12 games.
Bellefonte	55	DuBois	30	Kennedy had 8 baskets in 4 games.
Bellefonte	11	St. Francis	21	Carpeneto had 11 baskets in 8 games.
Bellefonte	92	St. Francis	16	Smith had 7 baskets in 8 games.
Bellefonte	35	Pitt University	30	Heim had 2 baskets in 3 games.
Bellefonte	54	Pitt Collegians	19	Swain had 1 basket in 2 games.
Totals	390		285	Elliott had 2 baskets in 4 games.
				Carlson made 60 fouls out of 135 attempts.

1913 Girls' Basket Ball Game

Pennsylvania State Champion 14-2 Basket Ball Team—Season of 1913-14
First row, L-R: Thomas Mangan, Forward; Captain P. Jones, Forward; John Pott, Guard.
Second row: Coach E. C. Weller; A. Heim, Forward; W. Elliott, Guard; Clifford Carlson, Center; Manager Robert Kann.

    The Blue and Gold scored 646 points to their opponents' 458.
    In 1914, Bellefonte played the Penn State College Frosh for the first time.
    The grand opening of the enlarged Bellefonte Y.M.C.A. took place on Friday night, November 21, 1913, from 7 to 9 p.m. The Tyrone band presented and furnished the music. There were speeches by Tyrone and Bellefonte people; also an exhibition of swimming by the Academy, State and Tyrone swimming teams; Japanese exhibit, and Gypsy village. The ladies' auxillary sold Japanese articles for 15 cents and up, and also served refreshments.
    The gymnasium was enlarged to almost twice its former size, making it one of the most perfect floors to be found for basket ball, indoor tennis, and volley ball. It could be rented for banquets, lectures, etc., for which purpose it was ideally fitted. It had a capacity of seating 700 people, including the galleries, making it the largest hall in town. The opening game of basket ball between Tyrone and Bellefonte took place from 9 to 10 p.m.

1914-15 Bellefonte Academy Basket Ball Team

Basket Ball Squad

Manager Ira Broadbent; Captain P. Jones, forward; Thomas Mangan, forward; John Lochrie, centre; Ernest Poole, guard; Bradley Downing,guard; Harold Davis, sub-guard; Duncan Berryman, sub-guard; James Curley, sub-guard; R, Lochrie, sub-centre.

Central Pennsylvania Champion 10-3 Basketball Five—Season of 1915-16
First row, L-R: Josephson, Guard; Kelly, Forward; Goodling, Guard. **Second row:** Jay Smith, Guard; Captain John Lochrie, Centre; Joe Brennan, Forward. **Third row:** Manager Spangler; R. Lochrie, Forward; Smoczynski, Guard; Coach Hartman. Not in picture: Ernie Poole.

The 1916 Cougars netted 531 points and gave up 356.

Pennsylvania State College, 1915

1917

The Academy went undefeated at 14-0 and won a Pennsylvania Prep Title. Bellefonte tallied 751 points to the losers' 346.

In a game with the Camden, New York Professionals, extra seats were provided; and admission was 50 cents.

Opponent Bethlehem Liberty was one of the fastest schools in the country.

Admission for the Tyrone YMCA game was 25 cents.

1920

The Tyrone Big 5 was a semi-professional team. Admission for the game with the Academy was 25 cents.

A game with Altoona High had a starting time of 2:30 p.m.

1920-21 Bellefonte Academy Basket Ball Team

Henry Clifford Carlson--Henry "Doc" Carlson was born on July 4, 1894 in Murray City, Ohio. He played high school football, basketball, and baseball at the Bellefonte Academy in 1910-14.

Carlson

Carlson played football, basketball, and baseball at the University of Pittsburgh from 1914-18, earning 4 letters in football, 3 in basketball, and 2 in baseball. He was a first team All-American end on "Pop" Warner's undefeated Pitt team of 1917 and a member of the 1916 team which claimed to be national champions.

Doc graduated from Pitt in 1918 and the Pitt Medical School in 1920. He joined the Cleveland Indians pro football team for 1 season; and was hired to coach the Pitt basketball team in 1922, while doubling as a physician for Carnegie Steel Company.

He was famous for his Figure 8 offense which many colleges copied. Legend has it that Carlson offered a basketball scholarship to Stan Musial, but "Stush" obviously chose baseball.

At the University of Pittsburgh, his coaching record was 367-247 from 1922-53. His 1928 team was 21-0 and won the Helms Athletic Foundation National Championship, and repeated in 1930. The 1941 team made the final four.

Carlson was inducted into the Helms Foundation Hall of Fame in 1949, the Naismith Basketball Hall of Fame in 1959, and the College Basketball Hall of Fame in 2000.

Doc was the Director of Student Health Services at Pitt from 1932-53. He died at his home in Ligonier, Pennsylvania on November 1, 1964 at the age of 70.

1922

The Penn State Freshmen basketball team, coached by Glenn Killinger was undefeated. Dr. W. Glenn Killinger was an All-American quarterback at Penn State in 1921.

The Academy topped Wyoming Seminary 30-29. Wyoming was 18-3 for the season with 2 of their losses at the hands of Bellefonte.

In a 7:30 p.m. game with Westmont High, the Academy Orchestra played during the game.

Everyone had a good time at the Athletic Banquet on March 17th.

Travelling was changed to a violation instead of a foul.

Killinger

The Champion Basketball Five—Season 1921-22

First row, L-R: Ash, forward; Schmidt, guard; Captain DeWaters, forward; Byer, guard; Berkes, guard. **Second row:** Coach Hamberger; Dare, forward; Kishbaugh, center; Manager Klein.

This team was one of the strongest in the history of the school, defeating such teams as Wyoming Seminary, Susquehanna University Reserves, the Stag Club of Lock Haven, Westmont High School of Johnstown, Dickinson Seminary and Bloomsburg Normal. Its only loss was to the unbeaten Penn State Freshmen Five.

Bellefonte Academy Basket Ball Squad for 1922-23
First row, L-R: Blackburn, Labelsky, Schmidt, Coleman, Hughes. **Second row:** Student Coach Van Hee, Berkes, Tate, Sweet, McCreedy, Preece, Manager Werster.

Bellefonte Academy Basket Ball Squad for 1923-24
First row, L-R: Lewis, F. White, Soisson, Captain Blackburn, Shively, Cutler. **Second row:** Manager Myers, Coach Snavely, E. Williams, J. White, Householder, O'Neil, Guarino, Coffey.
This team broke about even as to victories and defeats after a hard season.

1924-25 Bellefonte Academy Basketball Team
First row, L-R: Griffin, Whitmore, Slaven, Blackburn, Hill, Hood, Greeno. **Second row:**
Seitz, Vodrey, Bowers, Coach Snavely, Frick, Householder. Their 7 wins included victories
over Bloomsburg Normal 26-21 and Gettysburg Freshmen 29-28. Bloomsburg hadn't lost at
home in 2 years. Blackburn hit the game-winner against Gettysburg with time running out. The
Cougars also played California Normal of PA at 8:45 p.m. and Jersey Shore Central Shop.

Winners of
Academy
Basketball
League
circa
1926.
**First row,
L-R:**
Howard
Marks,
Guard;
Robert
Pflaum,
Centre;
Egbert
Sample,
Guard.

**Second
row:**

Robert Barnhart, Forward; Stuart Johnson, Forward; Alan Merrell, Manager; John Beatty,
Centre; Walter Crukovic.

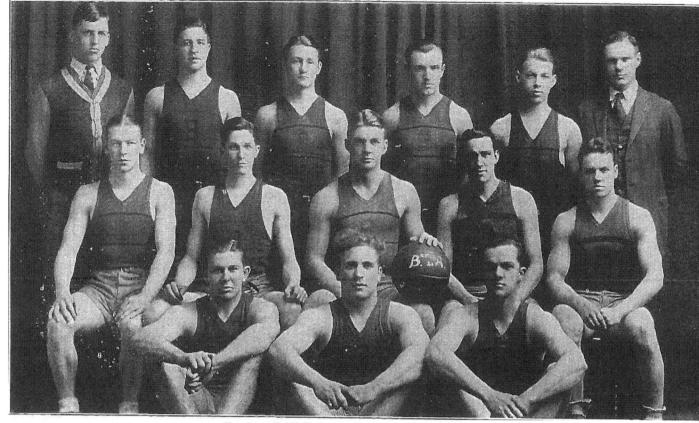

Basket Ball Squad, Season of 1925-26

First row, L-R: Hood, forward; Douds, guard; Householder, center. **Second row:** Robbins, forward; Myers, forward; Bowers, center; McGivern, guard; Rankin, guard. **Third row:** Manager Vodrey; Dougherty, guard; Morgan, guard; Goodwin, forward; Coach Snavely.

Coach Carl Snavely's first win came at the expense of the Yeagertown YMCA, and the Cougars topped St. Joseph's Academy of Williamsport. The Gettysburg College game drew a large crowd; and Bellefonte lost to the Bucknell Freshmen at the YMCA, 33-27.

Basketball was made a general school sport during the season of **1926-27.** Several teams representing the different floors of the different buildings composed a league. Two floors, 80 x 40, were laid out in the armory of Bellefonte where the league games were played. A general interest in the sport prevailed and many boys benefited. The winning team received letters.

In **1926**, Abe Saperstein formed a small basketball team called the **Savoy Big 5**, which eventually became the Harlem Globetrotters.
L-R: Asst. Coach Robert "Bobby" Anderson, Randolph Ramsey, Inman Jackson, William Watson, Tommy Brookings, Joe Lillard, William Grant, Walter "Toots" Wright, Lester Johnson, Mgr. /Coach Dick Hudson.
Circa 1927.

1929

The Academy outscored the Pitt Freshmen in the 2nd half 21-12; but fell to the young Panthers by a 32-19 score.

Against the Harmony Athletic Club, the Cougars were outscored 12-10 in the first period, but took a 24-13 lead into the halftime locker room. Bellefonte prevailed 54-34 in the game which began at 7:30 p.m. Admission was 50 cents.

Note: From 1901-1921, the Bellefonte Academy Basketball Team was 123-48.

1925 Bellefonte High School Girls' 6-2 Basketball Team

First row, L-R: Grace Cohen, Mary Robb, Catherine Farley, Lucile Smith, Kathryn Bullock, Mary Smith, Gale Mitchell, Martha Chambers, Johnston. **Second row:** Miss Josephine Hollingsworth, Martha Johnston. The season began on January 9th and ended on February 17th. **Wins:** Central State Normal (30-21 & 27-22); Philipsburg (27-16 &17-10); Lock Haven (22-14), Renovo (31-19). **Losses:** Renovo (21-20); Lock Haven (21-20).

1926: Catty Farley and Mary Smith sparked the Bellefonte High Girls to a 17-10 win over the Alumni. Mauvis Furey, Grace Cohen, Catherine Johnston, Margaret Taylor, Ann Gherity, Marjorie Way, and Nell Wolfe suited up for the Alums.

Don Best, C. Clark, and Dutch Waite were on Bellefonte High boys' squad.

1929-30 Bellefonte Academy Champion Basketball Team

1930-31 Bellefonte Academy Basketball Team

By 1930, the depression had become a national calamity.

In a close game all the way, the Cougars beat the Jersey Shore YMCA. The game was played at the Armory in Bellefonte at 8:30 p.m. Admission was 50 cents[9]. Very few games were played in the 1930-31 season .

---

[9] $8.00 today

Bellefonte Academy Basketball

Year	Pts. scored	Pts. allowed	Wins	Losses	
1902	31	24	2	0	incomplete
1903	48	44	2	1	incomplete
1904	150	148	4	5	incomplete
1905	98	134	3	3	incomplete
1906	30	143	0	3	incomplete
1907	188	135	5	3	incomplete
1908	240	148	6	1	incomplete
1909	423	214	8	2	incomplete
1910	296	232	6	2	incomplete
1911	700	320	8	3	complete
1912	532	436	9	4	incomplete
1913	389	288	6	4	complete
1914	646	458	14	2	complete*
1915	313	231	6	2	incomplete
1916	531	356	10	3	incomplete**
1917	751	346	14	0	complete***
1918	384	283	10	3	incomplete
1919	266	259	6	4	incomplete
1920	120	84	2	2	incomplete
1921	338	288	6	5	incomplete
1922	524	306	12	2	incomplete
1923	435	357	11	3	incomplete
1924	213	202	4	2	incomplete
1925	316	268	7	1	incomplete
1926	375	345	7	5	incomplete
1927					incomplete
1928					incomplete
1929					incomplete
1930					incomplete
1931	93	76	2	1	incomplete
1932	149	82	5	0	incomplete

*Pennsylvania State Champions
**Central Pennsylvania Champions
***Pennsylvania Prep Champions

Chapter 4
Bellefonte Academy Track & Field
1908-1932

1908
Harold Stevens was selected to be the Track Manager for the 1908 season.
Left: Captain Succop.   Right: E. Sprague

**Bellefonte Academy Champion Track Team of 1909
First row, L-R:** Miller, Sprague, Captain Succop, Yocum, Chambers. **Second row:** Sleppy, Coach Hall, Manager Stevens, Condo, Dillon.

On May 5th, the best men of the squad were sent to the Inter-scholastic Championship Meet at State College and took third place. Sprague took first in the high jump, second in the broad jump and 440 yard dash, third in the 220 yard dash, and won a Trustee's Scholarship for the best individual record in points. Yocum was second in the 2 mile run, Dillon third in the shot put, and Sleppy fourth in the 220 yard dash.

First row, L-R: Newell, Foster, Captain Sprague, Reiter, Yocum. **Second row:** Manager Colestock, Beattie, Brenneman, Weaver, Weston, Coach Evans.

Edward Sprague scored all 11 Bellefonte Academy points in a competition against Indiana Normal, Dickinson Seminary, Johnstown High, Canton High, Juniata Prep, Central Normal, Berwick High, Bloomsburg Normal, and Danville High at the Interscholastic Meet held at Penn State College on Friday, May 6th, 1910; and 10 points in a similar competition at Bloomsburg on Saturday, June 4th, 1910.

Captain Sprague was second in the 440 yard dash, second in the half-mile, third in the broad jump, and third in the high jump at State College. Indiana Normal won with 45 points. The 100 was run in 10 flat, the 220 in 22 flat, high hurdles in 15.6, and the low hurdles in 20 flat. The winning high jump was 5'7" and the pole vault was won with a height was 10' 6".

In the afternoon, Penn State College played Dickinson Seminary in baseball; and the Cadet Regiment gave a dress parade in the morning

Left: Coach Evans.   Right: Capt. Sprague

Leroy Colestock was the Manager of the 1910 track team.
The Penn Relays were on April 30.

1911
Lower left: Coach Kimble. Lower right: Captain Howard Neely.

Decker—100; Rockey—440; Reese—shot; Weekley—hammer throw; W. Smith—pole vault; Dillon—high jump; Gentzel—broad jump; Vaughn—half-mile; Loh—Manager.

145

1911 Track Team
L-R: Coach I. C. Kimble, Wilson, Captain Neely, Elliott, Brenneman, Hemperly, Taylor.

More than 250 schools were expected to compete in the April 29th, 1911 Penn Relays (National Collegiate Championship Meet) at Franklin Field in Philadelphia, including the Bellefonte Academy, Harvard, Michigan, Chicago, Princeton, Columbia, Illinois, Yale, Kansas, and host school Penn. Chicago will send Davenport (48.8 in the quarter and 1: 56.6 in the half mile); Michigan will send Craig (21.2 in the 220-a world's record); Harvard will send Foster (sprinting champion of 1909); Burdick of Penn, the Eastern Intercollegiate Champion, will meet the Western Champion French of Kansas in the high jump. Chisholm of Yale, the Eastern High Hurdle Champion, will meet Edwards, the Western Champion. Cornell is also expected to attend the championships which will include the100 yard dash, 120 yard high hurdles, shot put, hammer throw, discus, broad jump, high jump, and pole vault.

Left: High Hurdles at Franklin Field.

Twenty men reported to Captain Neely as candidates for the 1911 track team and their work was very satisfactory early on. The workouts were limited to road work only, since the runners were in need of more hardened ground.

Neely had a record as a quarter miler; Brenneman was the high jumper on last year's team; Reiter was also a quarter miler; and Hemperly, the weight man, formed a strong nucleus about which to build another fast team, such as the one that represented Bellefonte in the inter-scholastic meets last year.

The first scholastic meet for the season was to come off at Penn State College in the early part of May.

1912 Track Team

The proceeds from the annual Academy Minstrels this year were used in placing a new track around the athletic field on East Bishop Street. Work began during Easter vacation of 1912 and it was cindered in May. The track was one quarter of a mile around and enclosed both the baseball and football fields.

1912 Olympics in Stockholm, Sweden

1912 Bellefonte Academy Track Team

First row, L-R: Barritt, W. Irwin, Schneider, Heim, Creal. **Second row:** Coach Weller, Beer, Symes, Collopy.

The 1912 Bellefonte Academy track team participated in the annual Interscholastic Track and Field Meet held Friday, May 3rd, at Penn State College. Collopy was 3rd in the 100 yard dash and took a 3rd in the 220 yard dash. John Koch, a basketball standout, finished 3rd in the 440 yard dash.   In the running broad jump, Schneider won the event with a jump of 20 feet, 6 ½ inches; and Collopy copped 2nd. The Track Manager and Captain was Howard.

1913 Bellefonte Academy Track Team

On Friday, May 2nd, at Penn State College, the Academy and Bellefonte High School were among 16 schools competing at the Interscholastic Track and Field Meet. The Bellefonte contingency travelled in a special Bellefonte Central Railroad train. The 150 participants were split into High Schools and Academies; and the Bellefonte Academy competed with Bloomsburg Normal, Indiana Normal, and Mercersburg Academy. Schools from as far away as Harrisburg, Johnstown, and Beaver Falls made the trip to State College. School was dismissed at the Bellefonte Academy on account of the track meet. 50 students accompanied the team to State College.

Collopy finished 2nd in his 100 yard dash heat, and took a 4th in the event. Symes, Bellefonte's ace baseball pitcher, also came in 2nd in his 100 yard heat for the Academy.

The 8th annual Intercollegiate and Interscholastic Track and Field Meet took place the next Friday, May 9th at the Schenley facility at the University of Pittsburgh.   Out of 18 participating schools, mostly from the Pittsburgh area, the Bellefonte Academy was the only scholastic school invited. Collopy won his 100 yard heat in 11.4 seconds; but finished 4th in the final race. Schneider tied for 3rd in the running broad jump.

1914 Track Men—L-R: Harold O'Dea, Jacob Hildebrand, and Paul Nutt

Nutt was first in the broad jump at the Penn State, Pitt, and Westminister Meets. The Bellefonte Academy track team participated in the annual Interscholastic Track and Field Meet held Friday, May 1st on New Beaver Field at Penn State College. Jacob Hildebrand, a guard on the football team, placed 2nd in the Class A 12-pound shot put for the Cougars.

1915

Bellefonte Academy Track Team—Season of 1916

Left to Right: Coach Hartman, Speer, Kennel, R. Lochrie, Niles, Manager Powell.
Frank Speer broke the Interscholastic Record at the University of Pittsburgh Meet on May 20th in the 440-yard dash and won first place in the 440 dash at the Carnegie Tech Meet on May 27th, second in the broad jump and fourth in the 220.

Bellefonte Academy "The School in the Mountains." 111th year. For 100 young men, 15 and upwards. Individual attention, 4 buildings. No hazing. Hunting, fishing, Swimming pool, gymnasium, athletics. For catalog, address **JAMES R. HUGHES, A.M.,** Headmaster, Bellefonte, Pa.   –*The Literary Digest,* September 2, 1916.

1917

The annual Interscholastic Track and Field Meet was held Friday, May 12th at Penn State College. Class A consisted of the Bellefonte Academy, Bethlehem Prep, Mansfield Normal, and the Penn State Freshmen. The meet was hampered by a low number of entrants and Bellefonte finished 2nd to the Penn State Freshmen. However, the Blue and Gold were awarded a Class A cup for having the highest scholastic finish.

The 1921 Bellefonte Academy Track Team

The 1921 Bellefonte Academy walked away with the State Championship at the annual Penn State College Interscholastic Track & Field Championship on May 14th. Bellefonte far outdistanced Harrisburg Tech, Clearfield, Steelton, and Northeast Philadelphia High Schools. Over 220 athletes participated.

1921-22 Bellefonte Academy Champion Track Team

The Academy Cougars won the Schenley Oval Meet, placed second at Penn State College, and took first in the Pitt Relays in 1922. The 1922 Academy team won the Pennsylvania Interscholastic Track & Field Championship.

The Champion Track Team—Season 1922
First row, L-R: Howard Bash, Leroy Kelley, Harry Trout, Harry Byer. **Second row:** Coach Hamberger, Tyson Kishbaugh, Frederick Peterson, Linn, Manager Anderson.

This team won first place and a beautiful silver cup at the Carnegie Track Interscholastic Meet, held in Pittsburgh, May 6th, scoring 40 points. It also won first place and a beautiful silver cup at the University of Pittsburgh Interscholastic Meet held in Pittsburgh, May 20, scoring 45 points. Bellefonte took second place at the Pennsylvania State College Interscholastic Meet, held at State College, May 13th, scoring 31 points. The winner of that meet scored 35.5 points. Thirty schools competed at those meets.

1923 Bellefonte Academy Track Team
First row, L-R: Quinn, Bash, Captain Linn, O'Neil. **Second row:** Labelsky, Van Horn, Jennewine. Coach Kimble, Berkes, Preece, Knappenberger.

The 1923 track team won second place at the Carnegie Tech meet which was won by Mercersburg. Bellefonte won first place and a beautiful silver cup at the University of Pittsburgh meet.

1923 Relay Team
Left to right:
Millard Van Horn
Howard Bash
James Preece
Valen O'Neil

The relay team took first place at the University of Pennsylvania meet and the Carnegie Tech Meet. The silken banner prize is shown in this photo. The banner and the silver cup prize are shown in the above photo.

1924

"Gibby" Welch of Bellefonte was 2nd in the javelin and discus at the Princeton Track Meet. Donald Gwinn won the hammer throw with a heave of 170 feet.

The 15th annual Interscholastic Track Meet held at Penn State College on May 17th attracted over 300 athletes from Pennsylvania, New York, and New Jersey. Welch was the individual high scorer by finishing first in the broad jump, javelin throw, shot-put, and discus. Bellefonte's Welch shattered the javelin record with a heave of 177 feet, 6 inches; and broke the discus record as well, with a throw of 120 feet, 2/5 inches. Not to be outdone, Gwinn of the Academy broke the National Interscholastic 12-pound hammer throw record by 16 feet, tossing the ball 178 feet, 6 inches.

L-R: Welch, Coach Kimble, Gwinn

The track stars in the photo above won fourth place for the Academy in the Interscholastic Meet held at Princeton, N. J., on May 10th. The Lawrenceville School won third place beating out Bellefonte by a single point.

The same pair won 25 points at the 15th annual Interscholastic Meet held at Pennsylvania State College on May 17th, winning the second place Silver Cup. Harrisburg Tech won the meet with 26 points.

1925

1926 Bellefonte High School Track Team
Back row, L-R: Coach Jay Riden, ?, Dutch Waite, ?, ?, ?, ?. Front row: Coach E. K. Stock, ?, ?, ?, ?, ?, ?.

The 1926 Penn Relays

Penn University of Philadelphia sponsored a Relay Carnival on April 23rd, 1926 at Franklin Field; and a foursome from Bellefonte High School took second place in the high school mile relay with a time of 3 minutes, 41.4 seconds. The silver medalists were: Charles Merrill "Dutch" Waite, Alan Katz, John Shoemaker, and Jim McCullough. New Castle High came in first.

A the Interscholastic Meet, Bellefonte High's Don Best was 2nd in the broad jump and Jim MCullough placed 4th in the 100 yard dash.

Peter Timothy "Pete" Zaremba—Born in Aliquippa in 1909, where he excelled in football, basketball, and track, "Zar" turned down a basketball scholarship to Geneva College to attend the Bellefonte Academy. He starred in football and track in 1929-30, and went on to New York University where he won 3 letters as a tackle in football and earned 3 monograms in track. Zaremba made All-American in track and field at NYU in 1932-33; and won a bronze medal in the 16-pound hammer throw at the 1932 Olympics in Los Angeles with a toss of 170.53 feet. Patrick O'Callahan of Ireland took the gold at 176.125 feet. "Zar" (pic at right) received honorable mention All-American in football in 1933 and graduated from NYU with a degree in electrical engineering. He was inducted into the Aliquippa Hall of Fame in 1973 and the Beaver County Sports Hall of Fame in 1977.

Pete Zaremba's most memorable moment came in football when the New York University Violets played at Georgia University in 1933. The Governor of Georgia, Eugene Talmadge, came into the New York locker room prior to the game to get acquainted; and before he left, he bellowed "We're going to beat the hell out of you damn Yankees!" They did just that, to the tune of 25-0.

1927

The best track men being baseball players, a track team was not organized. It was the custom at the Academy to send good track men to interscholastic meets when they are not members of the baseball nine. Several beautiful silver cups and silken banners were won at Penn State College, University of Pittsburgh, University of Pennsylvania and other places by the track teams.

1931

The Bellefonte Academy participated in the Penn Relays at the University of Pennsylvania in Philadelphia; and Pete Zaremba placed first in the hammer throw.

1932

On April 8th, athletic scholarships were abolished to discourage high-powered athletic teams by direct order of James R. Hughes, Headmaster of the Academy.

Note: In 1921 and 1922, the Bellefonte Academy Track & Field Team won Pennsylvania Interscholastic Championships.

In 1924, the Academy lost the title by one point, albeit establishing numerous records.

Chapter 5

Bellefonte Academy Swimming, Boxing, Wrestling, Tennis, Golf Hockey, and Pool

Bellefonte Academy Tennis
1890-1931

Tennis began at Penn State College in 1890 and was called *Lawn Tennis* at that time. The crack college team of Phil Darlington and Price Johnson was defeated by Will Furst and Sam Hamill of the Bellefonte Academy 8-6, 6-2, and 6-5. Another set was played for the amusement of the spectators, and was won by the college boys, 6-1.

1906 Academy Tennis Tournament:

Frank Armstrong vs. Taylor 6-1	Browne vs. George Row 6-3
Hallie Jacobs vs. Driver 6-4	Alex Truitt vs. Riddle 4-6, 6-3
Oakley Pantall vs. Colestock 6-2	J.R. Hughes vs. C.S. Hughes 6-2

The Academy Athletic Association conducted an annual tennis tournament; and the 2 finalists would comprise the Academy tennis team which played outside schools. The tournament winner had his name engraved on a silver cup which was on display at the Academy.

In 1909, the cup was won by H.B. Hull over Leroy Colestock by the score of 6-2, 7-5, 6-3. In a tournament with Juniata College on May 29th, Colestock beat Emmert 6-2, 3-6, 6-4. Hull lost to Miller 2-6, 4-6; and in doubles, the Academy team lost by 8-6, 3-6, 4-6.

In 1910, the students at the Academy were warned to stay off the Tennis Courts unless they were members of the Tennis Association or pay a penalty for disobeying the law.

Leroy Colestock was the tennis manager and arranged 4 meets.

1911 Bellefonte Academy Tennis Team—L-R: Manager Philip Rose, Edward Eisenbeis, Captain Leroy Colestock, and Percy Eisenbeis.

1911: The annual Tennis Tournament of "singles" was completed for the year, Leroy Colestock of Butler winning the championship of the school; while he and Ed Eisenbeis, the man who finished second, made up the team that represented Bellefonte against Williamsport, Juniata, and the other schools of the tennis schedule secured by Mr. J. P. Rose, manager.
The outcome of the "doubles" tournament was not yet determined.

1912 Bellefonte Academy Tennis Team
L-R: James Beddall, Captain Hadesty, Manager Alvin Andorn, Victor Polansky, Fred Palmer.
Manager Philip Rose

Bellefonte Academy 1914 Tennis Team
Left to right: Clay Lindemuth, Theron Link, Manager Joseph Eisaman, Leroy Knight, Fred
Palmer. Gustave "Gus" Chartner served as a tennis manager.

The
Academy
Tennis
Team of
1922

**Left to
right:**
William
Frontizer,
Smith,
Richard
Frauenheim,
Miller,
Leroy
Kelley.

In the 1926-27 school year, the new tennis courts, all surrounded by wire netting, was the scene of a tennis tournament that was very interesting. The two best players were Paul Crawford, Wilkinsburg, PA, and William Hughes of Morgantown, W. VA. The former was awarded a fine tennis racquet offered to the best player by the Porter-Hoy Hardware Co.

1930 Bellefonte Academy Tennis

1931 Bellefonte Academy Tennis

161

Bellefonte Academy Boxing, 1909-31
1909
Leon Geyer and William Beckwith were light-weight boxers.
1927
Defeated the Bucknell University Freshmen, 5 to 2, at Bellefonte.
Lost to the State College Freshmen at State College, 3 to 4.
Lost to the Plebes of the U. S. Naval Academy at Annapolis, Md., 3 to 4.
Several meets were scheduled for the 1928 season.

1926 Bellefonte Academy Boxing Team
First row, L-R: John Manternach, Alex Ducanis, Coach & Captain Louis Mutzel, Thomas Gettings, Ed Sharp. **Second row:** Manager Charles S. Hughes, Louis Brehm, Gordon Hinkle, John Dreshar, Howard Chambers.

1927 Bellefonte Academy Boxing Team
First row, L-R: Robert Hedges, Ronald Johnson, Lou Mutzel (Coach), Edward Sharp, Louis Brehm. **Second row:** Charles S. Hughes (Manager), John Dreshar, John Adams, Alexander Ducanis.

1928 Bellefonte Academy Boxing Team. First row, L-R: Brickley, Tom Adams, Alex Ducanis, Egbert Sample, Richard Layer.

Second row: Manager Charles Hughes, Harry Temple, Jacques Croissant, Randolph Hubbell, Maxwell Diffenbach, Joseph Sindaco. The first match of the year was with Cook Academy.

1930 Bellefonte Academy Boxing Team. In 1930, Bellefonte beat Cook Academy 5-2 and Coal Township 5-2. A match was scheduled with West Point.

The regular annual meet with the Navy Plebes was scheduled for Saturday, March 8. Two weeks previous, an invitation was received by the Academy from the University of Virginia Athletic Council to participate in a boxing tournament sponsored by Virginia University on March 7 and 8. Seeing a good chance to advertise the strength of the boxing program, the Academy decided to split the squad, sending some to Annapolis and the others to Charlottesville, a 4-hour auto ride from Annapolis, and using 3 of those sent to Virginia against the Navy Plebes.

In the Virginia tournament, Bellefonte placed 3 men in the finals: Charles O'Day, Daniel McCabe, and Lucian Procino. Captain Paul Buckley lost to a Staunton Military Academy boy. In the fourth round, Augusta Military Academy advanced 4 men to the finals. Buckley, McCabe, and Henry Dreshar were driven to Annapolis to participate in the meet there. Talbot Southwick had to forfeit his bout to a Plebe since he was one pound overweight. Buckley, McCabe, and Spiegel won their bouts; but Dreshar lost to a Navy lad in the unlimited class, and Navy won the meet, 4-2. McCabe hurt his arm and had to forfeit his final bout at Charlottesville. Procino of Bellefonte won a gold medal in the 160-pound class, McCabe and O'Day received silver medals in the finals at Virginia University. Augusta Military Academy won the meet with 2 first places and 2 second places.

163

The 1931 team was 5-1, losing only one meet to Cook Academy. Defeated teams were: Cook Academy, Lewistown A.C., New York University Junior Varsity, Western Maryland Junior Varsity, and Penn Freshmen.

Bellefonte Academy Wrestling
1928

In the first match of the year, the Gamma Beta Iota Fraternity House of the Academy defeated the Main Building of the Academy, 19-17.

Bellefonte Academy Golf

1931

A Costly "Hole."

A South African golfer did a hole in one, or in golfing parlance, "shot an albatross" on the Durban Country Club course, but he learned that fame has its penalties. It cost him £40! He was advised by his partner to cut and run, and say nothing about it, but the hero insisted on observing his feat in the time-honoured way. The course was very crowded, and before all the thirsty players had refreshed themselves at his expense his hole-in-one had cost him £40.

Note: That would be over $3000.00 today.

The Golf Links were located at the Nittany Rod and Gun Club of Centre County, within a short autobus ride of Bellefonte.

164

Bellefonte Academy Swimming
1929-1931
1929
Former Academy swimmer Joe Bleckner captained the Penn Swimming Team.

1930 Bellefonte Academy Swimmers

At the pool—1931. Note the baseball field in the background.

1932

Snapshots at the Academy Swimming Pool on East Bishop Street in Bellefonte.

Hockey, 1911-21

The prospects for a good hockey team at the Academy for the 1911-12 season were the best there had been for some time, although not much attention was paid to the sport during the last few years. Due to the material on the team, it was expected to be worthy of consideration.

The students that composed the team: Negley, H. Eisenbeis, Myers, Maltby, E. Eisenbeis, Bemus, Collopy, and Balsinger. All those who wished to try out for the team were asked to hand their names to acting captain R. Myers before Thanksgiving vacation.

The team was expected to play 2 or 3 local games. Practice started at the Bellefonte Fair Grounds when weather permitted; and all candidates were asked to bring their sticks and skates to school with them after Thanksgiving vacation.

A good, healthy sport, hockey was expected to help break the monotony of the long winter months for those who were not out for basketball.

Myers filled both the captain and managerial positions until they could be filled by an election from the squad.

1921 Hockey Team

First Row, L-R: Miguel, Holmes, Stonemetz, Morrell, Whitman, Wilson. **Second row:** R. Putnam, P. Putnam, Burgess, Young, Provost. **Third row:** Mgr. Vose, Asst. Mgr. Small.

Pool

In September of 1910, a new pool table was installed at the Y.M.C.A. The cost for playing a game was one cent.

Pool was a popular sport among Academy students and the townspeople as well, evidenced by the fact that 3 distinct pool rooms existed in Bellefonte in the years 1911-13.

In 1911, the Academy 3rd floor pool team defeated the 2nd floor pool team in a fifty point game, 50-43.

168

Extra-Curricular Activities

1931 Academy Orchestra
1914 Weekend Social at the Academy

1930 Champions of the Bellefonte Academy Intra-Mural Basketball League

Deer Hunting in the Nittany Mountains

1928 Bellefonte Academy Winners of Intra-Mural Basket Ball League
Row 1, L-R: Robert Pflaum, center; Paul Storrie, forward; Egbert Sample, guard; Earl Trump, guard; Harry Smith, forward. **Row 2:** Ellsworth Houston, forward; John Joynt, guard; James Osborne, forward, Alexander Ducanis, center; Arthur Masters, forward; Paul Smith, forward; Walter Kozicki, guard; Frank Flizack, guard.

1921-22 Bellefonte Academy Orchestra
Herbert Jackson, Drums; Thomas Quinn, Clarinet; David Campbell, Piano; Leroy Kelly, Violin; George Johnson, Xylophone; Clyde Learn, Saxophone; Willard Van Camp, Banjo.

The Academy Orchestra played for many special dances throughout Centre County, especially at State College.

Left: The Garman Opera House. Right: The Garman Hotel (Do-De) .

1911 Bellefonte Academy Minstrels
First row, L-R: Harrington Smith, Oscar Deitrick, David Merrill, John Brenneman, Earl Winslow, Ellis Balsinger, Kenneth Chambers, Howard Neeley, Gerald Tiffany, Edward Maltby, Benjamin Taylor. **Second row:** President Frank Jamison, Purcell Beattie, Walter Crouse, James Fox, Elmer Phillips, Arthur Stahl, James Jr. Loh, Frederick Stead, Winfield Elliott, Albert Wilson, George McKee, Melvin Locke, Gustave Chartner, Arthur Goldsmith, Kenneth Vaughn, Charles Scheiber, Walter Shaffner, Frederick Clemson, John Taylor. **Third row:** Daniel Clemson, Louis Schad, Francis Thomas, Charles Scott, Carl Boas, I.C. Kimble, August Jr. Robinson, Manager Harvey Thompson, Edward Eisenbeis. **Note: Many athletes participated.**

Note: Proceeds from the 1912 Minstrel Shows went toward renovation of Hughes Athletic Field including the installation of a track. The Bellefonte Academy Minstrels which gave two successful performances in Garman's Opera House, May 19-20, 1922.
Note: The picture was taken on the Centre County Courthouse steps in Bellefonte. The Garman Hotel (Do-De) is in the background.

1805

Souvenir Program

of the

100th Anniversary Exercises

of

The Bellefonte Academy

June 15th and 16th

1905

**Bellefonte
Academy
Centennial
1805-1905**

THE DONORS OF THE PROPERTY ON
WHICH THE ACADEMY IS ERECTED.

Col. John Dunlop   James Harris

The Academy in 1840

Andrew G. Curtin, Dec'd   H. N. McAllister, Dec'd

Men Prominent as Trustees

E. C. Humes, Dec'd   James Harris

172

The First 100 Years—A Historical Sketch
1805-1905

In 1795, James Harris and James Dunlop laid out the town of Bellefonte. In so doing they had in mind three public necessities, first a public square dedicated to the official buildings of the new county they proposed to have erected, next a place of public worship for which they set aside two lots, and finally the cause of education. Since the highest grade of primary and intermediate educational work was found in the academies, which the close of the eighteenth century saw established in large numbers throughout the State, these founders of Scotch-Presbyterian stock, determined that their institution of learning should follow closely the lines of the kirk, hence the lots adjoining the church were marked on the original plan of the town, "For the Academy". However, later counsels changed this location and the summit of a high limestone ridge with the land sweeping away on every side was chosen as the site of the proposed building.

All this planning took place when scarcely half a dozen houses constituted the little village and it was not until ten years thereafter that their plans approached fulfillment. In 1799, when the erection of the new county was assured, it was agreed between the proprietors of Bellefonte and the legislative powers of the State that one half of all the money received from sales of the lots of their town should be paid over to the trustees of the county, one portion to be used for the construction of suitable county buildings in the public square and the other to be applied toward the proposed academy. In pursuance of this plan Centre County was erected early in the following year and Bellefonte designated as the "Seat of Justice," as the old papers put it.

During the next five years the accumulation of funds justified the preparation for a building project and on January 8th, 1805 the Bellefonte Academy was incorporated by the legislature with the following trustees constituting its first board of management, viz: H.R. Wilson, James Dunlop, Roland Curtin, William Petriken, Robert McClanahan and John Hall, all of Bellefonte; with William Stuart, Andrew Gregg and James Potter of Potter township; James Duncan, John Hall, and Jacob Hosterman of Haines township; John Kryder, of Miles township; Jacob Taylor, of Half Moon township; David Whitehill of Patton township; Richard Miles, Robert Boggs, Joseph Miles and John Dunlop, of Spring township; William McEwen and Thomas McCamant, of Centre township; and John Fearon, Matthew Allison and James Boyd, of Bald Eagle township. An additional set of assembly, passed in the following year, appropriated two thousand dollars to the building fund, on condition, however, that at least six poor children should receive two years' education at the new school free of expense.

Historical Sketch 1805-1905—cont.

During the year 1805 steps were taken toward the construction of a building which was soon under way. A rectangular, two-story limestone structure, occupying the ground between the north and south wings of the present building, was the first academy. Shortly after its completion the magnificent locust trees, which it was found necessary to remove some fifteen years ago, were planted and their steady growth matched the progress of the school. A dozen students registered for the first Academy.

Colonel James Dunlop, of Revolutionary fame, was the first president of the board of trustees. Thomas Burnside, afterwards Supreme Court Justice, was the board's first secretary. H. R. Wilson, the first regularly ordained minister of the gospel in this section of the state, was a member of the board, as were Roland Curtin, the great charcoal iron master, William Stuart and John Dunlop, prominent iron men and large land owners, General James Potter, Andrew Gregg, afterwards a Senator of the United States, and Richard and Joseph Miles, the founders of Milesburg, who were sons of Samuel Miles, one-time Mayor of Philadelphia. The members of the board of trustees of the Bellefonte Academy were always among the foremost citizens of the community and to the abilities of such men as those is due the credit of the survival of the school; for, of forty-one academies chartered by the State during the first five years of the nineteenth century, only five others survived in the struggle with the heavily endorsed public school system nourished by the patronage of the Commonwealth in 1834 and 1885.

The first acting principal of the Bellefonte Academy was the Rev. H.R. Wilson, the Presbyterian pastor who was succeeded in 1810 by his successor in the pastorate, Rev. James Linn. By 1815 the number of students had so largely increased that Thomas Chamberlain was engaged as principal and Mr. Linn selected as president of the board of trustees. Notwithstanding the many obligations of his church work and the burdens which naturally fell upon him as one of the prominent citizens of a rapidly growing community, James Linn time and again took up the work of instruction at the academy and many times acted as principal when the regular occupants of the office were disqualified by illness, or when the institution was unable to secure teachers. For over half a century he thus gave his services unsparingly for the benefit of education.

Robert Baird, afterwards celebrated as the founder of the Evangelical Christian Alliance, succeeded Mr. Chamberlain in 1818, and in 1820, J. B. McCarrell, later prominent in the Reformed Church, filled the position for two years. He was followed by J. D. Hickok, whose successor within a few months was H. D. K. Cross.

Historical Sketch 1805-1905—cont.

About this time one of the former students, whose name has not been preserved, presented the academy with a Spanish bell, engraved with the motto: "For Spain" and bearing a cross and the date 1802, which hung in the cupola until destroyed by the fire of 1904.

Alfred Armstrong of Carlisle was the first of the early principals to remain for a long term of years; and from 1824 to 1831 he made great progress with advancing age. Acting on his advice, therefore, the trustees selected his son as headmaster, retaining the father in the position of Principal Emeritus. Beginning with the new century, Mr. James R. Hughes developed the scope of the academy to its present high standing and has succeeded in making the boarding school department a principal feature in the success of the institution.

In the summer of 1904, a disastrous fire, the first in its history, destroyed the upper story of the main building. Trusting to the ability of the new regime to continue its remarkable success, the board of trustees decided to rebuild the academy in a manner befitting its past history and its coming centennial, and the present edifice with its beautiful Grecian columns was the result.

The academy of 1905 was a glorified image of the little old two-story building of a hundred years ago. Its future lay in the hands of the twenty-four trustees, some of the leading citizens of the town, and in the integrity and ability of Headmaster James R. Hughes, who had been twenty years in the service of the institution and who held the confidence of all who knew him. The place of the Bellefonte Academy in the educational system of the country has been made and those who hold it in charge should be competent to make its future more than equal it's past.

The hundred years' history of the Bellefonte Academy was comprised almost entirely within the span of the lives of two men, James Linn and James P. Hughes. The former's connection with the school was not severed until the day of his death in 1868, and the latter, at the age of seventy-eight, was still teaching in his old-time manner, of which nothing better has been said that "He could make a problem in arithmetic sound like a fairy tale."

Note: Andrew Gregg, one of the founders of the Bellefonte Academy, was born in 1755 near Carlisle, Pennsylvania. He served as a U.S. Representative from 1791-1807 and U.S. Senator from 1807-1813. He married Martha Potter, the daughter of General James Potter. He retired from the Senate during the War of 1812 and moved from Penns Valley to Bellefonte in order to get a better education for his children. He died in Bellefonte in1835 at the age of 79 and is interred in Union Cemetery.

In **1913,** the Bellefonte Academy was destroyed by fire and completely re-built in 6 months. The school opened for the fall term of the 1913-14 school year. The following is from a January 22, 1914 article in the Centre Democrat:

The beautiful little mountain town of Bellefonte, with its wonderful spring of pure, never-failing water, famous as the home of Governors and noted for its wealth and culture, has an institution in its midst that is doing more to put the town on the map than any one thing in its history. The reference is to the century-old institution of learning, the Bellefonte Academy, "The school among the mountains".

During its entire career the school has been steadily advancing although at times the way looked dark, but during the past year it has moved forward with leaps and bounds. Within the past 6 months it has been enlarged and remodeled at a cost of neary $60,000 and now ranks as one of the best, if not the best preparatory school for young men in this country. Hundreds of men in every walk of life have received their start at this famous old school and hundreds more will go out from its doors in the future to reflect credit on the school and town.

In January of 1914, a representative of the Centre Democrat visited the school and through the courtesy of the Head Master, James R. Hughes, was shown through the building and allowed to inspect its splendid equipment. In the first place, the school is ideally situated on an eminence commanding a view of town and surrounding country, where the air is pure and healthful.

Every stranger who comes to the town notices the handsome building of Grecian architecture with its broad columns in front and immediately wants to know what it is. This spring when the grounds are sodded and everything is bright and attractive, it will be one of the prettiest spots in town.

In former days you were compelled to climb a steep hill to reach the main building but this has been cut down until the ascent is so gradual you hardly notice it. The Acdemy property now consists of the main building, the headmaster's residence on the hill and the 2 dormitory houses on Spring Street at the foot of the hill.

1913 Bellefonte Academy—cont.

The main building with new wings now completed is 200 feet long, built of native limestone, the stone for the wings having been taken out of the hill itself, which is solid limestone rock.

The walls have been white coated and the exterior appearance of the building is beautiful. There are now about 115 students in attendance, 90 of which have rooms in the main building and 25 are located at the 2 dormitory buildings.

In the north wing on the first floor is located the main school room, a large, light and airy room whose cheerfulness commends itself to you at once. Adjoining it are recitation rooms in which classes in English history and Modern languages are heard. This is the classical department. In the large study hall is placed a sanitary drinking fountain for the convenience of the students.

In the basement of the north wing is a large room well-lighted and ventilated which will be used as a social hall. It is fitted up for basket ball and entertainments of a social character can be held there. Adjoining this hall is a well-equipped shower bath and next to that a small gymnasium. A pretty feature of the north wing is the handsome concrete porch and steps leading into it which, by the way, were designed by the Assistant Headmaster, A. H. Sloop. Many of the interior specifications and designs are the work of Mr. Sloop with the aid and assistance of Prof. Hughes and other members of the faculty, and reflect credit on the designers.

In the middle, or old building, is the business department including the business offices. As you enter the main hall you are struck by the cozy, home-like apprearance of the place and the many conveniences. Here are small boxes for incoming and outgoing mail, also parcel-post boxes. Those are placed there by the post office department. There is also a long distance Bell telephone booth which enables one to talk to any part of the country without leaving the building.

The school is equipped with a complete electrical system, controlled from the business office. In the centre section on the first floor are located the classrooms for higher mathematics and book-keeping.

On the first floor of the new south wing is located the scientific department. Here is carried on the study of biology, plant and animal life, physical geography, chemistry, and Miss Overton's class in elementary work. This department is in charge of Prof. A.H. Sloop and Prof. G.F. Reiter. Here is located the chemical laboratory completely equipped for both chemistry and physics. One room is set aside as a lectuare room for scientific demonstrations where the seats are raised from front to rear. A large demonstration table especially designed for lecture and demonstration work occupies the position immediately in front of the benches, where all important principles are practically shown in plain sight of every student. In the chemical laboratory is one of the latest chemical hoods to carry off the gases from the chemical experiments. In fact it is said that this chemical laboratory will compare in equipment with any second rate college in the country, and only surpassed by the big colleges.

In the basement of the south wing is located a large dining-room with 8 tables at which all the students can gather at one time. They are summoned to dinner by an electric bell in the dining room which rings bells in every room of the main building and dormitories. At one side of the room are individual lockers in which each student can keep his own napkins and napkin ring. In the kitchen where 2 big ranges are used to prepare the meals, will be found every convenience for saving labor such as a bread cutter, butter cutter, mechanical potato cutter and an electric motor for running the ice cream freezer.

1913 Bellefonte Academy—cont.

James R. Hughes residence

There is a cold storage room and a telephone just off the kitchen for the convenience of the matron in ordering goods. Students who are working their way through school wait on the tables.

Another pleasant feature of the school is the cozy room fitted up by Prof. Hughes in his residence, on the side next to the school, to be used as a Boys Club room. It is very cozy and homelike and here the boys can spend an evening reading books or magazines or in a quiet game of checkers. The room is finished in golden oak with high paneled wainscoating and has a fine brick fire place. Bookcases filled with good books, together with all the latest magazines and papers are to be found here. Some of the boys play and sing and there is also a piano for their use.

Leading off from the south wing is a room that is being fitted as a school infirmary. It will be furnished with 6 cots and be in charge of a nurse. The furnishings are the gift of Dr. and Mrs. R.G. H. Hayes.

The school is heated from its own private plant and is always warm and comfortable. The second and third floors of the main building are taken up with the students' rooms. The rooms are in suites, a bed room and sitting room with individual cots. On each floor there are several bath rooms equipped with tubs, shower baths, and all conveniences. A glance into the rooms shows them to be clean, tidy, homelike and cheerful. It seems as if every comfort possible is provided for the students attending this school.

The architect who designed the plans for remodeling the main building was J. Robert Cole, of Bellefonte, and the contractors were the well known firm of Gehret & Lambert.

On Friday evening, January 23, 1914, there will be a housewarming at the Academy from 8 to 10:30 p.m. and we urge everyone in town to go and see what a school we have in our midst. The new social hall will be formerly dedicated and you will have a chance to listen to the new $1000 Link endless roll piano just installed, which plays 15 different pieces from a roll 250 feet long. It is manufactured by E. A. Link, of Binghampton, N.Y., whose son Theron Link is a student at the Academy.

The approach for autos, sleighs or other vehicles is by Logan Street, stop in front of the main building, and exit by Bishop Street. Ushers will be available at every turn to direct visitors where they wish to go. An informal reception will be held in the basement social hall, and the young visitors may want to enjoy a little dancing. There will be music in the Boys Club room, Christy Smith's orchestra will play in the Xellentidea Editorial room adjacent to the main corridor and the new coin-operated piano, the finest of its kind in the world, will furnish the music in the social hall.

Refreshments will not be served. Children are not expected, unless accompanied by parents, but all interested in seeing the equipment of a modern up-to-date boarding school are most cordially invited to be present, whether residents of Bellefonte or any other part of the county. Many parents of the students from distant cities are expected.

Prominent Alumni

"The Bellefonte Academy has educated more public men…than any other school in Pennsylvania." *The Philadelphia North American*—1909.

Acheson, Edward Goodrich—A chemist and inventor of the Acheson Process, which is used to make silicon carbide. He became a manufacturer of carborundum and graphite. He was from Niagara Falls, New York.

Armsby, C. L. –Member of the Ohio State University Faculty at Columbus, Ohio.

Armsby, Charles L.--Graduate of Penn State College; Secretary & Treasurer of Chicago-Penn State College Alumni Association of Chicago.

Beaver, Gilbert—A leader in national YMCA activities.

Beaver, Hugh McAllister—Second son of Pennsylvania Governor James A. Beaver. He lived a short life, but was active in the activities of the YMCA. The gymnasium of the Bellefonte Y.M.CA. was named in his memory.

Blanchard, John—Judge. Was a prominent lawyer in Bellefonte and attorney for Penna. R.R.

Bolton, Clarence—Superintendent of Wheeling Mould Company of Wheeling, West Virginia; Southpaw pitcher for the Academy and was instrumental in winning games on the eastern trip of 1908.

Bower, John J., Esq.—Graduate of Franklin & Marshall College; Mayor of Bellefonte.

Brachbill, W.R.—One of the first graduates of the Bellefonte Academy under the principalship of Rev. James R. Hughes. Furniture dealer in Bellefonte in partnership with his father. Their store was one of the largest in central Pennsylvania.

Brisbin, Miss Daisy—Niece of Colonel Jackson Levi Spangler; became a teacher in an orphan school in Chester Springs. J. L. Spangler was a wealthy Bellefontian who invested in coal in Cambria County, Pennsylvania. The town of Spangler in Northern Cambria was named for him.

Burnside, James—Graduate of Dickinson College with highest honors; first Judge of the 25th Judicial District, appointed by Pennsylvania Governor William Bigler.

Cummings, Ralph—Graduate of Penn State College; Erecting Engineer with Allis-Chalmers Company of New York City.

Curtin, Andrew Gregg—Governor of Pennsylvania during the Civil War; U.S. Minister to Russia; U.S. House of Representatives. He was born in Bellefonte.

Curtin, Austin—Son of Roland Curtin; owner of a house, three lots, and a store in Bellefonte.

Curtin, Roland L.—Hero in the U.S Navy and was in charge of the ordinance and gunnery at the Naval Academy in Annapolis.

Dale, Arthur C.—District Attorney of Centre County in 1922; appointed Centre County Judge in 1924 by Governor Gifford Pinchot; Chairman of the State Workers' Compensation Board.

Decker, John—Graduate of Penn State College; Chief of the Signal Service System of the Michigan Central Railroad.

Dorworth, Charles—Editor of the *Bellefonte Republican* and appointed Pennsylvania Secretary of Forests and Waters. Played baseball for the Bellefonte Academy in 1894.

Fairlamb, George Ashbridge—Graduate of University of Pennsylvania School of Medicine, practiced in Bellefonte until the Civil War when he raised Company H, 148th Regiment Pennsylvania Volunteers. He suffered wounds and was a prisoner of war; returned to his Bellefonte practice after a post-war position at the Lazaretto Quarantine Station near Philadelphia.

Fleming, Montgomery Ward—Judge; Graduate of Haverford College and Pittsburg Law School; Attorney for Moshannon National Bank.

Foster, Rev. W.K.—Presbyterian Minister in Jenkintown, Pennsylvania.

Free, Dr. Edward—Editor–in–Chief of *Scientific American Magazine* and head of the Franklin Institute Lecture Bureau in Philadelphia. He was from DuBois.

Furst, Austin O.—Lawyer and President of Centre County Bar Association.

Furst, James, C.—Judge.

Furst, W.S.—Prominent lawyer in Philadelphia.

Gephart, John Wesley—President of Central Railroad of Pennsylvania. A law partner of former Governor James Beaver. Born in Millheim, Penns Valley, Pennsylvania.

Gephart, Wallace H.—Graduated from Princeton and became General Superintendent of the Central Railroad of Pennsylvania. Son of John Wesley Gephart.

Glenn, Reuben Meek—Manager of the College Hardware Store; started as an oil driller in Bradford, Pennsylvania, and transferred his operations to Texas when oil was discovered there.

Green, F. Potts—Attended Lewisburg University at age 13; dropped out to study pharmacy in a store in Lewisburg. Returned to Bellefonte in 1853 to work in the drug store of Rev. George Miles. Eventually he bought the store and became one of the leading pharmacists in Bellefonte.

Gray, John Purdue—Graduated from Dickinson College and earned his M.D. at the University of Pennsylvania; became acting superintendent of the Utica State Lunatic Asylum in New York State and became the permanent director of the institution after serving as head of the new Michigan State Asylum at Kalamazoo. He proved that Charles Guiteau, the assassin of President Garfield, was sane and able to stand trial.

Hackett, Ray—Judge.

Hall, H.G.—Former member of the Pennsylvania Legislature.

Hamilton, Peter J.—U.S. Circuit Court Judge for Puerto Rico; Took high honors at Princeton; A classmate of President Woodrow Wilson. Hamilton was from Niagara Falls, New York.

Harris, George—Physician and surgeon, a founder of the Bellefonte Hospital.

Harris, James—Banker, served on the Bellefonte School Board for 39 years.

Harris, J. Linn—Appointed to the Pennsylvania State Forestry Commission by Governor Tener.

Harris, Wilbur—Executive of Bethlehem Steel Corporation.

Hastings, Daniel H.—Born in Salona, Pennsylvania; was the Bellefonte High School Principal at age 18. Was 21st Governor of Pennsylvania, 1895-1899.

Hayes, Edmund—Son of Bellefonte's foremost physician, George Hayes; Employed by Dun & Bradstreet with headquarters in Chicago.

Hayes, Dr. George—Bellefonte's foremost physician; Graduate of University of Penn Medical College.

Hoy, Albert—President of John R. White and Warren Manufacturing Company in New York.

Hoy, Anna Harris—Professor at Bryn Mawr College.

Hughes, James R.—Headmaster and instructor at the Bellefonte Academy; played on the Academy football team for 13 years.

Keller, William—A lawyer and member of the Pennsylvania Supreme Court.

Leib, D.M.—Head of the Bellefonte Public School System.

Link, Edwin—Link Aviation; developed the whole field of flight simulation.

Mahoney, Ivan—Manager of the Company Store in Wilkes-Barre, Pennsylvania.

Marshall, James—Superintendent of Union Carbide Company in Niagara Falls, New York. Marshall hailed from Buffalo Run.

Martin, Edgar—Penn State College graduate; Commercial Engineer for Westinghouse Manufacturing Company of Columbus, Ohio.

McClure, Rev. A.J.—Head of one of the largest churches of Wyncote.

McClure, Charles—Princeton graduate; Prominent lawyer in Philadelphia.

McIntire, W.T.—Princeton graduate; Newspaper man in New York, Williamsport, Pittsburgh, and Newark; Special agent for the Department of Justice in investigations of sugar frauds in New York; Staff member of the New York *World;* Pitcher on the 1888 Academy baseball team.

Mitchell, J. Thomas—Bellefonte Attorney with offices in Temple Court; A member of the Bellefonte Academy Board of Trustees.

Olewine, James—Hardware business; Commercial Telephone; Chemical Lime & Stone Company; Centre County Agricultural Exhibiting Company; Bellefonte Trust Company.

Orbison, Agnes Louise—Professor of Bryn Mawr College.

Orbison, J. H.—Medical Missionary in India. He hailed from Bellefonte.

Orbison, Dr. Thomas—A noted psychiatrist from Bellefonte.

Orvis, Dr. Ellis L.—President of the United American Telephone Company; Trustee of Penn State, Leading Centre County Attorney, Judge of Centre County, Editor of the Centre Democrat, had an interest in brick-works in the town of Orviston, which bears his name.

Osmer, James H.—Born in Tenterden, Kent, England in 1832; immigrated to the U.S., settled near Bellefonte. Attended Mt. Pleasant College in Allegheny County and Dickinson Seminary in Williamsport; studied law at Elmira, New York, admitted to the bar of the Supreme Court of New York at Cortland; practiced law in Franklin, Pennsylvania; elected as a Republican to the 46th Congress of the United States from Pennsylvania's 27th Congressional District.

Palmer, Reverend John—first black to run for Pennsylvania Congressman-At-Large.

Porter, J.S.—Vice president of B &O Railroad in Baltimore.

Potter, George L.—General Manager of Pennsylvania Railroad and Vice-president of the Baltimore & Ohio Railroad.

Reynolds, William Frederick— Built the Armory at the corner of Lamb and Spring Sts. in 1894. Organized the Pennsylvania Match Company in 1900; Bellefonte Academy Trustee.

Rhoads, Rebecca—President of Centre County Woman's Christian Temperance Union; National Superintendent of Social Welfare Department of W.C.T.U.

Rhyman, James H.T.—Banker in Messoula, Montana; Member of the Board of Directors of the University of Montana. Rhyman was from Milesburg. He left a half million dollars to the University of Montana at his death.

Rowe, George—Officer of Wheeling Metal & Iron Company of Wheeling, West Virginia.

Shugert, John—Banker, President of Centre County Banking Company.

Shugert, S.T.—Editor of the *Centre Democrat*; Pennsylvania State Senator and House of Representatives.

Speer, Francis—Newspaper man in Bellefonte; Elected Recorder of Centre County.

Stone, John—Superintendent of Union Switch & Signal Company of Pittsburg.

Stover, John—U.S. House of Representatives.

Straub, James—Chemist, General Electric Company; Glidden Varnish Company; Niagara Electro-Chemical Company.

Valentine, Robert—Head of Valentine, Milliken & Company.

Valentine, Robert—Son of iron master Jacob D. Valentine; attended Westtown Friends School near West Chester; studied art at the Pennsylvania Academy of Fine Arts in Philadelphia and travelled extensively abroad. He specialized in local scenes, landscapes and portraits. He designed the emblem for the Bellefonte Anglers and Hunters Club. He was listed as a staff artist in a 1900 manuscript titled "The Addisonian Mirror", whose sketches show various activities at the Bellefonte Academy, personalities, and some particularly excellent sketches of horses.

Van de Vanter, Elliott—played baseball and football at the Academy; graduated from Cornell and became a civil engineer with Western Maryland Railroad Company.

Walker, Robert J.—Territorial Governor of Kansas; U.S. Senator from Mississippi influential in the annexation of Texas to the Union; U.S. Secretary of the Treasury under President James K. Polk; Lincoln's representative in Europe during the Civil War to keep England from recognizing the Confederacy.

Ward, Ferdinand—Partner in the firm of "Grant & Ward". The failure of the company caused Civil War General Ulysses S. Grant to write his famous "Memoirs" to pay off the firm's debts.

Weirick, Joseph—Principal of Howard High School.

Wetzel, John H.—Graduate of Franklin & Marshall College, College of Northern Illinois, and Law Department of the University of Iowa; Centre County Surveyor, Bellefonte Borough and Centre County Engineer; Elected to House of Representatives in 1898.

Woods, Joseph—Judge; crack baseball player at Princeton University.

Athletic personnel profiled in this book:

Doc Carlson	George McGee	Gerald Snyder
John Montgomery Ward	John Dreshar	Forrest Douds
Bud Sharpe	Charles Merrill Waite	Mose Kelsch
Pete Zaremba	W.E. Carroll Sleppy	Carl Snavely
Harp Vaughn	Doc McCandless	Lionel Conacher
Bill Ashbaugh	Hugh Sterling	Lefty James
Marty Kottler	Tiny McMahon	Franklin Hood
Jack McBride	Jake Stahl	Luby Dimeolo
Ed Matesic		

Dillon, Philip Coffey—A 4-year performer at the Bellefonte Academy in football, basketball, and baseball from 1908-12, Dillon, from Patton, PA, holds most of the football records:

Longest kick-off return for a touchdown—100 yards against the Tyrone Y.M.C.A in 1910.
Touchdowns in one game—5 against Altoona High in 1908.
Touchdowns in a season—20 in 1908.
Career touchdowns—36.
Longest field goal—35 yards against Williamsport High in 1911.
Career field goals—5.
Points-after-touchdown in one game—7 against the Bucknell Reserves in 1909.
Career points-after-touchdown—45.
Points/game—27 against the Bucknell Reserves in 1909 (4 touchdowns, 7 P.A.T.'s).
Points in a season—114 in 1908.
Career points—241.

Dillon had a 40-yard fumble return for a touchdown in 1908 in a 6-5 Bellefonte win against Penn State and captained the Cougars in 1909.

Having spent his youth in the coal regions of northern Cambria County, he enrolled in the School of Mines at the University of Pittsburgh in 1912 and earned 3 letters in football as well as 3 in baseball. Dillon led the Pitt football team in receptions in 1914.

After leaving Pitt, Dillon settled in Ellsworth, PA; a coal-mining community south of Pittsburgh in Washington County.

Headmasters of the Bellefonte Academy

View of Academy from the Big Spring

Being of the Scotch-Presbyterian faith, as were many of the early settlers, James Harris and James Dunlop (the founders of Bellefonte), believed that the proposed Bellefonte Academy should have a strong "kirk" (church) influence. Therefore the lot set aside for the Academy was initially adjacent to those for the churches. Shortly afterwards, the location was changed to the corner of West Bishop and Spring Streets. This site provided a picturesque setting on a high limestone ridge overlooking Bellefonte and the Big Spring.

Headmaster	Years Served	Total
Rev. Henry R. Wilson	1805-1809	4
Rev. James Linn	1810-1812	2
Closed during the War of 1812[10]		
Thomas Chamberlain	1815-1817	2
Robert Baird	1818-1819	<1
Rev. J. B. McCarrell	1820-1822	2
John H. Hickok	1823-1823	<1
Henry D.K. Cross	1923-1824	1
Alfred Armstrong	1824-1831	7
S. G. Callahan	1931-1831	<1
W. M. Patterson	1831-1835	4
W. H. Miller	1835-1837	2
J. B. Payne	1837-1838	1
John Livingston	1838-1845	7
David Moore	1845-1846	1
John Philips	1846-1847	1
Alfred Armstrong	1847-1853	5
Rev. F. A. Pratt	1854-1856	2
George Yeomans	1856-1862	6
Closed during the Civil War[11]		
Rev. James Potter Hughes	1868-1900	32
James Robert Hughes	1900-1934	34

James Potter Hughes, a mathematics teacher, was a staunch supporter of all kinds of athletic sports; and he and his horse were always a familiar sight at all kinds of games on the Academy athletic fields where competition began in 1890.

His love of sports rubbed off on his son, James R. Hughes, who provided the enthusiasm and direction necessary to produce championship teams at Bellefonte.

---

[10] The Academy Faculty enlisted in the armed services.
[11] Lack of qualified teachers.

Bellefonte Academy Students from Centre County, 1870-72

FEMALE MEMBERS

Bellefonte
Alexander, Alice
Alexander, Bertie
Barret, Emma
Boal, Nellie
Burnside, Sallie F.T.
Bush, Lizzie
Campbell, Mary
Crittenden, Mary
Devilling, Kate
Devilling, Mary
Faxon, Lizzie
Furey, Kate
Garret, Viola
Gehrett, Jennie M.
Gephart, Mary J.
Graham, Laura
Hale, Ella
Holmes, Ada
Hibler, Anna
Hoy, Ida
Hoy, Minnie
Hoover, Bella
Hughes, Emma S.
Leib, Ida
Milliken, Clara
Morrison, Mattie
Newman, Ella
Orbison, Agnes
Orbison, Nellie
Potts, Ella C.
Pruner, Clara
Rankin, Anna M.
Sands, Louise
Shaffer, Maggie M.
Sommerville, Bessie
Sommerville, May
Sommerville, Mary
Smith, Beile
Thomas, Mary
Thomas, Tammy
Valentine, Anna J.
Wylie, Laura
Wylie, Watsie

Bellefonte
Young, Clara B.
Young, Minnie
Milesburg
Butler, Elmira M.
Boggs, Amelia
Haupt, Anna
Kealch, Annie
Meminger, Sadie
Meminger, Emma
Moore, Rachel, J.
Stewart, Lizzie, M.
Stewart, Eda
Weaver, Lizzie
Jacksonville
Condit, G.C.
Snow Shoe
Minsker, Villa R.
Houserville
Mitchell, Maggie
Buffalo Run
Williams, Anna Q.
MALES—CONT.
Stormstown
Gray, J.R.P.
Snow Shoe
Loughry, Thomas
Mooney, Reese
Stewart, William S.
Centre Hall
Hoffer, Cris Z.
Keller, William
Moshannon
Holt, Charles
Pleasant Gap
Larimer, Rush
Buffalo Run
Leyden, J.A.
Millheim
Musser, F.P.
Zion
Rupert, W.W.
Jacksonville
Yearick, Cincero

MALE MEMBERS

Bellefonte
Adams, Thomas L.
Atwood, O.
Barnhart, William
Boalic, Edwin
Blanchard, John
Brachbill, William
Brew, H.C.
Breon, E.
Brockerhoff, Henry
Brockerhoff, Joe
Brown, Arthur
Brown, Edward A.
Burns, William
Burnside, G.W.T.
Burnside, William
Campbell, C.A.
Cook, George
Curtin, William J.
Dare, George S.
Duncan, John M.
Evans, J.M.
Foster, E.M.
Foster, W.K.
Garman, Edwin
Garman, A.
Gordon, J.N.
Gephart, J.W.
Green, Edward
Hagerman, J.I.
Harris, Wilbur
Hays, Harry A.
Henderson, R.J.
Hibler, J.A.
Hoffer, C.U.
Holmes, John
Hoover, A.M.
Hughes, J.R.
Humes, Edward
Humes, Irvin
Johnson, Thomas
Lane, James B.
Lieb, David
Lyon, John

Bellefonte
McCafferty, Charles
McCafferty, James
McClure, Charles H.
Orbison, Harris
Orvis, Ellis
Peck, William
Potter, George L.
Potter, James H.
Powers, Edward
Rankin, William
Ray, John
Reynolds, Wm. F.
Rishel, G.P.
Shaffer, Louis
Sommerville, Bond
Thomas, Clifford
Thomas, Richard
Todd, Robert
Twitmire, Thomas C.
Van Tries, George
Wetzel, Frank
Waddel, William W.
Weaver, J.C.
Williams, James E.
Wilson, Harry
Wylie, Samuel
Young, W.D.
Zimmerman, L.F.
Milesburg
Butler, Edwin
Butler, Emanuel
Jones, C.L.B.
Moore, H.A.
Poorman, E.C.
Roush, A.K.
Ryman, James H.T.
Roland
Curtin, J.G.
Philipsburg
Gano, George W.
Hoop, J. Walton
Williams, Harry C.
Williams, James H.

Bellefonte Academy Students from Centre County, 1892-95

YOUNG LADIES' DEPARTMENT

Bellefonte
Armor, Grace
Armor, Louise
Blanchard, Annie
Blanchard, Christina
Blanchard, Rebekah
Brew, Lusetta
Calloway, Louise
Cherry, Louise
Cook, Blanche
Crider, May
Curtin, Annie
Fiedler, Myrtle
Fisher, Mabel
Furst, Jennie
Gilmore, Madge
Hafer, Mary
Harris, Adeline
Harris, Jennie
Harper, Maud
Hastings, Helen
Henderson, Louise
Holz, Edith
Hoover, Katharine
Hoy, Lulu
Hughes, Ottilie
Lane, Patty
Laurie, Bertha
Laurie, Jessie
Malin, Helen
McCoy, Anna
Meek, Winifred
Meyer, Eva
Mitchell, Eleanor
Mitchell, Grace
Potter, Marguerite
Potter, Sara
Rowe, Edna
Shugert, Jennie
Shugert, Kate
Teats, Margaret
Valentine, Nellie

Bellefonte
Weaver, Elsie

Pleasant Gap
Bell, Mary

Milesburg
Boggs, Meta

Unionville
Buck, Alice
Davidson, Molly
Davidson, Ina
Griest, Mary

Oak Hall
Gilliland, Katharine

Buffalo Run
Reeser, Mary
Waddle
Sellers, Elsie
MEN-cont.
Marsh Creek
Confer, John
Zion
Cole, John
Fisher, Charles
Unionville
Davidson, Louis
Griest, Harry
Howard
Moore, Claude
Aaronsburg
Rogers, Coburn
Axe Mann
White, John
Roland
Curtin, John
Curtin, James
Curtin, Malcolm
Fillmore
Meek, Benner
Meek, Reuben

YOUNG MENS' DEPARTMENT

Bellefonte
Achenbach, Guy
Armor, George
Atwood, Francis
Beaver, Thomas
Blanchard, Fred
Bower, John
Brew, Thomas
Brisbin, Alfred
Buck, William
Butts, Fred
Campbell, Edward
Cook, Donald
Cook, James
Crider, Furst
Crider, Hugh
Curtin, Gregg
Derstine, Walter
Diskin, Patrick
Dorworth, Charles
Fiedler, Blaine
Fortney, Paul
Furst, James
Gallagher, David
Garman, Mart
Garman, Robert
Gephart, Wallace
Gephart, Wilson
Harris, Charles
Harris, Guy
Hassinger, Herbert
Hill, Louis
Holtz, Harry
Houck, Frank
Houck, Herbert
Hoy, Edward
Hoy, Randolph
Hughes, Edward
Hughes, Luther
Jackson, Maurice
Keller, Daniel
Kelley, David
Lane, James
McClain, Thomas

Bellefonte
McCoy, John
McClure, Edward
Miles, John
Montgomery, Fred
Munson, John
Osmer, Miles
Potter, Donald
Schofield, Edward
Shirk, Harry
Shugert, Frank
Teats, John
Thomas, Arthur
Thomas, Isaac
Thomas, Joseph
Thomas, William
Tonner, William
Valentine, Edward
Valentine, Robert
Waite, John
Walker, Lee
Weaver, Harry
Weaver, Philip
Woodcock, Jay
Woodring, Willis

Julian
Ardell, Robert

Buffalo Run
Baisor, Harry
Clark, John
Hastings, Enoch
Henderson, John
Longwell, Harry
Lutz, Charles
Roan, John
Rothrock, Eberick

Pleasant Gap
Bell, Roy
Eckenroth, Harry
Seibert, John
Smeltzer, Harry

Milesburg
Boggs, Clyde

Bellefonte Academy Students from Centre County, 1898-1901

YOUNG LADIES' DEPARTMENT

YOUNG MENS' DEPARTMENT

Bellefonte

Ardell, Eleanor
Ardell, Elizabeth
Beck, Helen
Blackford, Grace
Brisbin, Katherine
Bullock, Katherine
Bullock, Maud
Burnet, Katherine
Calloway, Magdalene
Conley, Nellie
Cook, Abbie
Cook, Anna
Cook, Grace
Crider, Mary
Dale, Ethel
Dale, Virginia
Garbrick, Cora May
Gephart, Elizabeth
Harper, Jennie
Harris, Annie
Harris, Eleanor
Harris, Mary
Hayes, Ellen
Lewin, Emily
Lewin, Miriam
Lingle, Marion
Locke, Mildred
Longwell, Helen
Loper, Lillian
Lyon, Anne
Lyon, Margery
McCoy, Anne
McFarlane, Mabel
Merriman, Augusta
Merriman, Christine
Merriman, Isabel
Mingle, Helen
Mingle, Roxie
Moore, Helen
Moore, Lida

Bellefonte

Noll, Rebie
Orvis, Anne
Orvis, Elizabeth
Potter, Janet
Potter, Sarah
Potter, Thomazine
Rankin, Adelaide
Rowe, Edna
Shaffer, Isabella
Shriner, Emma
Showers, Ida
Thomas, Lulu
Thomas, Margaret
Thomas, Mary
Valentine, Helen
Valentine, Rebekah
Waltz, Olive
Weaver, Mary
White, Helen
White, Josephine
Wolmersdorf, Helen

Unionville

Brown, Elizabeth

Waddle

Meek, Mary

Pleasant Gap

Miller, Elsie
Dale, Grace

Pine Grove Mills

Woods, Mary

Roland

Curtin, Katherine

Bellefonte

Aikens, Earl
Atwood, Francis
Baum, Maurice
Brachbill, Charles
Brisbin, Alfred
Conroy, Fenton
Corman, Alfred
Crider, Hugh
Curtin, Frank
Daggett, Lewis
Dale, Arthur
Dale, John
Decker, John
Dorworth, William
Eadon, Austin
Fleming, Ward
Furey, George
Furst, James
Furst, Walter
Garbrick, Clarence
Garbrick, Edward
Gephart, Wilson
Gilmour, Charles
Gray, Samuel
Harper, Clarence
Harris, George
Hayes, Edmund
Henderson, Miles
Hoy, Randolph
Jones, John
Joseph, Edmund
Kase, Charles
Keichline, Edward
Keller, Henry
Keller, Orvis
Kurtz, Leroy
Lane, Fred
Larimer, Fred
Larimer, Harry
Lewin, Lewis

Bellefonte

Lingle, Harold
Lingle, Raymond
Locke, Leroy
Lyon, Edward
Marshall, Allen
McCoy, John
Miller, Charles
Mitchell, Malcolm
Montgomery, Hassall
Orbison, Archie
Rankin, John
Rearick, Edgar
Sellers, Harry
Sellers, Willis
Thomas, Arthur
Thomas, Francis
Thomas, Joseph
Twitmire, Joseph
Valentine, Harry
Valentine, Stanley
Van de Vanter, Elliott
Walker, Robert
Ward, Arthur

State College

Armsby, Charles
Armsby, Edward
Armsby, Ernest
Armsby, Harry
Armsby, Sydney
MacDonald, Adams
O'Bryan, George

Mt. Eagle

Bathurst, Iber
Leathers, Erle

Howard

Bower, Charles

Eagleville

Quigley, Richard

Rock View

Saddington, Thomas

Student tickets at a reduced price could be obtained on all railroads coming into Bellefonte for pupils living out of town that were attending or planning to attend the Academy.

Bellefonte Academy Students from Centre County, 1898-1901—cont.
YOUNG MENS' DEPARTMENT

Unionville
Buck, William
Calhoun, Toner
Fisher, Harold
Holtzworth, Blair
McDonnell, John
Pratt, James
Van Valin, Ralph
Milesburg
Snyder, Clarence
Wright, Raymond
Zimmerman, Eddy

Martha Furnace
Thompson, Henry
Julian
Irwin, Arthur
Roland
Curtin, James
Curtin, Laird
Williams, Claire

Pleasant Gap
Hoover, Joseph
Spring Mills
Van Valzah, Robert
Hecla
McMullen, Ambrose
McMullen, Lawrence
Pine Grove Mills

Lemont
Long, Harry
Thompson, Irvin
Centre Hall
Van Pelt, John
Waddle
Meek, John
Meek, Reuben

Bellefonte Academy Students from Centre County, 1900-1902
YOUNG MENS' DEPARTMENT
Boalsburg: Meyer, George; Meyer, Marion

Hughes Hall of the Bellefonte Academy on South Spring Street, with the Academy Main Building is in the background. Hughes Hall was acquired in 1913, altered to a Master's House and used as a dormitory until 1933. The Charles Hughes family lived on the first floor. It was later converted to apartments; and Dr. Hugh Rogers had his medical offices there.

189

Bellefonte Academy Students from Centre County, 1900-1902—cont.

YOUNG LADIES' DEPARTMENT

YOUNG MENS' DEPARTMENT

Bellefonte
Ardell, Eleanor
Ardell, Elizabeth
Brisbin, Katharine
Brouse, Elizabeth
Brown, May
Cherry, Minnie
Clemson, Sara
Conley, Nellie
Cook, Grace
Crider, Mary
Curtin, Julia
Dale, Ethel
Dale, Virginia
Harper, Jennie
Harris, Anne
Harris, Eleanor
Harris, Mary
Hastings, Sara
Hayes, Ellen
Heinle, Elizabeth
Hoover, Rose
Lingle, Marion
Locke, Mildred
Longwell, Helen
Lyon, Anne
Lyon, Margery
MacFarlane, Mabel
Merriman, Augusta
Merriman, Christina
Meyer, Dora
Moore, Helen
Orvis, Anne
Potter, Janet
Powers, Pearl
Ryan, Maud
Shriner, Emma
Thomas, Mary
Valentine, Helen
Valentine, Rebekah
Williams, Lucretia
Unionville
Brown, Elizabeth
Davidson, Adalene

Unionville
Rumbarger, Marion
Pleasant Gap
Dale, Grace
Lemont
Mayes, Maud
Snow Shoe
Reese, Marie
Fillmore
Tressler, Anna

YOUNG MEN—cont.
Unionville
Holtzworth, Charles
McDonnell, John
Pratt, James
Van Valin, Ralph
Milesburg
Butler, Merrill
Thomas, Ralph
Buffalo Run
Clemson, Daniel
Clemson, Frederick
Martha Furnace
Cronister, Chester
Henry, Thomas
Roland
Curtin, Harry
Curtin, Laird
Parker, Trood
Zion
Eby, William
Stein, John
Stover, Joel
Fillmore
Fogleman, Robert
Tressler, Newton
Philipsburg
Fryberger, William
Waddle
Meek, John
Meek, Lester
Julian
Mattern, Randall

Bellefonte
Baum, Harry
Browne, Davenport
Chambers, Frederick
Daggett, Louis
Daggett, Randolph
Dale, Arthur
Dale, John
Furey, George
Furst, Walter
Gray, Durbin
Gray, Herbert
Gray, Samuel
Harris, George
Hayes, Edmund
Hayes, John
Joseph, Edmund
Joseph, Emanuel
Keller, Ellis
Keller, Henry, Jr.
Keller, Orvis
Kirk, Harold
Lane, Frederick
Lingle, Raymond
Locke, Leroy
Locke, Melvin
Lose, Strohm
Love, John
Lyon, Edward
McClure, Lawrence
McCoy, John
McGarvey, Paul
Meyer, Robert
Miller, Charles
Miller, Martin
Miller, Wilfred
Mitchell, Malcolm
Montgomery, Hassall
Quigley, Hugh
Rankin, John
Reynolds, Frederick
Rowe, William
Saylor, John
Schad, Louis

Bellefonte
Shivery, Andrew
Taylor, Frank
Taylor, Hugh
Taylor, James
Taylor, Joseph
Taylor, Vincent
Thomas, Francis
Valentine, Harry
Valentine, Stanley
Van de Vanter, Elliott
Walker, Lee
Walker, Robert
Ward, Arthur
Weaver, Frederick
Weaver, Philip
State College
Armsby, Raymond
Armsby, Harry
Graves, Carl
Hess, Samuel
Homan, Park
Reber, Hugh
Snyder, Cash
Weaver, John
Mt. Eagle
Bathurst, Iber
Leathers, Erle
Scotia
Baudis, Paul
Howard
Bower, Charles
McDowell, Willard
Muffley, Walter
Thomas, Pearl
Weirick, Joseph
Welch, Ronald
Pleasant Gap
Brooks, Paul
Unionville
Buck, William
Davidson, Louis
Fisher, Harold
Holtzworth, Blair

Bellefonte Academy Students from Centre County, 1901-1903

YOUNG LADIES' DEPARTMENT

Bellefonte
Ardell, Eleanor
Ardell, Elizabeth
Brisbin, Katharine
Brown, May
Cherry, Minnie
Clemson, Sara
Colborn, Hazel
Conley, Nellie
Cook, Grace
Crider, Mary
Curtin, Julia
Dale, Ethel
Dale, Virginia
Gephart, Elizabeth
Harper, Jennie
Harris, Anne
Harris, Eleanor
Harris, Mary
Hastings, Sara
Hayes, Ellen
Heinle, Elizabeth
Hoover, Rebekah
Lingle, Marion
Locke, Mildred
Longwell, Helen
Lyon, Anne
Lyon, Margery
McFarlane, Mabel
Merriman, Augusta
Merriman, Christina
Mingle, Roxie
Mingle, Helen
Myer, Dora
Moore, Helen
Orvis, Anne
Orvis, Caroline
Potter, Janet
Potter, Thamazine
Powers, Pearl
Ryan, Maud
Shriner, Emma
Thomas, Lulu

Bellefonte
Thomas, Margaret
Thomas, Mary
Valentine, Helen
Valentine, Rebekah
White, Helen
Williams, Lucretia

Unionville
Brown, Elizabeth
Davidson, Adalene
Rumbarger, Marion

Pleasant Gap
Dale, Grace
Miller, Elsie

Waddle
Gray, Ethel

Lemont
Mayes, Maud

Snow Shoe
Reese, Marie

Hecla
Rockey, Helen

Fillmore
Tressler, Anna

YOUNG MENS' DEPARTMENT

Bellefonte
Atwood, Francis
Baum, Maurice
Baum, Harry
Brachbill, Harry
Brown, Davenport
Chambers, Frederick
Crider, Hugh
Daggett, Louis
Daggett, Randolph
Dale, Arthur
Dale, John
Furey, George
Furst, James
Furst, Walter
Fleming, Ward
Gray, Durbin
Gray, Samuel
Harris, George
Hayes, Edmund
Hoy, Randolph
Joseph, Edmund
Joseph, Emanuel
Keichline, Edward
Keller, Henry, Jr.
Keller, Orvis
Kirk, Harold
Lane, Fred
Lingle, Raymond
Locke, Leroy
Locke, Melvin
Lose, Strom
Love, John
Lyon, Edward
McClure, Lawrence
McCoy, John
McGarvey, Paul
Meyer, Robert
Miller, Charles
Miller, Martin
Miller, Wilfred
Mitchell, Malcolm
Montgomery, Hassall

Bellefonte
Munson, John
Rankin, John
Reynolds, Frederick
Rowe, William
Saylor, John
Shivery, Andrew
Taylor, James
Thomas, Francis
Valentine, Harry
Valentine, Stanley
Van de Vanter, Elliott
Walker, Lee
Walker, Robert
Ward, Arthur
Weaver, Frederick
Weaver, Philip
Weaver, Robert

State College
Armsby, Edward
Armsby, Harry
Armsby, Sydney
Graves, Carl
Reber, Hugh
Weaver, John

Bellefonte Academy Students from Centre County, 1901-1903—cont.

YOUNG MENS' DEPT.—cont.

Milesburg
Butler, Howard
Snyder, Clarence
Zimmerman, Eddy
Boalsburg
Meyer, George
Meyer, Marion

Waddle
Meek, John
Scotia
Baudis, Paul
Haugh, Thomas
Martha Furnace
Cronister, Chester
Henry, Thompson
Roland
Curtin, Harry
Curtin, Laird
Parker, Trood
Williams, Obednego

YOUNG MENS' DEPARTMENT

Buffalo Run
Clemson, Daniel
Clemson, Frederick
Zion
Eby, William
Stein, John
Stover, Joel
Philipsburg
Fryberger, William
Fillmore
Fogleman, Robert
Gray, Herbert
Tressler, Newton

Howard
Bower, Charles
McDowell, Willard
Thomas, Pearl
Mt. Eagle
Bathurst, Iber
Leathers, Erle
Pleasant Gap
Brooks, Paul
Hoover, Joseph
Unionville
Buck, William
Calhoun, Toner
Davidson, Lewis
Fisher, Harold
Pratt, James
Holtzworth, Blair
Holtzworth, Charles
Pratt, James
Van Valin, Ralph

Note: Hastings, Pennsylvania, in northern Cambria County, is named for Daniel H. Hastings, Governor of Pennsylvania.

Bigler Avenue in the town of Northern Cambria, is named for William Bigler, Governor of Pennsylvania.

Headmaster's House (left) and the Bellefonte Academy (right) in 1903.

192

Bellefonte Academy Students from Centre County, 1902-1904

YOUNG LADIES' DEPARTMENT

Bellefonte
Allison, Catherine
Ardell, Eleanor
Ardell, Elizabeth
Barker, Emma
Brouse, Elizabeth
Brown, Mary
Chambers, Helen
Cherry, Minnie
Conley, Nellie
Cook, Grace
Curtin, Julia
Dale, Ethel
Dale, Virginia
Donachy, Susan
Harris, Mary
Hastings, Sarah
Hayes, Ellen
Heinle, Elizabeth
Hunter, Nancy
Locke, Mildred
Lyon, Anne
Lyon, Margery
Orvis, Caroline
Powers, Pearl
Rowe, Eleanor
Scott, Janet
Valentine, Helen
Valentine, Rebekah
Warfield, Mary
Williams, Lucretia

Snow Shoe
Reese, Marie

ELSEWHERE
Mill Hall
Yearick, Clarence

YOUNG MENS'-cont.
Milesburg
Carver, Andrew
Thomas, Ralph

Howard
McDowell, Willard
Muffley, Walter
Thomas, Pearl
Weirick, Joseph
Welch, Ronald

Buffalo Run
Clemson, Daniel
Clemson, Frederick

Zion
Eby, William
Stein, John
Stover, Joel

Martha Furnace
Cronister, Chester
Henry, Thompson

Roland
Curtin, Harry
Williams, Obednego

Mt. Eagle
Leathers, Erle

Boalsburg
Meyer, George
Meyer, Marion

Julian
Mattern, Randall

Waddle
Meek, Lester

YOUNG MENS' DEPARTMENT

Bellefonte
Baum, Harry
Browne, Davenport
Chambers, Frederick
Daggett, Boynton
Daggett, Louis
Daggett, Randolph
Dale, Arthur
Dale, John
Furey, George
Furst, Walter
Gray, Durbin
Gray, Herbert
Gray, Samuel
Hayes, John
Hunter, Graham
Jones, Lawrence
Joseph, Edmund
Joseph, Emanuel
Keller, Ellis
Keller, Henry
Keller, Orvis
Lane, Frederick
Locke, Leroy
Locke, Melvin
Love, John
Lyon, Edward
McClure, Lawrence
McGarvey, Paul
Meyer, Robert
Miller, Charles
Miller, Martin
Miller, Wilfred
Montgomery, Gordon
Montgomery, Hassall
Parker, Trood
Port, Blaine
Quigley, Hugh
Rankin, John
Ray, Calder
Reynolds, Frederick
Reynolds, Philip
Rowe, William

Bellefonte
Saylor, John
Schad, Louis
Scott, Charles
Shivery, Andrew
Taylor, Frank
Taylor, Hugh
Taylor, James
Taylor, Joseph
Taylor, Vincent
Thomas, Ashbridge
Thomas, Francis
Thomas, Richard
Valentine, Harry
Valentine, Stanley
Van de Vanter, Elliott
Walker, Robert
Ward, Arthur
Weaver, Frederick
Weaver, Robert
Williams, Mark

State College
Armsby, Edward
Armsby, Harry
Graves, Carl
Hess, Samuel
Homan, Park
Lawrence, John
Reber, Hugh
Snyder, Cash
Weaver, John
Philipsburg
Rowland, Howard
Unionville
Buck, William
Fisher, Harold
Holtzworth, Blair
Holtzworth, Charles
Fillmore
Tressler, Newton
Pine Grove Mills
Woods, George

Bellefonte Academy Students from Centre County, 1903-1905

YOUNG LADIES' DEPARTMENT

Bellefonte
Allison, Catherine
Ardell, Elizabeth
Barker, Emma
Beaver, Catherine
Brouse, Elizabeth
Brown, May
Chambers, Helen
Conley, Nellie
Cook, Grace
Curtin, Julia
Dale, Ethel
Dale, Virginia
Donachy, Susan
Harris, Mary
Hastings, Sara
Hayes, Ellen
Heinle, Elizabeth
Hunter, Nancy
Jacobs, Rebecca
Lingle, Marion
Locke, Mildred
Love, Catherine
Lyon, Anne
Lyon, Deborah
Lyon, Margery
McClure, Sara
Orvis, Caroline
Platts, Elizabeth
Potter, Janet
Quigley, Henrietta
Rowe, Eleanor
Scott, Janet
Valentine, Helen
Valentine, Rebekah
Warfield, Mary
Williams, Lucretia

Snow Shoe
Reese, Marie

MENS' DEPT.—cont.
Howard
McDowell, Willard
Muffley, Walter
Weirick, Joseph
Welch, Ronald
Waddle
Meek, Lester
Boalsburg
Meyer, George
Meyer, Marion
Philipsburg
Moore, Frederick
Rowland, Howard
Fillmore
Tressler, Newton
Pine Grove Mills
Woods, George

ELSEWHERE
Mill Hall
Yearick, Clarence

YOUNG MEN'S DEPARTMENT

Bellefonte
Chambers, Frederick
Daggett, Boynton
Daggett, Frederick
Daggett, Louis
Daggett, Randolph
Dale, Arthur
Dale, John
Furey, George
Furst, Walter
Gray, Herbert
Gray, Samuel
Hayes, John
Hunter, Graham
Jones, Lawrence
Joseph, Edmund
Joseph, Emanuel
Keller, Ellis
Keller, Henry
Keller, Orvis
Lane, Frederick
Lingle, Raymond
Locke, Leroy
Locke, Melvin
Love, John
Lyon, Edward
McClure, Lawrence
Meyer, Robert
Miller, Charles
Montgomery, Gordon
Parker, Trood
Platts, Edward
Port, Blaine
Quigley, Hugh
Rankin, John
Ray, Calder
Reynolds, Frederick
Reynolds, Philip
Rowe, William
Saylor, John
Schad, Louis
Scott, Charles

Bellefonte
Shivery, Andrew
Taylor, Frank
Taylor, Hugh
Taylor, Joseph
Taylor, Vincent
Thomas, Ashbridge
Thomas, Francis
Valentine, Harry
Walker, Robert
Weaver, Frederick
Weaver, Robert
Williams, Mark

State College
Armsby, Edward
Armsby, Harry
Hess, Samuel
Homan, Park
Lawrence, John
Reber, Hugh
Snyder, Cash
Milesburg
Carver, Andrew
Thomas, Pearl
Zion
Cole, Nevin
Eby, William
Hockman, Harry
Schaffer, Charles
Stein, John
Stover, Joel
Axe Mann
Connaghan, John
Roland
Curtin, Harry
Williams, Obednego
Unionville
Holtzworth, Charles
Julian
Mattern, Randolph

In 1904, the Bellefonte Academy capacity was 160 students—30 male boarding students and 130 day students. There was a faculty of 12, all college graduates.

Bellefonte Academy Students from Centre County, 1905-1907

YOUNG LADIES' DEPARTMENT	YOUNG MENS' DEPARTMENT	
Bellefonte	**Bellefonte**	**Howard**
Allison, Katherine	Brown, Davenport	Bower, Haupt
Beaver, Catherine	Cole, Ralph	Condo, Archibald
Brown, May	Daggett, Frederick	Muffley, Walter
Conley, Nellie	Daggett, Randolph	
Cook, Grace	Dale, Arthur	**Milesburg**
Cook, Janet	Gamble, MacDonald	Carver, Andrew
Crider, Emily	Gray, Samuel	Thomas, Ralph
Dale, Ethel	Hayes, John	
Davis, Isabel	Hayes, Thomas	**Zion**
Donachy, Susan	Hughes, Arthur	Hockman, Frank
Hastings, Sara	Hunter, Graham	Hockman, Harry
Hayes, Ellen	Joseph, Edmund	Yarnell, Rush
Hughes, Carolyn	Joseph, Emanuel	
Hughes, Margaret	Keller, Ellis	**Axe Mann**
Hunter, Nancy	Keller, Henry	Connaghan, John
Jacobs, Rebecca	Krumrine, Charles	Williams, Mark
Krumrine, Annabel	Lingle, Raymond	
Lingle, Marion	Locke, Melvin	**State College**
Locke, Mildred	Love, John	Hess, Samuel
Love, Catherine	Lyon, Edward	
Lyon, Anne	Lyon, Jack	**Unionville**
Lyon, Deborah	Montgomery, Gordon	Irvin, Boyd
McClure, Sara	Montgomery, Jack	
Miller, Isabel	Platts, Edmund	**Julian**
Musser, Mary	Port, Blaine	Mattern, Randolph
Platts, Elizabeth	Quigley, Hugh	
Potter, Janet	Reynolds, Frederick	**Philipsburg**
Quigley, Henrietta	Reynolds, Philip	Moore, Fred
Quigley, Mary	Saylor, John	
Rowe, Eleanor	Schad, Louis	**Pine Grove Mills**
Scott, Janet	Scott, Charles	Woods, George
Sebring, Henrietta	Shaffer, Paul	
Warfield, Mary	Sheldon, Gregg	ELSEWHERE
Williams, Lucretia	Shields, Edward	**Barnesboro**
	Struble, Leland	Bender, Edward*
State College	Taylor, Frank	Miller, Charles
Grove, Vianna	Taylor, Hugh	Wagner, John
Ishler, Mabel	Taylor, Vincent	
	Thomas, Ashbridge	**Mill Hall**
Centre Hall	Valentine, Harry	Yearick, Clarence
Potter, Delinda	Walker, Robert	
	Weaver, Robert	*1909 grad.

40 members of the 1906 Bellefonte Academy made up 3% of Penn State's 1907 enrollment.

Bellefonte Academy Students from Centre County, 1907-1909

Bellefonte
Cole, Ralph
Daggett, Frederick
Daggett, Randolph
Dale, Arthur
Decker, Miles
Fox, James
Gamble, MacDonald
Gray, Samuel
Hayes, John
Hayes, Thomas
Hughes, Arthur
Joseph, Edmund
Joseph, Emanuel
Keller, Ellis
Krumrine, Charles
Locke, Leroy
Locke, Melvin
Love, John
Lyon, Edward
Lyon, George
Lyon, Jack

Bellefonte
Mensch, Thomas
Montgomery, Gordon
Montgomery, Jack
Morris, Elliott
Platts, Edward
Port, Blaine
Quigley, Hugh
Reynolds, Frederick
Reynolds, Philip
Rhinesmith, Samuel
Schad, Louis
Scott, Charles
Shaffer, Paul
Sheldon, Gregg
Shields, Edward
Shugert, George
Struble, Leland
Taylor, Frank
Taylor, Hugh
Taylor, Vincent
Thomas, Francis
Walker, Robert
Weston, Richard
Williams, Mark

Howard
Bower, Haupt
Condo, Archibald

Unionville
Fisher, William
Irvin, Boyd

Hecla Park
Hockman, Frank

Pine Grove Mills
Woods, George

Note:
    Barnesboro is the home town of Hugh Duffy Daugherty, former head football coach of the Michigan State Spartans.

Zion
Cole, Nevin
Gentzel, Earl
Yarnell, Rush

State College
Foster, Harold
Hess, Samuel

Snow Shoe
Redding, James

ELSEWHERE
Barnesboro
Bender, Philip
Wagner, John

Bellefonte Academy Students from Centre County, 1910-1912

Bellefonte
Carpeneto, Joseph
Daggett, Frederick
Daggett, Randolph
Decker, Jack
Decker, Miles
Fox, James
Gray, Samuel
Hayes, John
Hayes, Thomas
Hughes, Arthur
Hughes, James
Jamison, Frank
Jamison, Paul
Joseph, Emanuel
Katz, Joseph
Kline, Erick

Bellefonte
Kline, Harrison
Krumrine, Charles
Locke, Leroy
Locke, Melvin
Long, Elmer
Love, John, Jr.
Lyon, George
Lyon, Jack
Mensch, Thomas
Montgomery, Gordon
Montgomery, Jack
Morris, Elliott
Parrish, Joseph
Platts, Edmund
Ray, Philip
Reynolds, Frederick

Bellefonte
Reynolds, Philip
Rhinesmith, Samuel
Schad, Frederick
Schad, Louis
Shaeffer, Paul
Scott, Charles
Sheldon, Gregg
Shugert, George
Smith, Calvin
Straub, James
Taylor, Frank
Taylor, Robert
Thomas, Francis
Walker, Robert
Weston, Richard
Zion
Gentzel, Earl

Milesburg
Ashe, Paul
Kohlbecker, Aloysius
McCullough, Claude
Centre Hall
Allison, Gross
Baird, Lester
Bradford, William
Lambert, Earl
Stormstown
Clemson, Daniel
Clemson, Frederick
Pleasant Gap
Coldren, Roy
Keller, Ray
Noll, Harry

Students from Centre Co., 1910-12—cont.

Howard
Condo, Archibald

Muffley, Harry

Unionville
Irwin, Boyd

State College
Foster, Harold

Hess, Samuel
Holmes, Frank

Snow Shoe
Redding, James

Bellefonte Academy Students from Centre County, 1911-1913

Bellefonte
Carpeneto, Joseph
Daggett, Frederick
Daggett, Randolph
Decker, Jack
Decker, Miles
Gettig, Donald
Hayes, John
Hayes, Thomas
Hughes, James
Jamison, Frank
Jamison, Paul
Kline, Esick
Locke, Melvin
Love, John
Mensch, Thomas
Montgomery, Gordon
Montgomery, Henry
Montgomery, Jack
Morris, Elliott
Quigley, Hugh

Bellefonte
Reynolds, Philip
Schad, Frederick
Scott, Charles
Sheldon, Gregg
Shugert, George
Smith, Calvin
Straub, James
Taylor, Robert
Walters, Sydney

Zion
Gentzel, Earl
Hoy, Austin

Centre Hall
Baird, Lester
Bradford, William
Lambert, Earl
Mitterling, William

Milesburg
Ashe, Paul
Kohlbecker, Aloysius
McCullough, Claude
Robison, Austin
Smith, Clair

Mount Eagle
Leathers, Clarence

Pine Grove Mills
Decker, Wilbur

Pleasant Gap
Noll, Harry
Noll, Ray
Noll, Samuel

State College
Holmes, Frank

In 1911, the Bellefonte Academy was 2nd in the State out of 32 schools in the Number of Freshmen admitted to Penn State College with 16. Northeast Manual Training High School of Philadelphia was first with 21. Ranking below Bellefonte were: Central Manual Training High School of Philadelphia; Harrisburg High School; Philadelphia Central High School; Mercersburg Academy; York High School; Reading High School; Scranton Central High School; Harrisburg Tech High School.

197

1912 Annual Academy Minstrel Parade
Passing through the Bellefonte Public Square led by the Pennsylvania State College Band
Below: Bellefonte Academy Graduates, June, 1913, Forty-One in Number
First row, L-R: Francis, Scranton; Collopy, Jamestown, NY; Balsinger, Pittsburgh; Schneider, Wilkes-Barre; Loucks, York; McClure, Pittsburgh; Geyer, Pittsburgh; Lindemuth, York; Scott, **Bellefonte**; Irwin, Ben Avon. **Second row:** Diehl, Lehmaster; Hadesty, Pottsville; Ellis, Philadelphia; Mullen, Shamokin; Gay, Warren; Lines, Luthersburg; Smith, **Bellefonte**; Gentzel, **Zion**; McKee, Pittsburgh. **Third row:** Ashe, **Milesburg**; Latshaw, Pittsburgh; Epright, Altoona; Weisenburn, Hazelton; Hunter, Oakmont; Goldsmith, Scranton; Irwin, **Unionville**;

Andorn, Bridgeport, OH; Shaffner, Wheeling, W. VA; Beddall, Pottsville. **Fourth row:** Messerly, Warren; Decker, Scranton; Eisenbeis, Pittsburgh; Bemus, Jamestown, NY; Dalrymple, Warren; Smith, Connellsville; Bloyd, Moundsville, W. VA; Kennedy, Freeport; Swain, Sheffield.

In 1913, the Academy bought the Philip Beezer home and it became a Frat House, replacing the one on N. Allegheny St.

Bellefonte Academy Students from Centre County, 1913-1915

Bellefonte
Bertram, Edward
Carpeneto, Joseph
Charlton, Leonard
Daggett, Frederick
Fulcomer, Spurgeon
Gettig, Donald
Grove, Edwin
Hayes, John
Hoy, Allen
Hughes, James
Locke, Melvin
Montgomery, Gordon
Montgomery, Henry
Montgomery, Jack
Quigley, Hugh
Schad, Frederick
Sheldon, Gregg
Shugert, George
Straub, James
Taylor, Robert
Walters, Sydney

Bellefonte
Montgomery, Gordon
Montgomery, Henry
Montgomery, Jack
Quigley, Hugh
Schad, Frederick
Sheldon, Gregg
Shugert, George
Straub, James
Taylor, Robert
Walters, Sydney

Axe Mann
White, Ray

Centre Hall
Baird, Lester
Bradford, William
Mitterling, William

Howard
Snyder, Jason
Weber, Walter

Milesburg
Ashe, Paul
Kohlbecker, Aloysius
McKinley, James
Robison, Austin

Philipsburg
Rowland, Charles
Rowland, Edward

Pine Grove Mills
Decker, William

Pleasant Gap
Noll, Ray

State College
Alexander, Carey

Zion
Hoy, Austin

Bellefonte Academy Students from Centre County, 1919-1921

Bellefonte
Beezer, Herbert
Hughes, Charles
Hughes, James
Kilpatrick, Clayton
Rider, Donald
Shaeffer, Paul

Howard
Holter, Willard
Zaleski, Stephen

Julian
Bullock, George

State College
Alexander, Carey

Zion
Clevenstine, Frederick
Clevenstine, Malcolm
Hockman, Charles
Noll, Kermit

On June 26, 1913, James R. Hughes bought the Bellefonte Academy at a sale by Sheriff Arthur B. Lee for $11,000. Improvements were commenced that would cost $40,000.

Tobogganing on the bluff in 1921

Bellefonte Academy Students from Centre County, 1920-22

Bellefonte	Julian	Zion	Hublersburg
Hughes, Charles	Bullock, George	Clevenstine, Frederick	Faust, William
Hughes, James		Clevenstine, Malcolm	
Rider, Donald	**State College**	Gates, Daniel	
Shaeffer, Paul	Alexander, Carey	Noll, Kermit	

Bellefonte Academy Students from Centre County, 1921-23

Bellefonte	State College	Zion	Howard
Gray, Carl	Alexander, Carey	Clevenstine, Frederick	Holter, Willard
Hughes, Charles		Clevenstine, Malcolm	
Hughes, James			
Rider, Donald			
Schad, Franklin			

Bellefonte Academy Students from Centre County, 1923-25

Bellefonte	Bellefonte	Howard	Zion
Bilger, Herbert	Kurtz, Frederick	Holter, Willard	Clevenstine,Frederick
Chipley, Carroll	Martin, Basil		Clevenstine, Malcolm
Curtin, John	Rider, Donald	**Port Matilda**	
Gray, Carl	Schad, Franklin	Harshberger, Samuel	
Harvey, M.E.	Waite, William	Williams, Donald	
Harvey, Orvis			
Hughes, Charles		**Snow Shoe**	
Hughes, Graham		Chambers, Howard	
Hughes, Virginia		Uzzle, James Jr.	

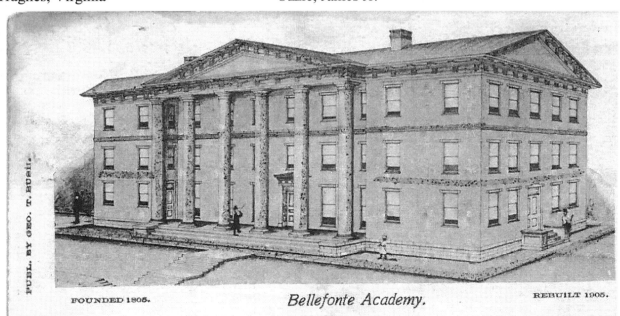

PUBL. BY GEO. T. BUSH.

FOUNDED 1805. *Bellefonte Academy.* REBUILT 1905.

The rebuilt **Academy Building of 1905** was designed by Robert Cole of Bellefonte.

W.   Master's   Hughes
Bishop   House   Hall
St.   (Overton Hall)
Entrance   **Bellefonte Academy Grounds circa 1925**

Master's House (Overton Hall) on the corner of S. Spring Street and W. Bishop Street Academy Entrance.

Bellefonte Academy Students from Centre County, 1925-27

Bellefonte	Bellefonte	Snow Shoe	State College
Chipley, C.	Hughes, V.	Uzzle, James	Campbell, Clifton
Cohen, Alfred	Kurtz, Frederick		Crawford, Newton
Curtin, John	Morris, Alexander		Kerstetter, Clarence
Evey, Gerald	Schad, Franklin		
Gingery, Joseph	Spangler, V		
Harvey, M.	Waite, Charles Merrill		
Harvey, Orvis	Zettle, Frederick		

Bellefonte Academy Students from Centre County, 1927-29

Bellefonte	Bellefonte	Aaronsburg	Osceola Mills
Beaver, James	Hughes, D.	Otto, Morgan	Ricketts, John
Cohen, Alfred	Kersavage, Michael		
Curtin, William	Locke, David	**Snow Shoe**	ELSEWHERE
Evey, Gerald	Montgomery, Jack	Kachik, John	**Spangler***
Fleming, John	Morris, Alexander		Dumm, Robert
Gingery, Joseph	Rossman, Hubert		
Harnish, Lawrence	Taylor, Philip		
Harvey, Louis	Wagner, George	*Former Major League Baseball Umpire	
Heverly, Cameron	Zettle, Frederick	Augie Donatelli attended Spangler High.	
Hughes, Graham			

Bellefonte Academy Students from Centre County, 1928-30

Bellefonte	Bellefonte	Aaronsburg	Linden Hall
Beaver, James	Spangler, Jackson	Otto, Morgan	White, Stanley
Bickett, Philip	Spangler, L.		
Burns, John	Taylor, Philip	**Osceola Mills**	**Snow Shoe**
Burns, V.	Wagner, George	Ricketts, John	Kachik, John
Capers, Burnside			
Curtin, William	**State College**	ELSEWHERE	ELSEWHERE
Fleming, John	Markle, Hugh	**Spangler**	**Aliquippa**
Furst, Austin		Dumm, Robert	Zaremba, Pete
Harnish, Lawrence	ELSEWHERE		
Heverly, Cameron	**Windber**		
Hood, Robert	Klena, Matthew		
Hughes, D.			
Hughes, Graham	**Notes:**		
Katz, Allen			
Kelleher, Philip	Spangler, PA, was named for Colonel Jackson Levi Spangler		
Kersavage, Michael	of Bellefonte, who invested in coal in northern Cambria Co.		
Leathers, William	Matthew Klena is the father of Tom Klena, a former dentist in		
Locke, David	in Penns Valley.		
Montgomery, Jack	Pete Zaremba is an uncle of Marty Ilgen, former athlete of		
Morris, Alexander	Penns Valley High School.		
Rossman, Hubert	The Dumm family owned and operated a lumber company and		
Schlow, Frank	Reo Dealership in Spangler, PA, which along with Barnesboro,		
	presently comprises the borough of Northern Cambria.		

Bellefonte Facts and Factoids

In 1799, when Centre County was about to be formed, Milesburg, a town just north of Bellefonte, was the logical place for the County Seat since it abutted on a navigable stream, the Bald Eagle Creek. Bellefonte's Spring Creek was not navigable to any craft much larger than a canoe; but the Bellefonte town fathers ingeniously loaded a small flatboat with furniture and other goods and had mules drag it up Spring Creek. They promptly dispatched a messenger to the State Legislature, proclaiming that the freight season had begun—in Bellefonte; and consequently Bellefonte became the seat of government in Centre County.

In the state of PA, Bellefonte has the best fire companies, the cleanest streets, the best bow hunting and trout fishing, and the best Italian food.

Bellefonte is the home of seven governors:
William Bigler—Pennsylvania—1852-54.
John Bigler—California—1852-56.
Robert J. Walker—Kansas—1857.
William F. Packer—Pennsylvania—1858-60.
Andrew Gregg Curtin—Pennsylvania—1861-66.
James A. Beaver—Pennsylvania—1887-90.
Daniel H. Hastings—Pennsylvania—1895-98.

Bellefonte is the home of the grandfather (William Mills) and father (John "Pike" Mills) of a singing group known as the Mills Brothers. William cut hair at 213 W. High Street from 1871-1931. Pike Mills played football for Bellefonte High School and joined the singing group when one of his sons died in 1935.

In the battle of Lake Erie, Bellefonte supplied some of the cannonballs used by Commodore Perry against the British in 1813.

The song "After the Ball is Over" was first sung in Bellefonte.

In 1783, Abraham Lincoln, President Lincoln's grandfather, and John Winters, returning to Kentucky on foot, travelled through Bellefonte and paused on the bluff overlooking the Big Spring to admire the view.

A Bellefonte man commanded the guard at the execution of Lincoln's assassins.

Parisian bookseller-publisher Sylvia Beach's father, Robert Sylvester Beach, taught Latin at the Bellefonte Academy. Her grandmother lived in Bellefonte, whom she visited. Silvia hosted literary greats such as Ezra Pound, Ernest Hemmingway, and F. Scott Fitzgerald, and published James Joyce's "Ulysses".

Madison, Kentucky, the fictional setting for David Morrell's Rambo books, is based on Bellefonte.

As early as 1807, a subscription school[12] was functioning in Bellefonte under Miss Sarah Tucker, a Quakeress. She served the community as a teacher for about 20 years.

In 1839, the Bellefonte Female Seminary was begun at the Academy with State aid from the 1838 supplement, but the school only existed until 1845 after the repeal of the common school act.

In 1856 Bellefonte High School transferred to the North Wing of the Bellefonte Academy. In 1862 the Bellefonte High School Board and the Academy trustees consolidated the high school and the Academy.

At the outbreak of the Civil War, J.D. Wingate opened a Grammar School in the Bellefonte Academy building; and by 1862 the property was leased to the Bellefonte School District. On May 20, 1910, the Grammar School of the Bellefonte Academy closed its doors.

In 1868 the Bellefonte Academy trustees took possession of the Academy, and James Potter Hughes was elected headmaster. The high school purchased a lot at the corner of Lamb and Spring Streets. The Sechler private school was established at that location in 1868, but had just a few pupils. It was torn down in 1908.

In 1888, the Bellefonte Academy was plagued by growing pains and finances; but was kept afloat due to the generosity of J. Dunlop Shugert, great-grandson of James Dunlop, one of the founders of Bellefonte.

Bellefonte had the state's largest swimming pool, 322 feet by 80 feet.

Bob Shaeffer of Bellefonte was 15 years old when he witnessed a B-17 bomber crash into a tree on the Garbrick Farm just beyond the airfield circa 1939.

---

[12] Patrons in the community who wanted their children educated in the school paid the bill.

Terry Brisbin of Bellefonte played football at the Bellefonte Academy with James. R. Hughes and went on to the U.S. Naval Academy at Annapolis, Maryland. Brisbin's father, General James S. Brisbin, took command of the 7th Calvary after General George Custer was wiped out at Little Big Horn.

The 1924 Bellefonte Academy football team outscored its 9 opponents by a 456-0 margin, the greatest number of points scored by a college, normal, prep, or high school that year. Their 25-yard line was not crossed all season.

In the 3 years 1924-26, the Bellefonte Academy football team outscored its opponents by a score of 1362-56 in winning 3 United States Prep Championships.

The second wife of Bellefontian Charles McCafferty was the model for Lady Liberty on the Morgan silver dollar, first minted in 1878.

Ed Hughes, son of Bellefonte Academy Headmaster James P. Hughes, helped the Wright Brothers get off the ground at Kitty Hawk, North Carolina, in 1903. He gave the Wright Brothers some magnetic wire for their generators that enabled the aircraft to generate enough power to stay aloft. Ed played baseball for the Bellefonte Academy.

The ice cream cone made its American debut at the St. Louis World's Fair in 1904. In 1905, Thomas Clayton Brown, the owner and operator of a shooting gallery in Bellefonte, made the first ice cream cones in Pennsylvania in his small oven and served them to his customers. Brown later became the head of Bellefonte's leading motion picture theatres where ice cream cones were available.

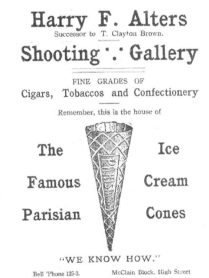
Above: A 1912 Advertisement.   At right: A 1911 Advertisement.

A synthetic lubricant invented by Dr. Edwin Acheson, who attended the Bellefonte Academy, inadvertently helped the Germans prolong World War I when his factory in Belgium was captured.

According to Hugh Manchester, late editor of the Centre Democrat and resident historian, Bellefonte was responsible for the Cracker Jack box, the electric light switch, the automatic voting machine, the Tom Collins, and the naming of Miles City, Montana.

With a population of close to 1000 in the mid-1830's, Bellefonte was an early player in Pennsylvania's mineral and metal industries due to its abundance of timber, coal, limestone, iron ore, and an excellent supply of water.

Bellefonte had a jail by 1802 and hanged its first murderer, Daniel Byers, on December 13th of that year.

By 1810 Bellefonte had 5 pig-iron furnaces, 4 forges, and at least one iron mill, which begat wealth; and more wealth begat influence and power.

In 1806, Bellefonte became a borough and water became a necessity for the town. James Smith, the owner of the Big Spring, gave Bellefonte the right to take water from the spring. The borough installed a pumping station and built a stone and concrete reservoir on Academy Hill which supplied water to town residents via a wooden pipe system. Prominent people had a hydrant located in front of their homes. The reservoir was covered with heavy iron sheeting; and when the Academy added a north wing, it was built over the reservoir.

In 1853 the town fathers successfully petitioned the state legislature, beating out stiff competitors from Pittsburgh and Philadelphia and several other counties, to build the Farmer's High School—a precursor to Penn State University—in Centre County. The Presbyterians of Bellefonte, who wielded much influence in the community, did not want the school to be in Bellefonte proper; so it was established 11 miles to the southwest in the present town of State College.

Eugene Weik was the first principal at Bellefonte High School.

In 1868 the first telegraph office in Bellefonte was located at the drugstore of F. Potts Green.

Dr. R.G. Hayes started the first hospital in Bellefonte, located in Rogers' Apartment House Building on South Spring Street, adjacent to the present VFW.

In 1888, the Collins Brothers established the first hot blast, coke-fed iron furnace in Bellefonte. A nephew, Thomas Shoemaker, managed the Bellefonte Iron Works. The Shoemaker family was the first in Bellefonte to have electric lights on their Christmas tree.

In 1814, Bellefonte's first newspaper, *The American Patriot,* was edited and published by Alexander Hamilton through 1817.

Charles F. Schad, a German immigrant, first settled in Pittsburgh and later came to Bellefonte where he established a glass works along the road to Coleville, near the present site of Warner Company Operations. The area around the glass factory became known as "Glassworks Meadow", a fenced-in site where many early baseball and football games were played by local teams.

Bellefonte Academy graduate Robert J. Walker was the first resident of Bellefonte, possibly the first resident of Pennsylvania to have his picture appear on a piece of U.S. paper currency when he was the U.S. Sect. of the Treasury from 1845-49.

John Montgomery Ward, born in Bellefonte and a player for the Bellefonte Academy and Penn State, is the only man in history to win 100 games as a pitcher and collect over 2000 hits. Ward was the first successful curveball pitcher. He visited the Academy on May 22, 1912; and persuaded by James R. Hughes, spoke to the baseball team during the 11:10 period. In 1912, Ward was President of the Boston Nationals Baseball Club.

In 1892, John Montgomery Ward, as a player/manager for Brooklyn, began the custom of having Southern towns pay to have Northern teams train within their boundaries. While in Ocala, Florida, his Brooklyn team played games against State League teams. Ocala even furnished his players with various free railroad tickets around Florida. The previous year, Brooklyn had paid Ocala $350 for the use of their baseball grounds, which is equivalent to $9200.00 today.

The post office in Bellefonte was established on April 1, 1798 with James Harris as the postmaster.

When the Academy burned in 1913 and was rebuilt, the new gym was the setting for Friday and Saturday evening socials. Academy students and young ladies from the Bellefonte area danced in the gym to the music of a Link Electric Piano, a product of Binghampton, New York. The piano was said to be the finest of its kind in the world.

Frederick Douglass visited Bellefonte and spoke at the Undine Fire Hall in 1870 on the need of fair civil rights for freed slaves. He eloquently championed the rights of African Americans around the nation during and after the Civil War.

Actor Jonathan Frakes was born in Bellefonte and most recognized for his role as William Riker, second in command of the USS Enterprise in the acclaimed 1990's television series Star Trek, The Next Generation.

Football player Todd Christensen was born in Bellefonte while his father, a college professor, was working on a doctorate at Penn State University. Todd played in the National Football League from 1978-1988 and is best known for his performance as a tight end for the Oakland Raiders and Los Angeles Raiders.

Thomas Edison visited Bellefonte. He was a stock owner in the Edison Electric Illuminating Company of Bellefonte which was chartered in 1883. During his visits to Bellefonte, Edison reportedly stayed in the Bush House Hotel.

The first woman registered architect in Pennsylvania, Anna Wagner Keichline, was born in Bellefonte and lived in Bellefonte. She designed 24 commercial buildings and residences spanning central

Pennsylvania, Dayton, Ohio, and Washington, D.C. including the Plaza Theatre in Bellefonte which had one of the largest stages of any theatre in Pennsylvania.

The United States Government established an aero-mail station on the Woodrow Wilson Aerial Service Line connecting New York City with Chicago. Bellefonte was the first main stop after two hours flight from New York. It was the only regular stop in the State of PA; and was in operation from 1918-25.

On September 30, 1920, while flying to Bellefonte with a cargo of mail, pilot F.A. Robinson struck a cable over the Susquehanna River near Millersburg, and dropped to his death. It was thought the pilot lost his direction and was following the river on his way to Bellefonte.

James R. Fink, born in Bellefonte, was the pilot of a B-17 during World War II and flew 35 bombing missions over Germany as an Army Air Force Lieutenant with the 322nd Squadron of the 91st Bombardment Group based in Bassingbourn, England and survived; although the plane was shot down by the Germans in April of 1945 on its 128th mission.

Henry Petriken, born in 1798, was the first white child born in Bellefonte. He was a printer, and became editor of the Bellefonte Patriot. A member of the State House from 1828-30, a State Senator from 1831-35, Deputy Secretary of the Commonwealth from 1839-42, and Superintendent of the railroad around the inclined plane from 1845-48.

On August 1, 1821, the steeple of the court house in Bellefonte was struck by lightning. The rod happened to be broken opposite one of the windows, causing the current to divide—part entered the building, making a considerable hole, and the other part went down the wall, killing 8 sheep which were browsing nearby.

Hugh Taylor Manchester, born in Bellefonte, was the editor of the Centre Democrat and a resident Bellefonte historian. He graduated from Bellefonte High School and Penn State with a Bachelor of Science centennial degree in political science. He was a veteran of WWII, a speech writer and staff assistant to Congressman James Van Zandt, and had a weekly column in the Centre Daily Times. He was a 12-year member of the Bellefonte Borough Council, served as mayor of Bellefonte on seven occasions while the office was vacant, and had a pilot's license.

Charles C. Brown, Jr., a Senior Judge on the Centre County Court of Common Pleas in Pennsylvania was born in Bellefonte and lives in Bellefonte. His undergraduate degree was earned at Juniata College and he received his Juris Doctor degree from New York University. He was Centre County District Attorney; a Partner in the firm McQuaide, Blasko & Brown as well as the firm Wilkinson, Brown & Blasko, and an Associate in the firm of Love & Wilkinson. His father, also a Juniata College alumnus, was the Manager of the G.C. Murphy Store on the diamond in Bellefonte.

Epilogue

For 200 years, the Academy Building stood majestically on a limestone bluff overlooking the Big Spring in the town of Bellefonte, Pennsylvania. The magnificent portico, built in 1905 with columns that stood 3 stories high, was a reminder until 2004 that an exceptional institution once occupied the site.

A 200 ft. long grassy mound where the Main Building once stood, a dilapidated Headmaster's House, and 2 stone monuments at the S. Spring Street entrance are all that remain from the 2004 fire that destroyed the main building of a school that produced numerous prominent graduates and national prep football championships.

Except for local residents who were on athletic scholarships, a Victorian classic education was offered to those in a high income bracket. The cost of an education at the Bellefonte Academy became unaffordable* during the Great Depression; and with bankruptcy staring over his shoulder, Headmaster John R. Hughes labored on until he eventually sold the property to a corporation known as the "Bellefonte Academy and School of Aeronautics, Inc." A year later, in 1934, a sheriff's sale rendered the imposing white building lifeless.

In the fall of 1936, hopes were raised that another organization would purchase the Academy property along with the athletic field for a co-educational college; but those plans never materialized, ending a proud and glorious history.

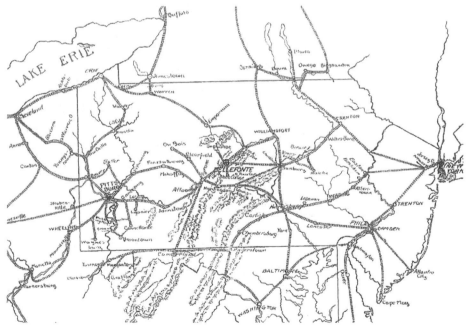

*1930-31 school year: $900 included tuition, boarding, furnished room, light and heat. $5 lab fee for science students. A corner room was $950.

1931-32 school year: Expenses for boarding students rose to $1000 and $1050 depending on location. Lab fee remained at $5.

A liberal deduction was made in favor of Ministers' children and pupils studying for the ministry.

Bellefonte was accessible by the Bald Eagle Valley Branch of the Pennsylvania Railroad, connecting Tyrone, on the main line, with Lock Haven, on the Philadelphia and Erie R. R. and the Northern Central. It was also connected with the Lewisburg & Tyrone Branch of the P.R.R.

William Ralph Gray

Ralph Gray was born in the coal-mining town of
Mosscreek, Barr Township, Cambria County, Pennsylvania
on April 27th, 1939, the son of coal miner Blanford Gray and
Anna Alessi Gray, a 1930 high honor graduate of Spangler
High School. He attended Barr Twp. Elementary School in
Marsteller, and in 1953, enrolled in Barnesboro High School,
where he made the varsity football team and was ranked first in the freshman class.

In 1954 Spangler and Barnesboro High Schools formed a jointure under the
name of Northern Cambria. He made the starting team as a sophomore and played
three years for the Black and Gold. As a senior in 1956 he captained the team, was
a nominee for the Point Stadium Award, made Johnstown High School's All-
Opponent Team, and received the Joseph A. Daugherty Award as the team's most
valuable player. In 1957 he graduated from the Barnesboro Unit of Northern
Cambria High School.

George Washington University, in Washington D.C.,was chosen from several
scholarship offers, and after one year, transferred to Indiana State College in
Indiana, PA. After sitting out a year, he was a 2-year starter at halfback on both
sides of the ball and graduated in 1961 with a B.S. Degree in Education.

He then taught mathematics at Bellefonte High for 20 years, was the Head of
the Department, and coached high school and legion baseball in Bellefonte for 19
years. A M.Ed. in Mathematics was earned from Penn State University in 1965,
and in 1981 joined the staff at Penns Valley Jr.-Sr. High School where he became
Math Dept. Head and taught college level Calculus as a certified instructor of the
University of Pittsburgh. He was a P.I.A.A. Football Official for 30 years.

He retired in 1997, and has written articles for the Barnesboro Star, The Star
Courier and Plymouth Magazine. He is the editor of the annual newsletter for the
Class of 1957 of Northern Cambria, Barnesboro Unit. He compiled a yearbook for
the 50th Reunion of his high school graduating class; and is the author of *The
Armistice Day Classic*, a history of the Barnesboro-Spangler football rivalry; *They
Came Together,* a book about the end of the rivalry and the beginning of the
Northern Cambria era; *Champions Along the West Branch, Volumes I & II,* books
about the championship seasons of Barnesboro, Spangler, and Northern Cambria;
A Mission in the Valley, a history of Saint Kateri Tekakwitha Catholic Church in
Penns Valley; and *The Battle of Benner Pike,* a history of the Bellefonte-State
College football rivalry.

Academy Acknowledgements

Kaitlyn Bush
Bob Hines
Rebecca Brutlag
Kay Taylor Gray
Charles Waite, Jr.
Harry Breon
Fred Smith
Donna Clemson
Bruce Manchester

Denny Leathers
Lori Naylor
Marty Ilgen
Connie Bjalme
Cathy Horner
Joe Pearce
Dick Knupp
Vonnie Henninger
Zachary Brodt

Dick Leathers
Joe Furin
Carl Bjalme
Jim Wierbowski
Miriam Meislik
Galen E. Dreibelbis
Charles C. Brown, Jr.
Bill Santin

THE ACADEMY. BELLEFONTE, PA.

Bibliography
The Beaver County Times
The Brooklyn Daily Eagle
The Pittsburgh Press
The New Castle News
The Centre Daily Times
The Bellefonte Republican
The Democratic Watchman
The Centre Democrat
The Los Angeles Times
The *Alhambran*
New York University Archives
California Interscholastic Federation
Los Angeles Public Library
The Beaver Falls News-Tribune
The Bellefonte Academy *Xcellentidea*
The Battle of Benner Pike, by Ralph Gray
Wilkinsburg High School Library
Bellefonte Academy Catalogues
A Clever Base-Ballist, by Brian DiSalvatore
The Altoona Mirror
The Williamsport Grit
Memories from another Era, by Charles A. Mensch
Roland Encyclopedia of Football, Third Edition
Princeton Alumni Weekly, Volume 50
The Pittsburgh Gazette Times
The Weekly Keystone Gazette
University of Pittsburgh Archives
The Centre County Historical Society
The Bellefonte Academy 1805-1923, by Fred Smith
The Penn Stater Magazine
Columbia University Archives
The Literary Digest
Oklahoma Historical Society
History of Centre and Clinton Counties, Pennsylvania, by John Blair Linn
Centre Hall, by William W. Kerlin

**Master's House
(Overton Hall)**

213

Index

214

Eisenbeis, 14, 16, 17, 19, 20, 21, 23, 26, 27, 94, 99, 100, 101, 102, 117, 118, 119, 120, 121, 122, 123, 124, 125, 158, 167, 171, 198
Eisenbrown, 29
Eisenhower, 28
Eldridge, 3
Elliott, 9, 14, 19, 27, 29, 32, 100, 102, 103, 104, 128, 129, 131, 132, 146, 171, 183, 188, 190, 191, 193, 196, 197
Ellis, 24, 26, 102, 171, 182, 186, 190, 193, 194, 195, 196, 198
Ellsworth, 169
Elsey, 13, 14, 93
Emmert, 98, 158
Engelhart, 98
English, 7, 177
Entrekin, 16, 17, 92, 119, 122
Epright, 198
Evans, 16, 17, 27, 76, 77, 93, 95, 96, 118, 145, 186
Evey, 202
Ewing, 3
Fahringer, 99
Fairlamb, 180
Fanker, 13
Farabaugh, 5, 6
Farles, 3
Farley, 141
Farwick, 68
Fausel, 98
Faust, 200
Fawcett, 33
Faxon, 186
Fay, 1
Fearon, 1, 173
Feit, 48
Ferguson, 87, 88
Ferrel, 22
Fessler, 68
Fiedler, 187
Field, 42
Fink, 209
Fisher, 3, 108, 187, 189, 190, 192, 193, 196
Fisk, 16, 17, 19, 121
Fiske, 20, 121
Fitch, 51
Fitzgerald, 204

Fleming, 5, 7, 16, 19, 20, 38, 39, 70, 107, 127, 180, 188, 191, 202
Flizack, 56, 58, 59, 65, 67, 69, 169
Fluck, 126, 127
Fogleman, 190, 192
Foresman, 14, 67
Forsythe, 96, 99, 110
Fortney, 187
Foster, 1, 16, 17, 20, 23, 56, 58, 59, 61, 95, 118, 122, 145, 146, 180, 186, 196, 197
Fox, 28, 54, 171, 196
Frakes, 208
Francis, 12, 27, 33, 34, 42, 43, 55, 77, 91, 101, 102, 103, 104, 128, 131, 171, 183, 187, 188, 190, 191, 193, 194, 196, 198
Franciscus, 11
Frauenheim, 39, 44, 107, 160
Fravel, 38
Frawley, 42
Fray, 26
Free, 52, 180
Freedman, 70
French, 146
Frick, 139
Fried, 29, 32, 33
Friedman, 68
Friesell, 54
Frontizer, 160
Fry, 55
Fryberger, 190, 192
Fulcomer, 199
Fullerton, 12, 91, 116, 119
Fulmer, 122
Fulton, 97, 105, 126
Fultz, 17
Furey, 141, 186, 188, 190, 191, 193, 194
Furin, 212
Furst, 158, 180, 187, 188, 190, 191, 193, 194, 202
Gallagher, 187
Gallaudet, 3
Gallup, 70
Gamble, 19, 20, 21, 195, 196
Gano, 30, 186
Garbrick, 5, 55, 188, 204
Garman, 170, 171, 186, 187
Garret, 186
Garver, 97

Hughes, 1, 2, 3, 4, 5, 17, 18, 20, 22, 23, 24, 26, 28, 31, 33, 39, 40, 42, 45, 51, 55, 59, 62, 67, 70, 76, 77, 96, 98, 105, 106, 112, 126, 138, 150, 157, 158, 160, 162, 163, 171, 175, 176, 177, 178, 179, 181, 185, 186, 187, 189, 195, 196, 197, 199, 200, 201, 202, 204, 205, 207, 210

Hull, 42, 158
Hullihen, 24, 29, 32, 33, 77, 104
Humbers, 119
Humes, 96, 186
Hummel, 117

Hundertmark, 70, 112
Hunter, 26, 27, 33, 85, 97, 99, 193, 194, 195, 198
Hutchinson, 123
Hutton, 56
Hylman, 2
Ilgen, 202, 212
Irvin, 186, 189, 195, 196
Irwin, 20, 24, 26, 27, 39, 40, 56, 57, 78, 94, 95, 96, 97, 98, 99, 100, 107, 116, 123, 148, 189, 197, 198
Iseman, 48, 56
Isenberg, 65, 69
Isett, 67
Ishler, 195
Ivy, 52, 54, 64
Jackson, 44, 140, 170, 179, 187, 202
Jacobs, 10, 88, 90, 158, 194, 195
James, 64, 109
Jamison, 24, 92, 93, 94, 95, 96, 97, 98, 99, 100, 101, 102, 103, 104, 171, 196, 197
Jeffries, 51
Jennewine, 41, 154
Joesting, 68
Johns, 94
Johnson, 38, 39, 44, 119, 139, 140, 158, 162, 170, 186
Johnston, 70, 141
Johnstonbaug, 97
Jones, 25, 26, 27, 29, 32, 36, 47, 48, 58, 68, 70, 90, 102, 104, 107, 108, 111, 128, 129, 130, 131, 132, 133, 186, 188, 193, 194

Jordan, 11, 28
Joseph, 29, 90, 92, 104, 140, 159, 163, 173, 174, 184, 187, 188, 189, 190, 191, 192, 193, 194, 195, 196, 197, 199, 202, 211
Josephson, 105, 134
Joyce, 204
Joynt, 65, 67, 69, 70, 71, 72, 73, 169
Kachik, 202
Kaer, 68
Kane, 54
Kann, 26, 27, 29, 102, 132
Karle, 56
Kase, 188
Katz, 156, 196, 202
Kealch, 186
Keichline, 8, 9, 77, 86, 87, 115, 122, 188, 191, 208
Keiser, 98
Keith, 52
Kelleher, 52, 53, 202
Keller, 181, 186, 187, 188, 190, 191, 193, 194, 195, 196
Kelley, 6, 17, 153, 160, 187
Kellogg, 36
Kelly, 33, 86, 96, 105, 134, 170
Kelsch, 33, 34, 105, 184
Kennedy, 102, 103, 104, 129, 131, 198
Kennel, 150
Kerlin, 213

Kerr, 87
Kersavage, 202
Kerstetter, 202
Killen, 8
Killinger, 136
Kilpatrick, 199
Kimble, 17, 18, 20, 76, 77, 96, 100, 121, 122, 123, 124, 146, 154, 155, 171
Kineder, 70
King, 39, 86
Kinley, 13
Kinsella, 88
Kirk, 190, 191
Kishbaugh, 40, 44, 137, 153
Klein, 25, 137
Klena, 202
Kline, 8, 18, 22, 23, 38, 67, 93, 96, 97, 99, 100, 196, 197

Osborne, 56, 58, 169
Osman, 11
Osmer, 182, 187
Otto, 4, 6, 7, 8, 17, 65, 69, 85, 86, 87, 88, 90, 94, 202
Overton, 177, 201, 213
Owens, 28
Pace, 98
Packer, 203
Page, 3
Painter, 13
Palmer, 5, 67, 102, 104, 159, 182
Pantall, 11, 12, 13, 14, 90, 158
Paraduex, 52
Park, 70
Parker, 190, 192, 193, 194
Parks, 11
Parrish, 196
Parshall, 44
Parsons, 13
Pashall, 39
Patterson, 119, 185
Patton, 58, 173
Pauxtis, 72, 74, 76, 77
Payne, 185
Pearce, 212
Peck, 13, 186
Penty, 12
Pentz, 12
Perry, 203
Peterson, 153
Petriken, 22, 173, 209
Pflaum, 56, 58, 59, 111, 139, 169
Philips, 185
Philliber, 14
Phillippe, 92
Phillips, 19, 20, 23, 68, 171
Pileonis, 72
Piper, 3, 19, 96, 101
Platt, 130
Platts, 119, 194, 195, 196
Pleck, 88
Poco, 70
Poe, 52
Pokorny, 48
Polansky, 102, 104, 159
Pollock, 3
Pondelik, 68

Poole, 29, 33, 133, 134
Poorman, 186
Porach, 56
Port, 193, 194, 195, 196, 200
Porter, 160, 182
Post, 60, 68
Poteet, 58
Pott, 104, 123, 132
Potter, 5, 85, 96, 173, 174, 175, 182, 185, 186, 187, 188, 190, 191, 194, 195, 204
Potts, 6, 36, 43, 181, 186, 206
Pound, 204
Powell, 33, 104, 150
Powers, 186, 190, 191, 193
Pratt, 113, 185, 189, 190, 192
Preece, 41, 138, 154
Preston, 22
Prichard, 40, 42
Prindle, 22, 126
Probst, 119
Procino, 163
Prolette, 100
Provost, 167
Pruner, 186
Putnam, 167
Putt, 98
Quarrier, 68
Quigley, 3, 17, 111, 115, 188, 190, 193, 194, 195, 196, 197, 199
Quinn, 40, 41, 154, 170
Rabe, 42
Radish, 70
Ramsey, 140
Randall, 68, 190, 193
Rankin, 48, 52, 110, 140, 186, 188, 190, 191, 193, 194
Rappie, 127
Raschella, 40, 44, 107
Rathmeyer, 93
Raught, 110
Ray, 12, 69, 181, 186, 193, 194, 196, 197, 199
Ream, 98
Rearick, 188
Reber, 190, 191, 193, 194
Redding, 92, 196, 197
Redman, 36
Reed, 1
Rees, 3

30926214R00133

Made in the USA
Middletown, DE
12 April 2016